The Scandinavian Middle Classes 1840–1940

Edited by Tom Ericsson, Jørgen Fink and Jan Eivind Myhre

Unipub forlag
Oslo Academic Press
2004

© Unipub/Oslo Academic Press and the authors, 2004

ISBN-13 978-82-7477-136-9
ISBN-10 82-7477-136-2

The book was published with the support of The Council for research in the humanities in the Nordic countries (NOS-H)

All rights reserved. No part of this book may be reproduced in any form or by any electronic or mechanical means, including information storage or retrieval systems, without permission in writing from the publisher

Cover design: Lene K. Jonasson
Cover photographs by A.B. Wilse and Fredrik Emil Faye
© Norsk Folkemuseum/Norwegian Museum of Cultural History

Printed in Norway by AiT e-dit

For further information, please contact:
Unipub/Oslo Academic Press
Phone: + 47 22 85 33 00
Fax: +47 22 85 30 39
E-mail: post@unipub.no
www.unipub.no

Preface

This book has emerged from the growing interest among European historians in the history of the middle class, and in particular its lower strata. Studies of this social group were long rather narrowly connected with twentieth-century fascism, but the focus has changed and much broader perspectives have developed. The lower middle class has been identified as an important segment of society whose social, economic and cultural significance in European societies demands attention irrespective of its political character.

This book has developed in the context of a Nordic research project, 'The Middle Class in the Nordic Countries, 1840-1940', which was organised in the middle of the 1990s and financed by the Council for Research in the Humanities (NOS-H). During three round tables in Århus (Denmark), Umeå (Sweden) and Helsinki (Finland), historians from the Nordic countries presented and discussed their research on the Nordic middle class. The first part of the book contains three major essays on Denmark, Sweden and Norway, based on the authors' own research and that of other historians. They are written by Jørgen Fink, Tom Ericsson and Jan Eivind Myhre, respectively.

The second part of the book contains thematic essays on the history of the Scandinavian middle class. The thematic essays deal with many different themes where the core of the lower middle class, small businessmen (master artisans and shopkeepers) and expanding groups of white-collar workers, plays an important role. Lars Edgren discusses craftsmen and political consciousness. Jørgen Fink analyses the Conservative Democratic Party and its defence of the middle class. Christina Florin focuses on female white-collar workers, and the gender perspective also emerges in Hanne Rimmen Nielsen's article on Danish female teachers. Hanne sadly died during the preparation of this book. Teachers also form the theme of one of Jan Eivind Myhre's articles. His focus is on their self-appraisal and strategies to improve their social standing and standard of living. The geographical space of the lower middle class is discussed in Jan Eivind Myhre's essay on suburban life in Norway, and in Jørgen Smidt-Jensen's, the social character of Danish retailers is studied in the context of four representative streets in the city of Århus.

Over the years many people were involved in the discussions at the round tables, which strongly influenced the character of the discussions. The editors especially want to thank Henrik Stenius and Tore Pryser, and Geoffrey Crossick in particular, for their invaluable contributions to different aspects of the work involved in the writing of this book. The editors also want to thank the Council for Research in the Humanities (NOS-H) for making a generous contribution to the costs of publication. Finally the editors are grateful to Oslo Academic Press, and in particular Rune Rambæk Schjølberg, for their help.

November 2003,

Tom Ericsson, Umeå,
Jørgen Fink, Århus
Jan Eivind Myhre, Oslo

Contents

Preface	3
Tom Ericsson, Jørgen Fink and Jan Eivind Myhre	
Introduction	7

Part 1
NATIONAL PERSPECTIVES

Tom Ericsson
A Silent Class. The Lower Middle Class in Sweden, 1840-1940   19

Jørgen Fink
The Middle Class in Denmark 1840-1940   57

Jan Eivind Myhre
The Middle Classes of Norway, 1840-1940   103

PART 2
THEMES

Lars Edgren
Craftsmen and Political Consciousness in Sweden 1850-1900   149

Jørgen Fink
In Defence of the Middle Class. But who and how?   185

Christina Florin
Multiple Identities. Female Professional Strategies
in an Historical Perspective   199

Jan Eivind Myhre
Middle Classes and Suburban Lives:
Norway 1840-1940 in a Comparative Perspective   217

Jan Eivind Myhre
Uncertain status: Norwegian Teachers between
Professions and Middle Classes   237

Hanne Rimmen Nielsen
Gender, Class and Culture. Danish Female Teachers, their Cultural
Influence and Integration in the Local Community 1900-1950   261

Jørgen Smidt-Jensen
Retailers in a Danish Town: The Streets of Århus 1860-1900   293

Contributors   313
Index   315
Extended Table of Contents   318

TOM ERICSSON, JØRGEN FINK
AND JAN EIVIND MYHRE

Introduction

The emergence of the middle class was an aspect of the rise of class society. The history of the middle class is the history of the transition from the old traditional society of estates and guilds to a modern class society. This transition took place all over Western Europe, and the Scandinavian countries were no exception. On this level, there was no Scandinavian *Sonderweg*.[1] Instead the historian will find the general Western European pattern of development: a demographic transition from high to low birth and death rates, urbanisation, the introduction of capitalist economy, a transport revolution, industrialisation, secularisation, political democratisation, and the spread of literacy.[2] On a more detailed level, however, the three Scandinavian countries followed somewhat different courses. The Norwegian historian Francis Sejersted actually employed the term *Sonderweg* to describe the domination of small and middle-sized (and therefore middle-class) entrepreneurs in Norwegian economic modernisation, people who needed the active participation of the state in order to establish the economic infrastructure they wanted.[3]

It is necessary to say a word or two at the outset about the term 'middle class', mainly because of its different usage between the countries. The main problem concerns its upper limits. In England, for example, the middle class encompasses rich entrepreneurs as well as modest clerks. In this book, we do not attempt to deal with the upper ranks of the bourgeoisie (German *Bürgertum*, Scandinavian *Borgerskap*). However, the question of how to delimit the middle class, upwards as well as downwards (and for that matter sideways, into rural society), will be a part of our discussion. This is also the case with the recurrent question as to whether there is more than one middle class. Both terms, 'the middle class' and 'the middle classes', will be employed by the authors, sometimes synonymously.

How did all the major social changes in the century between 1840 and 1940 affect the middle class? The emergence of a class society created both the middle class and the middle-class problem. The problem of the middle class was that it had to adapt to a class society into which it did not fit very well. The working class was an homogeneous one (at least comparatively speaking) and the bourgeoisie of managers and entrepreneurs was an homogeneous class (at least in relation to the working class), but the middle class was not. The very problem of class and class adherence created inner divisions within the middle class, weakening its capacity for political and social action.

The class conflict between capital and labour became the dominant social tension at the end of the nineteenth century, and the middle class had to face this as a reality. Attempts were made on a European basis to create a middle class movement centred on The International Bureau of the Middle Class at Brussels. However, it proved unsuccessful.[4] A mass movement of the middle class was never established. Nevertheless the middle class was conceived of as a reality and became an object of great concern to many European contemporaries, particularly intellectuals and politicians. Among social conservatives, democratisation created a desperate need for mass movements that could cope with the labour movement, and much writing and many suggestions arose out of this need. Thus the middle class to some extent became a manipulated class and was rather a class *an sich* than *für sich,* if we are to use the terms of Marx (following Kant). But even more, to extend the terms a little, the middle class became a class *für andere.*

The three Scandinavian countries present three varieties of the European pattern, and it is the aim of this book to analyse these varieties. The Scandinavian middle class has been more or less invisible in historical research.[5] When historians in the Scandinavian countries have studied the emergence of modern society in Denmark, Norway or Sweden, much more attention has been paid to other classes or social groups, such as farmers and workers. In a majority of the historical studies dealing with the political, economic, cultural and social history of the Scandinavian countries, those social groups that formed the core of the middle class are seldom treated as a class. They appear as individuals, occupational groups or as members of social organisations, voluntary associations, political parties or craft associations.[6] A clerk will be treated either as an employee in a firm or as a member of the local or national bureaucracy, the independent artisan as a member of a local temperance association or the association of master artisans of the provincial town in which he lives. The shopkeeper will be seen either as a member of the local Baptist Church, or as a member of the local municipal council. The clerk, the independent artisan and the shopkeeper have seldom been analysed as part of a middle class with distinctive political, economic and social interests. Scandinavian historians in general have analysed master artisans or shopkeepers more as separate social groups or occupations than as part of the middle class. The same is true if we look at historical research concerning different white-collar occupations.[7]

A tale of three nations

From the perspective of an outsider the Scandinavian countries seem to be relatively homogeneous. A majority of the population lived in the countryside until well into the twentieth century. Denmark, Norway and Sweden belonged to the group of nations whose industrialisation took place roughly between 1850 and 1920, which is rather late compared to the more developed nations on the European continent and the United Kingdom. Catching up with the pioneering industrialised nations was not easy, and the road to modernity followed by the Scandinavian countries had its own specific characteristics.[8]

However, there were differences among the countries themselves. The most salient feature of the middle class in the Scandinavian countries lay in a paradox: these societies were distinctively coloured by their middle classes, and yet these groups represented a shadowy and almost anonymous presence in both contemporary and historical analysis. The aim of this book is to explore and explain the circumstances that brought about an undramatic yet rather successful social and economic development. Consequently the middle classes are analysed from a broad national perspective, as part of the evolving fabric of their societies. This introduction will place the development of the Scandinavian middle class in its wider context.[9]

The book starts with three national histories, where the particular perspectives of Denmark, Sweden and Norway are placed within a broader European context. They reveal many similarities, but at the same time the development of each country was distinctive, characterised by its special national features. Stability, responsibility and moderation were often seen as middle-class virtues in countries like Germany, Belgium and France, but in Denmark they were seen as national virtues. The Danish nation was imbued with middle class values, but they were not conceived in such terms. In a sense, the Danish middle classes disappeared as their values became seen as national characteristics rather than as distinctive class features. In Norway and Sweden the middle classes seem to have played a more anonymous role, because of their relative political weakness on the national scene. The major issue in Norwegian politics in the nineteenth century was formal national sovereignty and national identity, leaving questions about the middle class in the shade, although the concept of middle class was sometimes invoked in connection with questions about democracy.

The middle classes of Sweden and Norway were also socially squeezed between the bourgeois elite and the working class. The *Bildungsbürgertum* of senior civil servants was particularly strong in Norway during the nineteenth century, and the *Wirtschaftsbürgertum* of economic and business elites in Sweden in the twentieth century. In Denmark, the urban middle class seems to have followed wider European patterns with the old group of small businessmen going into a relative decline and the new middle class of employees expanding to become, in the inter-war years, an increasingly important part of society. The battle for the loyalty of employees became the most important political issue of the inter-war years. In Sweden and in Norway, at an early stage, at the beginning of the twentieth century, sizeable sections of the new middle class of employees in the private and public sectors were absorbed into the socialist political movement, and therefore never formed a strong united political force.

Other sections of the middle class in Sweden, the traditional small businessmen, did not play a significant role at all after the First World War. When the Social Democratic Party came into power they favoured other groups in society, particularly the trade unions, the co-operative movement and big industry. While the middle class in many European countries formed its own political parties, the same did not happen in the Scandinavian countries (with a few exceptions). In Denmark, however, the Conservative Democratic Party, founded during the First World War, was an attempt at creating a political party of the middle class. It did not have followers in the other countries. In Sweden, sections of the lower middle class tried to form political alliances in local politics, but in most cases these were short-lived and played no significant role. When the middle class formed organisations, they were in most cases non-political. The Swedish *Medelklassens riksförbund* [National Association of the Middle Class] even stated that it was 'a politically neutral organisation for the benefit of the economic middle class and for the protection of its social and economic interests.' Pure economic and social interests were often stated as a reason for organisation, while political ambitions were seldom pronounced. In Denmark this was particularly true, because neither the urban nor the rural middle class seems to have experienced a threat to their middle class status, and therefore common organisational actions were normally not needed.

The themes

The thematic essays in this book deal with three of the most central themes involved in the study of the middle class: ideology and politics, gender and family, and social and spatial differentiation. On the European continent the most visible one was the ideological and political expression of the middle class. It has often been described as a journey from a radical left to a defence of conservative ideas including extreme right wing ideas and anti-semitism. Lars Edgren, in his essay on master craftsmen in Sweden, tries to advance our understanding of this process. His argument is that we have to pay more attention to the surrounding circumstances to understand why both radical and conservative ideologies appeared at the same time. Organised master artisans would generally be opposed to economic liberalism, seen as posing a threat to their privileges. Instead they would argue for state regulation of the crafts. However, this opposition to free market principles must not be taken to signify that masters could not participate in other issues in liberal political movements. Therefore, the Swedish craftsmen's movement has to be studied in a comparative perspective, and it displays similarities to its German counterpart. Edgren's essay lends support to interpretations that stress the survival of corporate traditions and their importance in shaping the attitude to the state of masters in late nineteenth-century Sweden.

A major political problem of the middle class in the Scandinavian countries was its political representation. Very few spokesmen emerged from their own ranks, and that was particularly true regarding the old middle class, the small businessmen in handicrafts and retailing. It meant that those politicians who acted as spokesmen were often seen as strangers and intruders rather than friends. Jørgen Fink explores this problem in a case study of the Conservative Democratic Party. The party was formed in 1915, and the name itself was a compromise between the right wing of the party, who had wanted the name 'Conservative Party' and the left wing of the party, who had wanted the name to be 'the Democratic Party' (*Folkepartiet*, literally 'the people's party'). The left wanted the party to establish itself as a party of the middle class. The three leading politicians of this wing of the party nonetheless held different opinions about the middle class they sought to represent. They disagreed about which groups belonged to the middle class and how they could serve it. This became evident when an anti-monopoly Act was presented in the Danish parliament. This Act caused a deep division within the left wing of the party, and revealed the frailty of its position. The leading politicians of this wing tried to act as spokesmen of the middle class, but the social group they sought to represent did not acknowledge them and did nothing to prevent their political downfall.

The second of the themes concerns the importance of gender and the role of the family in middle-class life. Middle-class women played an important role in the development of the Scandinavian countries. New family patterns and work opportunities moved middle-class women from the household to the public sphere. Many occupations became middle-class occupations because so many women originated socially from the middle class. Occupations such as schoolteachers, telephone and telegraph operators, and traditional occupations like nurses were totally dominated by women with a middle-class background, in some cases even a bourgeois or upper-class background. New educational opportunities for women increased during the period and promoted this development. The appearance of women, however, created conflict in various occupations. In Denmark this was visible among female schoolteachers. Hanne Rimmen Nielsen argues that a clash between the modernity of the new middle class and traditional values occurred when female teachers took up work in the countryside. They were female in a male society, urban in a rural context, middle-class in pre-class surroundings. They were normally alone, in the sense that they had no female colleagues in their immediate vicinities, and thus felt themselves isolated and in need of integration into their local communities. Under these circumstances they adopted different strategies. One was through marriage, which normally meant giving up work and a middle-class identity. Another was through political and associational activity, and the last was through adopting a fierce self-discipline, which demanded immaculate moral conduct and strict celibacy. To explore the fate and the conditions of this social group Hanne Rimmen Nielsen has undertaken a series of case studies.

Uniquely female strategies seem to have developed in many of the new female occupations. In her article, Christina Florin, studying schoolteachers, nurses, clerks, secretaries, midwives and dairy officials, reveals that women in white-collar and lower professional occupations needed to develop different techniques because of gender differences between men and women. Did these techniques differ from one occupation to another, or were there common gender strategies independent of the occupation and work environment? Is it possible to apply traditional gender and professionalisation theory to an analysis of white-collar employment?

Questions of middle class, professions and gender meet in Jan Eivind Myhre's contribution on Norwegian primary school teachers. The article takes the reader right up to the end of the twentieth century in order to show the consequences of teachers trying to ride two horses at the same time. They wanted to achieve middle-class living standards through a union-like strategy, while simultaneously striving to create a profession, mainly through adopting pedagogy as their scientific basis. The sinking salary and status of teachers is interpreted as the occupation falling between a tough trade union strategy and an unsuccessful craving for professional status.

The third general theme concerns social and spatial differentiation. As can be seen from much of the historiography of the European middle class, social differences between classes and within classes seem to have been important. The lower middle class in particular, whether we speak about the traditional small businessmen or the new middle class, has often been described in terms of its lack of internal coherence. For example, there existed major economic and social differences between a wealthier shopkeeper in a town's high street and a poor artisan working in his backyard, and between the teacher in an urban secondary school and the female clerk in a small private office. The internal social and economic differences are revealed in Jørgen Smidt-Jensen's essay on retailers in the Danish provincial town of Aarhus. The number of shops in the town increased immensely between 1850 and 1900, creating a distinct social hierarchy. From quite early on, the world of shopkeepers contained three social subgroups. The wealthy shopkeepers were to be found in the city itself where new shopping streets had come into existence. They kept servants, owned their own houses, and voted solidly for the political right. Those in the middle group of shopkeepers were also to be found in the shopping streets of the city, but in less central locations. Not all of them had servants and they tended to be tenants rather than owners of the houses they occupied. Their political leanings were less stable. The lowest group of retailers lived in the new working-class districts on the outskirts of the town. They did not employ servants and often ran their businesses in order to supplement other sources of income. They voted for the Liberal Party at first, and later for the Danish Labour Party when it began to participate in elections.

The rise of the middle class and the rise of modern suburbs in Norwegian urban society between around 1870 and 1940 went hand in hand, as Jan Eivind Myhre shows in his essay on the middle class and suburban life. The suburban movement, involving mainly the construction of villas but also of houses for two or four families, was partly an escape from what was considered a dreary urban environment. The movement, however, was not confined to the middle classes, as workers (mainly better-off skilled workers) moved out of town in considerable numbers, especially after the beginning of the twentieth century. The different classes shared a worship of the natural environment, as the names of the houses show. Both were commuters to the city and certainly adhered to nuclear family values. A communal, even a collective, attitude to the many practical and social tasks of the suburban neighbourhoods was evident among middle-class and working-class suburbanites alike. Often, however, the two groups were spatially separated, since suburban areas were either created by occupational associations or followed the logic of land and house-market prices. Middle-class housing schemes would have restrictions to keep workers out. Although the majority of suburban dwellers were middle-class, and although middle-class people were the ones to take suburban lifestyles to the extreme, the suburban movement was a cross-class affair.

We intend the ten essays in this book to show both the common patterns and the diverging paths taken by the Scandinavian middle-class experience in its most formative period, the century between around 1840 and 1940. Where the patterns resembled each other, it was due to the countries going through roughly the same process of modernisation. Where they differed, the reasons were mainly dissimilar social, political and economic structures, although these tended to become more alike in the twentieth century.

Notes

[1] For the *Sonderweg* [special path] debate in Germany see Jürgen Kocka, 'German History before Hitler. The debate about the German "Sonderweg"', *Journal of Contemporary History*, vol. 23, 1988, pp. 3-16. David Blackbourn and Geoff Eley, *The Peculiarities of German History: bourgeois society and politics in nineteenth-century Germany*, Oxford 1984. Richard J. Evans, *Rethinking German History*, London 1987. The debate is also documented in *'Historikerstreit'. Die Dokumentation der Kontroverse um die Einzigartikheit der nationalsozialistischen Judenvernichtung*, München 1987.
[2] For a modern comparative history of the Nordic countries see Harald Gustafsson, *Nordens historia. En europeisk region under 1200 år*, Lund 1997.
[3] Francis Sejersted, 'Den norske "Sonderweg"', *Demokratisk kapitalisme*, Oslo 1993, pp. 163-208.
[4] Geoffrey Crossick and Heinz-Gerhard Haupt, *The Petite Bourgeoisie in Europe 1780-1914. Enterprise, family and independence*, London 1995, p. 145; Tom Ericsson, *Mellan arbete och kapital. Småborgerligheten i Sverige 1850-1914*, (Umeå Studies in the Humanities, 86), Stockholm 1988, p. 8.
[5] There are some exceptions. For Sweden, see: Ericsson, 1988; Tom Söderberg, *Två sekel svensk medelklass. Från gustaviansk tid till nutid*, Stockholm 1972. For

Denmark: Jørgen Fink, *Middelstand i klemme? Studier i danske håndværksmestres økonomiske, sociale og organisatoriske udvikling 1895-1920*, (Skrifter udgivet af Jydsk Selskab for Historie, nr. 46), Aarhus 1988; Jan Eivind Myhre, 'Finding the Middle Class. Norway in a comparative perspective, c. 1870-1940', *Scandinavian Journal of History*, 3, 1994, pp. 237-249.

[6] This is particularly true when we look at the historical literature on voluntary associations in the Nordic countries. See Sven Lundkvist, *Folkrörelserna i det svenska samhället 1850-1920*, Uppsala 1977; Henrik Stenius, *Frivilligt, jämlikt, samfällt. Föreningsväsendets utveckling i Finland fram till 1900-talets början med speciell hänsyn till massorganisationsprincipens genombrott*, Helsingfors 1987; Vagn Wåhlin, Omkring studiet af de folkelige bevegelser, *Historisk Tidskrift*, vol. 1 1979; *NOU(Norges offentlige utredninger) 1988: 17 Frivillige organisasjoner.*

[7] See for example Mats Greiff, *Kontoristen. Från chefens högra hand till proletär*, Lund 1992; Gro Hagemann, *Skolefolk. Lærernes historie i Norge*. Oslo 1992; Christina Florin, *Kampen om katedern. Feminiserings- och professionaliseringsprocessen inom den svenska folkskolans lärarkår 1860-1906*, Umeå 1987; Åsmund Arup Seip, *Rett til å forhandle. En studie i statstjenestemennes forhandlingsrett i Norge og Sverige 1910-1965*, Oslo 1997; Åsmund Arup Seip, *Lektorene. Profesjon, organisasjon, politikk 1890-1980*, Oslo 1990.

[8] The literature on the emergence of the welfare state in the Scandinavian countries is extensive. See, for example, Gösta Esping Andersen, *Politics against Markets*, Princeton, N.J. 1985; Peter Baldwin, *The Politics of Social Solidarity*, Cambridge 1990; Klaus Misgeld et al., *Creating Social Democracy: A Century of the Social Democratic Labour Party in Sweden*, University Park, Pa. 1992; Anne-Lise Seip, *Sosialhjelpstaten blir til 1720-1920*, Oslo 1984.

[9] The historical literature on the middle class, including the petite bourgeoisie and white-collar workers, has increased during the last decades. However, the most recent literature on the classical *petite bourgeoisie* is Geoffrey Crossick and Heinz-Gerhard Haupt, *The Petite Bourgeoisie in Europe 1780-1914. Enterprise, Family and Independance*, London 1995. On white-collar workers in a comparative perspective, see Jürgen Kocka, *Angestellte im Europäischen Vergleich. Die Herausbildung angestellter Mittelschichten seit den späten 19. Jahrhundert*, Göttingen 1981, which still gives the best introduction to the subject.

PART 1
NATIONAL PERSPECTIVES

TOM ERICSSON

A Silent Class. The Lower Middle Class in Sweden, 1840-1940

Introduction

In 1923, the chairman of the Nobel Prize Committee, Professor Henrik Schück, made a speech in which he claimed that the achievements of science were closely related to the progress of the middle class. However, at the same time he argued that the glory days of science were over, because the middle class was in decline, and its interest in the cultural aspects of life had disappeared. Instead its thoughts were preoccupied with everyday matters such as clothes and food.[1] Schück's description indicates that the middle class had lost its position in society, and like the working class it had to think about its daily bread. He was probably right to say that the social and economic gap between the middle class and the working class had narrowed, but he was definitely wrong if he thought that the middle class had declined in numbers. However, Schück did not give a clear definition of what he really meant by the concept of 'middle class'. The only indications he gave were that a majority of European scientists had been recruited from the middle class, and that the middle class had a common interest in the cultural aspects of life. By that, Schück probably meant that the European middle class had at least one thing in common, namely its members' educational background. However, his definition was rather vague, and the historian has to ask who these people were who actually belonged to the middle class in Sweden in the early 1920s. What can be said about the definitions of 'middle class' in currency at that time? Which social groups or occupational strata were regarded as middle class groups in Swedish society during the period from 1840 to 1940? By taking a closer look at what people from that period had to say about the social structure in Sweden, and particularly at what they meant when they used the concept of middle class, it is possible to catch

19

the meaning of the concept and see to what extent it changed over time.

Early understandings of the lower middle class

It is necessary to begin with the observation that the word 'middle class' (in Swedish, *medelklass*) first seems to have appeared in the Swedish vocabulary in the late eighteenth century, while the concepts of 'upper class' and 'lower class' are much more recent. The latter concepts became more frequently used in Sweden when the author August Strindberg published his book *Tjänstekvinnans son* in the late nineteenth century.[2] However, one of the first to use the concept of middle class was Erik Gustaf Geijer (who later became professor of history at Uppsala University) in his letters from his travels in England in 1810.[3] In his description of the social environment he observed in England, he pointed out that certain people he met belonged to the middle class. It is not clear from his observations whether he used the term 'middle class' in the same way as it was used in Britain. When Geijer adopted it to describe the social structure of Sweden at the beginning of the nineteenth century, he did it in such a way that it excluded many of the social groups that later formed the core of the Swedish middle class, namely small businessmen in manufacturing, handicrafts and retailing, white-collar workers and minor professionals. It seems as if Geijer used the concept to describe his own social environment in Sweden consisting of saw mill owners and ironmasters.

Until the beginning of the nineteenth century the most common word to describe those social groups that were later regarded as the lower middle class was *medelståndet*, which was an exact translation of the German *Mittelstand*. It was another way of classifying those occupational strata that belonged to one of the four estates in the Swedish parliament [*Riksdag*], the Estate of the Burghers [*borgarståndet*], namely the urban population consisting of master artisans, shopkeepers, wholesalers, factory owners and other industrialists. However, it was not until the last decades of the century that the concept of middle class was more generally used in descriptions of the Swedish social structure.[4] It was also then that its meaning changed depending on the person who used it, and on the social framework to which it was applied.

The historian and political scientist Pontus Fahlbeck, a professor at Lund University, and a conservative politician and member of the parliament, belonged to a group of academics and intellectuals who played an important role in the debate on social issues in late nineteenth-century Sweden. In 1892 he published a book on the history of social classes. He was very well aware that the very concept of class was problematic, and that the borders between different classes could be very difficult to delineate. He pointed out that transitional stages between different classes were particularly difficult to observe. Fahlbeck expressed this observation in the following way: 'A spectator who puts himself too close to the object he wants to study might not see its complexity (diversity). It is when you first look at the object (class) from a distance that the separate groups will appear.'[5] Fahlbeck identified up to three classes in the Swedish society of his time, and one of them was the middle class. According to Fahlbeck, the middle class included the traditional urban small businessman, like the shopkeeper, the master artisan and other small tradesmen, but he also regarded farmers as a part of the middle class. Fahlbeck's definition fits those groups in society that historians and social scientists usually regard as the lower middle class very well.

The problem with identifying the middle class is also evident in a book on social classes and political parties by E.H. Thörnberg, published during the First World War.[6] His argument was that the middle class in Sweden at the turn of the century could not be regarded as a single social class, but rather could be divided into two distinct ones. One consisted of the well-to-do representatives of industry, trade and commerce, and the other was the petite bourgeoisie, which included master artisans and small shopkeepers. The latter social groups, according to Thörnberg, were homogeneous and characterised by their distinct political and social interests. The political attitudes of the master artisans and small shopkeepers tended towards an old liberalism, which meant that they were sceptical of the established church, the military and the bureaucracy. This mentality also meant that their social interests were closely connected with the working class.[7] This part of the middle class was also characterised by its desire to climb the social ladder. Thörnberg expressed this in the following words: 'Among petit bourgeois families in Sweden, in the large cities and the small towns, as well as in the countryside, efforts are made to move upwards. They have two goals. One concerns the family as a whole. They want to climb, because the parents have themselves often moved up from a lower stratum. Their second goal is to provide their children with the economic and intellectual wherewithal to gain them a place among the upper class.'[8]

Even among those occupational groups that belonged to the lower middle class, opinions were vague about which groups should be included in it. However, instead of discussing the actual concept of middle class or lower middle class, many representatives of the small entrepreneurial group preferred to use the word *Mittelstand* to describe themselves. A good example was an article published in the journal *Det Nya Sverige* [The New Sweden] in 1908 by C.J.F. Ljunggren, the chairman of *Sveriges hantverksorganisation* [Swedish Handicrafts Association]. In this article, Ljunggren discussed the concept of *Mittelstand*, which the Swedes had borrowed from Germany. He wrote that '*Mittelstand* is used to describe that section of the population which is active with a greater or lesser degree of independence in retailing and the handicrafts, or more generally within one of the many branches of small-scale economic enterprise.'[9] For Ljunggren, the key words were 'independence' and 'small-scale'. It was these characteristics that distinguished the *Mittelstand* from other social groups. This definition excluded employees, whether white-collar or blue-collar workers, and also the representatives of large-scale industry and commerce. Ljunggren's definition approximated quite closely to what was called the 'old *Mittelstand*' in Germany, a term used to describe the small owners of capital within retailing and the handicrafts.

Carl Correus, a prominent member of *Sveriges Minuthandlares Riksförbund* [Swedish Retailers' Association], had a considerably wider definition of *Mittelstand*, which he also used instead of middle class. However, Correus distinguished between the old and the new *Mittelstand*. He wrote that, 'It is possible to speak of an old and a new *Mittelstand*. The latter includes salaried employees, craftsmen, those living on small amounts of interest or pensions, some foremen and officials employed in agriculture, trade and industry. The old *Mittelstand* is the independent master artisans and shopkeepers.'[10] It is obvious that Correus had a more modern view, when he regarded the emerging group of white-collar workers in public and private employment as an important part of the lower middle class or the *Mittelstand*, as he preferred to call it. The use of '*Mittelstand*' instead of 'lower middle class' also had connotations that went beyond ideological affinity. It brought to mind a corporatist tradition, the pre-industrial society in which the social order had rested on status rather than class. This was no coincidence. An important aspect of the *Mittelstand* movement in Sweden and elsewhere was to replace the class society with a social model that borrowed its main characteristics from a corporatist, pre-industrial tradition dominated by small master artisans and shopkeepers, the guilds and trade societies. On the other hand the concept of class acknowledged that modern society was organised on other economic principles.

It is interesting to note that those occupational groups described by others as 'the new *Mittelstand*', such as clerks, managers and schoolteachers, never seem to have expressed their social place in society in terms either of a specific class position or of being a part of the *Mittelstand*.[11] They seem to have lacked a clear terminology. However, there were other expressions of social behaviour that placed them in a sense closer to the working class than to the elite. Already in the late nineteenth and early twentieth century, many occupational groups in the public and private sectors began to form trade unions. However, these organisations were often very eager to point out that they were different from those of the working class. They presented their organisations as respectable, they wanted to co-operate with employers, and strikes and confrontation were banned from their agenda. They did not want to be identified with the ideology or behaviour of the working class.[12] By showing this loyalty towards their employers, and at the same time making a clear ideological and social distinction between themselves and the working class, the new *Mittelstand* placed themselves in the middle in society. This intermediate position could also be seen in other contexts. At least master artisans and shopkeepers saw themselves as representing the centre in political life, a buffer between a radical left and a conservative right.[13] Especially among the old middle class, master artisans and shopkeepers, metaphors and history seem to have played a much more important role in shaping their own images of themselves and their social position in society.[14] At the beginning of the twentieth century they were still trying to convince Swedish society that they constituted the social stratum that could balance the forces of capital and labour, and that they were immune to socialism and other general threats to society. They regarded themselves as a model for the rest of society, the healthy core adjusted to a harmonious social development.[15]

The lower middle class in official statistics

Sweden has a long tradition of keeping track of its population. Already in the middle of the eighteenth century the state founded its first National Bureau of Statistics [*Tabellverket*] which collected information on important demographic and social changes in each Swedish parish annually. From the resultant data it is possible to get a fairly clear picture of the population of Sweden from 1749 onwards. However, the official statistics do not supply the historian with an adequate analysis in terms of class. Instead each general trade is divided into specific types of occupations, and from these figures the lower middle class occupations can be calculated reasonably accurately. Swedish society experienced very strong population growth during the hundred years that form the focus of this essay. At the middle of the nineteenth century the population was around 3.5 million. It increased during the second half of the century to 5.1 million in 1900, and it continued to grow to 6.4 million in 1940.[16]

The development of Swedish society during the nineteenth century favoured the growth of the lower middle class. Industrialisation, urbanisation and the decline of the corporate state together contrived to expand the number of lower middle class occupations. Local, regional and national authorities increased in size when their areas of competence grew, and at the same time industry and other areas of private employment expanded and took on more administrators.[17] Like many other countries in Europe, Sweden did not experience a rapid decline among the traditional lower middle class occupations within the handicrafts and the retail trade. On the contrary, the number of master artisans and shopkeepers increased after the abolition of the guilds in 1846 and the introduction of free trade in 1864.[18] Official statistics for the period 1870-1910 show a steady increase in the retail trade, which was particularly strong during the 1870s and the 1890s. However, this development was much stronger in rural areas. During the 1870s the growth in rural areas was 72 per cent, while urban areas showed an increase of 21.6 per cent. The reason for this strong rural growth was initially closely linked to the introduction of free trade legislation in the 1860s. Shops were previously excluded from the countryside, and people had to buy their goods in markets or travel to the nearest town. The growing urban population favoured the growth of the retail trade.

The handicrafts, too, were characterised by a strong increase, and between 1865 and 1910 the number of independent artisans' workshops rose from about 15,000 to around 60,000.[19] However, industrialisation probably did more than any relaxation of government regulations to provide the handicrafts with competition of a kind that forced them to react if they were not to go under. The response they made varied from one craft to another. Some of the leading master artisans accepted the challenge from industry and installed new machines in their workshops. Other master artisans discontinued production altogether or relegated it to secondary importance, establishing themselves instead in repair and service enterprises, often selling industrially produced goods as well. A third group specialised in the luxury goods end of the market, tending more and more towards quality craftsmanship.[20]

Industrial expansion during the second half of the nineteenth century and the beginning of the twentieth, along with the development of the public sector, resulted in considerable structural occupational changes. One of the most important changes was the increased proportion of the population engaged in non-manual occupations, the white-collar work force, or, as many contemporaries preferred to call it 'the new *Mittelstand*'. In 1870 about 3 per cent of the population was involved in white-collar employment. During the following five decades the proportion of the population involved in white-collar employment increased to 11 per cent. This meant an increase from 44,500 to 287,000 in absolute numbers (Table 1). The growth became particularly strong after the turn of the twentieth century.

Table 1. White-collar workers in the private and public sector in Sweden, 1870-1920

Year	Public sector	Private sector	Percentage of the total occupational workforce
1870	22,200	22,400	3.1
1880	27,700	32,700	3.7
1890	36,000	40,000	4.4
1900	44,400	59,100	5.3
1910	60,900	111,100	7.9
1920	82,700	203,800	11.0
1930	103,200	253,400	12.7
1940	171 900	413,900	19.4

Source: Sten Carlsson, *Yrken och samhällsgrupper*, Stockholm, 1968, p. 255, table 1.

A comparison between the private and public sectors shows that the number of white-collar workers in each was very similar in 1870. Up to the turn of the century, the growth of white-collar workers in the private sector was slightly higher than in the public sector. However, after 1900 the increase within the private sector became much greater, and in 1920 the number of white-collar workers in the private sector was around 71 per cent of the overall total. The rise of the white-collar worker also favoured the growth of female lower middle class occupations.

Table 2. Female white-collar workers in Sweden 1870-1920

Year	No.	Percentage of all white-collar workers
1870	5,400	12.1
1880	10,300	17,0
1890	17,700	23.3
1900	29,500	28.5
1910	60,400	35.1
1920	117,100	40.9
1930	165 000	45.0
1940	253 000	43.5

Source: Carlsson, *Yrken och samhällsgrupper*, p. 267, table 2.

In 1870 women constituted 12 per cent of the white-collar work force, while in 1920 their share had increased to almost 42 per cent (Table 2).[21] Female lower middle-class occupations were particularly dominant in the public sector, and in 1920 female white-collar workers outnumbered their male counterparts, constituting 53.6 percent of all white-collar workers.[22] As in most other

53.6 percent of all white-collar workers.[22] As in most other European countries, women dominated in those areas of the public sector where salaries were low, in occupations such as clerks, telephonists, telegraph operators, teachers, and nurses. However, the number of female white-collar workers in private employment was higher still, being especially significant in the retail trade (as clerks and shop assistants), in banking and assurance (as clerks), and in small businesses (as secretaries and clerks).[23]

Finally, it is possible to draw some more general conclusions from official Swedish statistics on the development of the middle class, which shows that the chairman of the Nobel Prize Committee did not have to worry about the decline of the middle class. The number of people with lower middle-class occupations increased during the whole period under study, and both the old and the new *Mittelstand*, as contemporary observers named them, recorded a steady growth.

Social mobility and recruitment

The growth of the lower middle class in Sweden was also characterised by high social mobility. This was particularly visible within the traditional lower middle class occupations. Swedish retail trades and handicrafts tended to reproduce the wider European pattern of insecurity. Mobility was widespread between different petit bourgeois occupations and between the petite bourgeoisie and other classes in society. On the one hand, there was a steady stream of people moving in and out of the occupations that were the core of the petite bourgeoisie: those who had saved a small amount of capital, making it possible for them to open a small workshop or a retail outlet, and those returning to the status of wage earner (or worse) in the wake of business failure. Secondly, people who at one time were master artisans and owners of small workshops, might later leave production for retailing, thus effectively transforming themselves into shopkeepers. Thirdly, there were those who managed to increase their capital and extend their business. Small shops grew bigger and became part of larger complexes of shops, chain stores or department stores, or the small workshop grew and became a small factory. These people often left the restricted world of small business for the social milieu of the bourgeoisie proper.[24]

In the expanding sawmills of northern Sweden, the economic problems faced by shopkeepers and master artisans were similar to those of their European cousins. In the last few decades of the nineteenth century, many shopkeepers and master artisans were forced by bankruptcy to wind up their careers as small businessmen. Between 1874 and 1885 the local court of Härnösand dealt with 145 bankruptcies, 45 per cent of them involving shopkeepers, 19 per cent master artisans and 10 per cent factory owners and wholesalers. In comparison with other occupations, shopkeepers and master artisans represented a much higher percentage than their proportion of the population as a whole.[25] However, we do not know why these master artisans and shopkeepers went bankrupt. In his study of the town of Eskilstuna, the Swedish historian Bo Öhngren reveals that, during the economic depression in the 1880s, many shopkeepers and master artisans did not pay their taxes and therefore went bankrupt. When times were hard they were unable to convert their assets into cash.[26] In the town of Örebro in central Sweden, small business was characterised by the same high degree of instability throughout the nineteenth century. Between 1830 and 1840, almost 50 per cent of retail shops and workshops closed down within 10 years of their opening, and 30 years later the figures were much the same. The prospects were no better at the turn of the century. Local population registers often bear an annotation indicating that a small businessman had become impoverished.[27] By comparison, in Härnösand about 70 per cent of businesses were founded only 6 years before the year of bankruptcy, and 25 per cent of businesses were only 2 years old before the shopkeeper or master artisan went out of business.[28] In Örebro between 40 and 50 per cent of retailers ceased to trade within 10 years.[29] One could argue that shopkeepers and master artisans appearing in the bankruptcy files were a specific group, different from those who did not appear in the registers. It is important to recognise that those who went bankrupt constituted an important part of the total number of shopkeepers and master artisans, and therefore it is possible to look at bankruptcies as a reflection of the economic conditions in the retail trade and handicrafts in the late nineteenth century. The French historian Jean-Claude Martin argues that high rates of bankruptcy were the norm. Almost any small businessman could be affected.[30] In Sweden, shopkeepers and master artisans often reopened their businesses only a couple of years after bankruptcy. The life cycle of the small businessman was rarely smooth and was often punctuated by sudden changes, making the future unpredictable.

What little is known about the pattern of recruitment to handicrafts suggests that it was more occupationally cohesive than the retail trade. Part of the reason for this was probably to do with its inheritance from the guild age, which had created a specific artisan milieu where the artisan family and its employees constituted a social and cultural unit. Sons did not necessarily go into the same trades as their fathers, but it was likely that the family tradition was continued in an artisan occupation of some kind.[31]

However, the recruitment pattern in the retail trade was different. The social background differed very much and people who opened shops were drawn from various occupations.[32] The occupation of shopkeeper seems only seldom to have been handed down from one generation to another, but as has been shown from a study of the town of Sundsvall, sons of shopkeepers who managed to establish themselves as shopkeepers were generally successful.[33] It is likely that the expansion of the town into a large centre for trade and commerce in the sawmill district opened up possibilities that never presented themselves in other towns in Sweden. Nearly 40 per cent of the sons of master artisans, not counting those who ended up as journeymen, remained in the same trade and they seldom left the handicrafts. Sundsvall's expansion into a major commercial centre also meant that public and private employment grew rapidly. Therefore, remaining in the same economic sector as their fathers was easy for the sons of white-collar workers. The expansion also created excellent opportunities for occupational and social advancement. In Sundsvall, sons of clerks often advanced into the upper echelons of white-collar employment. At the same time, the white-collar sector served to rescue those from other middle class occupations who would otherwise have experienced social degradation.[34]

Politics and ideology

The political pattern has to be analysed from two different perspectives, the national and the local. First, on the national level, where there were no political parties before the beginning of the twentieth century, the politics of the lower middle class was closely related to the local community. The economic and social position of the lower middle class, especially master artisans and shopkeepers, gave them a unique political platform as long as the guild system existed. Their political power was particularly strong in local politics. In a majority of the towns in Sweden, master artisans and shopkeepers dominated the political constituency, and their associations functioned as important political pressure groups. The political influence of master artisans and shopkeepers was a consequence of the liberties of the guild system. The abolition of the guilds and the introduction of free trade did not immediately change the political power of the small entrepreneurs. On a national level the abolition of the parliament of four estates did not mean a significant change or radicalisation of national politics. Conservative and socially reactionary forces were afforded new scope for their activities in the lower chamber, which was directly elected by the people. It is not surprising that conservatism was widespread there since the franchise was restricted to only about 25 per cent of the adult male population, and was based on annual income. Membership of the upper chamber was by indirect election that involved meeting the minimum income and property requirements enforced at elections to county and municipal councils. In consequence, the wealthy groups were strongly overrepresented in the upper chamber, a disproportion that was even more pronounced since affluence was required for inclusion on the electoral rolls. The right to vote in elections to the lower chamber was dependent upon possession of an annual income of at least 800 crowns or the ownership of real property valued at not less than 1,000 crowns.[35]

The struggle for parliamentary reform during the nineteenth century was intended to create more room for economic liberalism and for those groups that sustained the new industrialisation. It also opened the doors to political advancement for the landowning farmers, while many small businessmen and white-collar workers were excluded from parliament, as was the great majority of the working class. The significance of the reforms for these groups was that those who wielded economic power over them became able to exercise more political power too.

Among the lower middle class there were various groups that could only seldom earn enough to meet the income requirements. Bo Öhngren has shown that in 1885 the median income for shoemakers in the town of Eskilstuna was 700 crowns, for carpenters 600 crowns, and for masons 500 crowns. At the top of the income scale were painters with a median income of 2,000 crowns and bakers with 1,500 crowns.[36] In the town of Helsingborg, Gregor Paulsson noted that the medium income of an master artisan was 600 crowns, or the same as a skilled worker.[37] Within the handicrafts, large groups were excluded from the franchise, including some of the biggest such as shoemakers and carpenters.

However, much more important political institutions for the lower middle class were the local councils. When new political reforms were introduced at the beginning of the 1860s, a majority of the urban political councils were dominated by master artisans and shopkeepers. In the towns of Norrköping and Linköping, 50 per cent of the members of the local councils were small businessmen.[38] The same pattern can be seen in other small towns such as Östersund, Jönköping and Nyköping.[39] In bigger cities, with much more differentiated social and economic structures, small businessmen had to give way to other social groups. In Gothenburg, the city council consisted of 50 members, of whom only 7 were small businessmen, while a majority (29) were wholesalers.[40] However, the political power of master artisans and shopkeepers began to decline during the 1870s. In Östersund, the number of small businessmen on the municipal council decreased by 50 percent between 1862 and 1877, and by 50 percent again between 1877 and 1911. A similar pattern appeared in the town of Enköping.[41] It was first of all the number of master artisans that decreased, but shopkeepers too disappeared in favour of representatives of big industry, wholesalers and senior officials.[42] In the town of Gävle, there were eight master artisans on the municipal council in 1862. Two decades later there were only two or three master artisans.[43]

Despite these changes, urban political development in Sweden during the last decades of the nineteenth century did not result in the lower middle class lacking political representation. In many towns they were over-represented in proportion to their share of the population. There were many reasons for this. The income requirement played a significant role, and this was particularly apparent during economic crises. During the 1880s many shopkeepers and master artisans were disqualified because they were liable to income tax, and their problem was bad liquidity.[44] When times were hard it was difficult to turn assets like claims and properties into cash, and bankruptcy was often the only way to solve the problem. In the town of Sundsvall in northern Sweden, 35 per cent of shopkeepers, and 17 per cent of master artisans went bankrupt in 1894 because they had not paid their municipal or state taxes.[45] For many master artisans and shopkeepers, exclusion from participation in parliamentary elections because of low incomes could be compensated for by the fact that they owned a property, which included both a dwelling and a shop or workshop. The ownership of property among small entrepreneurs had other political dimensions, affording them a favourable position in local society. Most house owners were organised into local house-owner associations [*fastighetsägarföreningar*] which influenced local politics in many ways, particularly when it came to questions relating to taxes, keeping public places clean, and refuse collection and disposal.[46] At the end of the nineteenth century around 3 per cent of the electorate based their franchise on house ownership. In small towns the proportion could be much higher, which can be seen from the examples of Gävle and Enköping in 1892, where 14 and 12 per cent respectively based their franchise on house ownership.[47] In the nine house-owner associations that were founded before the turn of the century, small entrepreneurs occupied a very dominant position. Some 42 per cent were master artisans and 16 per cent were shopkeepers.[48] In Stockholm, too, small businessmen were dominant among house owners. In 1876, 36 per cent were master artisans and 13 per cent were shopkeepers.[49] However, it is important to ask whether the lower middle class formed political parties of their own or if they joined already existing political parties.

The political role of the lower middle class, particularly master artisans and shopkeepers, reveals different patterns. During the early days of the house-owner associations there were close political links to the political left, that is liberalism. The Swedish political scientist, Pär-Erik Back, argues that house-owner associations were based on a liberal tradition, the freedom to form associations, which was a consequence of the disintegration of the guild system. House-owner associations also had close links to the working class, and they were engaged in one of the most debated questions at the end of the nineteenth century, namely 'the issue of the working class'. In the local house-owner association in Stockholm, members often discussed questions of public health, suspensions of inn and tavern licences, and improvements in working conditions, which indicates that these associations formed by sections of the lower middle class had their roots in the Swedish reform movement after 1848.[50]

However, the situation in Stockholm was not unique, and close political links to the political left of the day could also be seen in towns such as Gävle, Malmö and Helsingborg.[51] The radicalism of these associations seems to have evaporated around the turn of the century. Instead they showed a much more conservative outlook. One major reason for this political conversion is probably the increasing political power of the labour movement and the emergence of the Social Democratic Party. The Social Democrats demanded, among other things, that there ought to be restrictions on property ownership, which was fundamental to large segments of the lower middle class. These clashes between the middle class and the working class follows a European political pattern, which meant that the lower middle class, and small businessmen in particular, abandoned liberalism because of the increasing power and demands of the working class movement.[52]

There also existed other political alternatives for house-owner associations where they could articulate their political interests. It was very common for house-owner associations to have their own lists of candidates at the municipal elections. This did not mean that all the candidates were house owners, but at least it meant that the candidates favoured the political demands of the house owners. It was also common for a local house-owner association to work in concert with other local associations, such as associations of retailers or master artisans, in municipal elections. In parliamentary elections they often used the same political strategies, with the difference that the candidates did not necessarily have to be house owners. The political role of house-owner associations was only one aspect of the political dimension of the lower middle class. A similar function was also played by local associations of retailers and craftsmen. It is important to note that the borderline between these associations is very difficult to delineate in a clear way. Many small businessmen might be members of two or more of these associations.

There were also many instances where the lower middle class reacted very strongly to the politics of the established political parties in municipal elections. Master artisans and shopkeepers in particular reacted strongly when their interests did not occupy a central position on local political agendas. At the turn of the century, small businessmen in retailing and the handicrafts often sought a more prominent role in local politics. In an appeal to its members in the town of Jönköping in 1906, the local association of shopkeepers said: 'When we see how other groups in the town act to get their people elected, it is necessary for the shopkeepers to do the same'.[53] A similar appeal was made from the town of Umeå in a letter from the local association of shopkeepers to the association of master artisans and the house-owner association, although the retail association in Umeå also put forward its own political standpoint: 'A majority of shopkeepers, master artisans and house owners are not satisfied with the narrow and radical policy of the Liberals, and we do not want to follow the Conservatives and their reactionary policy. The centre is the true and natural political place for the burghers'.[54]

After the turn of the century, it became more common for small entrepreneurs to argue for a more active political role in municipal elections and local urban politics, and master artisans and retailers were also supported by their national organisations in this. At the same time there existed an opinion among small businessmen that it was necessary to keep a low political profile, which meant that a more active political role had to be characterised by restraint. The ideal would be that shopkeepers and master artisans would be neutral with regard to the political ideologies of the Conservatives and the Social Democrats. In the journal *Hantverks-*

och Industritidning, which represented small industry and the handicrafts, the editor O Th Huldén opined: 'Without having to make their associations into local political organisations or national campaigning organisations, the associations of master artisans should not neglect the importance of questions related to local and national politics'.[55] In both this statement and that from the retail association of Umeå can be seen a view of the role of the small businessman in contemporary society that was very typical for Europe after the turn of the century.

Members of the lower middle class looked upon themselves as constituting a moderate political force. They argued that the main conflict in society was between the two extremes, the working class and large-scale capital. The *Mittelstand* (sometimes the broader concept of middle class was used) stood in the middle between these two protagonists serving as a cohesive force supporting the existing social order and as a guarantor of society's development in a sound and positive direction. White-collar workers held a similar opinion, that their place in society was in the middle, between the employers and the workers.[56] This kind of position was very typical of the petite bourgeoisie at that time, and was often expressed in continental Europe during this period.[57] There was a belief that if the right economic and social direction were followed, that is to say, if regard was paid to the demands of small businessmen, the foundations for a stable economic, social and political development would be laid in which class conflict had no place. In 1908 this point of view was expressed in an illuminating way in the monthly journal published by *Sveriges allmänna handelsförening* [General Trading Association of Sweden]. Its editor, Conrad Palm, like many other shopkeepers and independent artisans, saw the small businessman as the core of the middle class, writing that, 'The *Mittelstand* is perhaps the most noble group that sustains society. It receives and deflects blows from both sides, as befits a buffer. However, in addition the *Mittelstand* and the middle class as a whole hold the balance in society politically, socially and economically. The economic adaptability of the *Mittelstand* enables it to survive crises better than both large-scale capital and the masses of the industrial working class. The *Mittelstand* is the group within the population that saves most and its savings constitute the basis for any country's capital accumulation and resources. The political and social utility of an affluent and self-confident middle class is probably beyond dispute.'[58]

For Palm, as for many other spokesmen of the Swedish *Mittelstand* movement, the *Mittelstand* was a model of economic and social self-discipline. It was the only group in society that was not imprisoned within the system of unrestrained laissez-faire capitalism and that did not treat class antagonisms as of central importance. Instead, it represented the healthy core element in Swedish society, since it was the social group that stood for the harmonious development of society without class conflict. The upper class and the working class were, for the representatives of the ideas of the *Mittelstand* movement, the greatest threats to the calm and sensible development of society. The criticisms that the lower middle class, in particular the traditional small businessmen in retailing and handicrafts, directed at the upper and working classes often assumed a very sharp tone. O.T. Huldén argued that class antagonisms created unrest within society, leading to moral decline. He went on to say that 'when the existing form of society breaks down because of an over-cultivated upper class that has degenerated through its love of pleasure and a ruthless lower class that is devoid of non-material interests, salvation will come from the sound, healthy core of society, the true middle class.'[59]

Huldén's statement also had a direct political significance. The *Mittelstand* was seen as a group that sustained the state and society, that was neutral in the struggle between capital and labour and that was virtually immune to socialist currents of thought and other threats to society. The *Mittelstand* acted with the best interests of society at heart. Shopkeepers and master artisans saw themselves as sustaining society because they belonged to an old tradition with its roots in the past, whereas capital and labour were the products of modern industrial society. History was often used to demonstrate that the *Mittelstand* had been and ought to be an important force in society.[60] However, by presenting this historical argument shopkeepers and master artisans faced a serious problem, since the *Mittelstand* also included within it the white-collar workers, and they were clearly also the products of modern industrial society. However, this division within the lower middle class does not seem to have been acknowledged. On the other hand, as been argued earlier, there existed among the old lower middle class of shopkeepers and master artisans an opinion that white-collar workers formed the same social stratum as themselves.[61]

The historical argument presented by shopkeepers and master artisans was often referred to as a model for society and other classes in society. The ideology that emerges was closely linked to the nineteenth century picture of the family as the cornerstone of society. In this context, the family was symbolised by the small master artisans and small shopkeepers and their independence was necessary in order for society to rest on the best and most secure foundations. A good example from the time just before the outbreak of the First World War can be found in *Svensk Hantverkstidning* [Swedish Journal of Handicrafts], where the very typical strong nationalistic feelings of the small businessmen are also apparent. 'The dominant role that craftsmen and artisans played in the social life of earlier times has long since passed to other groups in society. However, artisans still constitute a considerable and important factor in society. The old, honourable handicrafts have to be sure given way to large-scale industry, but they continue to occupy a position by the side of industry that fully demonstrates their value and indispensability. The handicrafts create interest among its practitioners in their work and the success of their work, and awaken a love for their workshops and for their hearths and homes. Within society, the handicrafts serve to preserve honourable, genuine labour and a love of neighbourhood and fatherland.'[62] In 1906 O Th Huldén made a similar statement, when he said that 'among the Swedish master artisans there is a strong feeling of national sentiment.'[63]

The nationalistic sentiments of master artisans and shopkeepers manifested themselves in a number of different ways. It was clearly expressed in connection with the propaganda against door-to-door peddling. The peddlers were often identified with foreign, and especially Jewish, trading interests, and this evoked not only a generally unfavourable attitude to foreigners but also strongly anti-semitic currents of thought. Such nationalistic and anti-semitic attitudes were particularly prevalent among shopkeepers.[64] From the eighteen-eighties onwards the nationalism of the shopkeepers was linked with demands for a strongly protectionist policy designed to shield domestic trade from the import of foreign goods. From the eighteen-eighties onwards shopkeepers constituted an important source of support for conservative groups in the Swedish parliament which pursued a protectionist policy under the slogan 'Sweden for the Swedes'.[65] The foremost spokesman for protectionism was Per E. Lithander, who was both a member of parliament and the chairman of *Sveriges allmänna handelsförening*. Until his death Lithander pursued a strongly nationalistic and anti-semitic campaign in support of the interests of the shopkeepers through many parliamentary motions and pamphlets.[66]

There was also an element of nationalistic thinking in the attacks on consumer co-operatives. Shopkeepers saw consumer co-operatives as part of the Swedish labour movement, since they had developed out of the consumer co-operatives set up by the workers in the middle of the nineteenth century. However, there were representatives among the shopkeepers who went further in their agitation and argued that consumer co-operatives were part of the attempt of the international labour movement to spread socialism in Sweden. Consumer co-operatives served as a vanguard of the Social Democratic Party in its efforts to obtain political power in Sweden.[67] This was, of course, a considerable exaggeration, but this line of argument played an important part in the attempts of shopkeepers to gain a hearing for their demands. In all probability this line of argument was drawn from foreign models. Certainly the debate within the petite bourgeoisie on the continent was influenced to some degree by the threat of what was called 'the unholy alliance between socialism and Jewish capital'.[68]

It is clear that the traditional lower middle-class groups around the turn of the century experienced difficulties in obtaining a response to their political demands. Their spokesmen often argued that their interests were disregarded both by the state authorities and within the political decision-making process. Small shopkeepers in particular believed that their influence over developments within their own sector of the economy was very slight. Their attacks were directed both at existing economic organisations (such as the chambers of commerce) and at national and local political authorities. In 1908, writing in the journal *Meddelanden från Sveriges minuthandlares riksförbund* [Communications from the Swedish Retailers' Association], a shopkeeper argued that the failure to give shopkeepers an opportunity of influencing the development of the retailing sector was to be regarded as a virtual declaration that they were incapable of managing their own affairs.[69] Shopkeepers like many other small businessmen wanted to take care of their own interests, but the reality was very different. As in so many other contexts, it was for the shopkeepers a question of morality and justice. Economic and political influence over the development of the retailing sector had in their view been placed in the hands of groups that lacked experience and knowledge of the special problems the sector experienced. The position of the small shopkeeper was weak, not least within the chambers of commerce that were established around the turn of the century. As the *Malmö detaljistförening* (Malmö Retailers' Association) pointed out, it was necessary to establish special retailers' organisations on the French and German models if retailers were to gain any real influence. The chambers of commerce were primarily spokesmen for the large-scale traders.[70]

The weak political position of the lower middle class at the beginning of the twentieth century continued into the following decades, and when the Social Democrats came into power. One of the major obstacles for the shopkeepers' associations, and other associations of small businessmen, was the fact that they represented only a small number of all businessmen. In 1918 about 9,600 shopkeepers were members of *Sveriges Köpmannaförbund* [National Organisation of Swedish Retailers], or about 20 per cent of all retailers. During the next 10 years the number of members rose to slightly more than 11,000, and continued to gradually increase through the early 1930s to about 15,000 in 1936. However, the percentage of organised shopkeepers seems to have been almost the same from the end of the First World War up to the middle of the 1930s. Local associations of small businessmen often enjoyed a far greater level of support than that of the national organisation.[71]

The Social Democrats introduced new procedures into the decision-making process, which were an important element in what later came to be regarded as 'the Swedish model'.[72] The Social Democrats introduced a system where different interest groups were represented in all major official reports preceding parliamentary and governmental decisions; that is different interest groups co-operated with the state. Traditionally, state commissions and committees were dominated by experts, which in a sense favoured the argument of the traditional lower middle class. Instead the interests of the citizens in the administration of the state were guaranteed by the influence of organised interest groups. However, for the representatives of small business in particular, their influence in the decision-making process did not change during the 1920s and 1930s. The reason for this was that they were squeezed between different interest groups, and at the same time very few members of parliament represented small business.[73] Because of historical links and a common ideology, the trade unions, the co-operative movement and big industry were favoured by the Social Democratic government, while the representatives of small business could only find support among certain segments of the bourgeois parties. Other parts of the lower middle class seem to have been more successful in their co-operation with the state and the Social Democratic governments, at least after 1920 when their organisations were recognised after decades of trade union struggle.[74] At the same time certain groups within the white-collar workforce, and especially school teachers, were over-represented in the second chamber of the *Riksdag*. However, the relationship between the lower middle class and the state remains an area to which historians in Sweden have paid little attention.

Very few political attempts were made to organise the middle class. At the end of the First World War the Centre Party was formed after a split within the Conservative Party. According to the Centre Party, the middle class was neglected by the Conservatives, and instead they had begun to join the Social Democrats. However, the Centre Party had a very vague definition of the middle class, and it seems as if they were most eager to organise farmers and other small entrepreneurs. Another organisation, *Medelklassens politiska organisation* [Political Organisation of the Middle Class] was founded on more liberal grounds. The organisation proclaimed that the middle class was squeezed between large-scale capital and the working class, and while the wages of the workers were increasing, the middle class had begun to proletarianise. In 1918, *Medelklassens riksförbund* [National Organisation of the Middle Class] was founded by Alf von Löwenstern, and according to its regulations it would be 'a politically neutral organisation for the benefit of the economic middle class and for the protection of its social and economic interests.'[75] This organisation too had a very vague idea of its electorate. They talked about those with middle incomes, who during the years of economic crises had 'sunk deeply under the income level of the worker'.[76] The organisation seems to have been primarily a local political organisation in Stockholm, and its members could be found among senior officials and businessmen, but not among people with lower middle-class occupations. All these attempts to organise the middle class failed, and the organisations lasted only a couple of years. According to Tom Söderberg, the foundation of these middle-class organisations was a response to the disinclination of the bourgeois parties to organise their parties on a class basis, and therefore identify themselves with the lower classes in society.[77] The idea of a specifically middle class politics did not totally die out, and at the end of the 1920s new attempts were made to create a middle-class party based on the interest organisations of shopkeepers, master artisans and house owners, as had the *Mittelstand* movement at the beginning of the century. However, even though these attempts came at a time when corporatist ideas were popular and widespread both in Swedish society and on the European continent, lower middle-class groups seemed to have been difficult to organise outside the traditional political parties. The attempts that were made to organise the lower middle class politically had one thing in common. They happened at a time when Sweden had experienced severe economic crises characterised by high inflation and falling salaries among a majority of lower middle-class occupations.[78]

The relationship between the Social Democrats and classes other than the working class has received little attention. However, from its very beginning the Social Democratic Party was never a socially exclusive labour party, and never really recognised or responded to the fact of the remarkably high degree of union organisation among Swedish white-collar workers compared with that among the workers who formed the majority of their supporters. The Swedish sociologist Göran Therborn has put forward three hypotheses about this relationship. First, he argues that there have been strong links between the Social Democratic Party and the salaried employees movement, but even if the Social Democrats have been open to other groups in society, they have been labelled a labour party. Secondly, the social integration of the large classes, the tradition of the Swedish people standing together against the powers-that-be, has been expressed politically in ways other than voting for the Social Democrats. The most accessible alternative for the lower middle class has been the development of and support for similar social democratic policies in other parties, which means that the Agrarian Party, the Liberal Party and even the Conservatives could be viewed as social reform parties. Thirdly, Therborn claims that the Swedish party system has provided the radical middle class with a very similar alternative to social democracy, and the Liberal Party in particular has gained political support among white-collar workers.[79]

Popular movements and the lower middle class

The analysis of politics and ideology shows that up to 1909 when universal suffrage for men was introduced, large segments of the lower middle class were excluded from the franchise because the right to vote was tied to an individual's income or property ownership. However, there existed organisations (namely the popular movements) where the lower middle class could find a place to express its political demands, and where its members could meet people from other classes of society who had experienced the same lack of political influence. In this way, the lower middle class became involved in a broader social and political community. The popular movements, and particularly the temperance movement and the free churches, became a melting pot where the lower middle class was confronted with other social classes, especially the working class. Therefore, lower middle-class values and ideas could influence working-class ideology and vice versa. Religion and temperance served as catalysts for different class interests, and at the same time allowed traditional social relations to continue between the lower middle class and the working class. The popular movements have played a central role in modern Swedish history from the time they were founded in the middle of the nineteenth century onwards. At the turn of the century 15 per cent of the Swedish population above the age of 15 were members of the free churches, the temperance movement or the labour movement, and at the beginning of the First World War this had increased to 25 per cent. The main objects of the popular movements, beside their idealistic activities, were the struggle for democracy and equality. They wanted to change society in a radical way. Their demands were many, freedom of assembly, freedom of expression and social reforms, but most of all they wanted universal suffrage to achieve these goals.[80]

It is obvious that lower middle-class groups increased their share of membership in the popular movements, which might mean that lower middle-class political conditions became more and more identified with those of the working class in late nineteenth-century Swedish society. In the town of Karlskoga, the number of master artisans in the local free church increased between 1880 and 1900 from 13.7 per cent to 22.3 per cent, the number of shopkeepers increased from 3.1 per cent in 1880 to 20.3 per cent in 1890, and the number of white-collar workers increased from 8 per cent to 15 per cent between 1880 and 1890, but their share decreased from then until the turn of the century.[81] The lower middle class seems to have been over-represented among the members of the free churches compared to their proportion of the population. In the town of Uppsala in 1880, over 50 per cent of the members in two of the larger congregations of free churches belonged to the lower middle class, while the lower middle class share of the population was around 20 per cent. The same pattern could be found in the towns of Eskilstuna and Karlstad.[82] Within the temperance movement the lower middle class also played a significant role, which can be seen from its share of the membership. However, local temperance associations show very different figures, although the number of master artisans was always high. In Uppsala's local association of the International Order of Good Templars, 72 per cent of the members were master artisans between 1884 and 1900, and in the Swedish Order of Good Templars in Karlstad, 31 per cent of the members were master artisans.[83]

The political influence of the popular movements increased both in local communities and at a national level during and after the 1880s. Already in 1911 almost 20 per cent of the members of the second chamber in the *Riksdag* belonged to a free church, and two thirds of the politicians were members of the temperance movement.[84] In local elections, the role of the popular movements was related to the strength of the local free churches and the temperance movement. In towns where the local associations had many members their political power increased. However, as long as the franchise was based on income many members of the popular movements were excluded from voting. Instead they had to join forces with other groups in society, even the more traditional political ones. By doing so it was possible to increase their influence and get their members elected. It might seem a little odd that the traditional political forces welcomed these popular movements, but they strongly believed in a corporatist society, and therefore thought that the new groups should be represented.[85]

Family and the urban environment

The life of both the old and the new Swedish lower middle classes was closely related to the urban environment from the middle of the nineteenth century to the Second World War. However, it was a constantly changing environment that influenced the different occupational groups constituting the lower middle class. During the second half of the nineteenth century, changes were noticeable for small businessmen in handicrafts and retailing, and particularly visible was the breakdown of the traditional social milieu within the handicrafts. In many Swedish towns the master artisans had to move from their old artisans' *quartiers* in the centre of the town to more outlying areas which had been built to receive the masses of urban newcomers. Those master artisans who still lived in the old quarters also experienced a growth in urban immigration. Many urban immigrants, especially the workers, settled down in the old artisans' quarters, which meant that the social structure became much more heterogeneous. In the new artisans' quarters on the outskirts of the towns population density greatly increased. In smaller Swedish towns the number of inhabitants in each house was as high as that in many European cities.[86] In the quarter called *Denmark* in the town of Helsingborg, where a majority of the houses were built during the 1860s and 1870s, in 1886 there were 25 houses shared between 150 households, meaning that each house lodged 6 families. The houses were two-storey buildings divided into four flats. The flats were small , and most had two rooms and a kitchen. So in fact, there was more than one family living in each flat.[87] In this particular quarter in Helsingborg, most people were workers and artisans, while only 12 households were those of shopkeepers and lower white-collar workers, and 12 were those of widows and unmarried women. Despite their changes of location, the new artisans' quarters still had something in common with the old ones. They kept their popular outlook. People knew each other, and their social and economic conditions were almost the same. It also shows that people within the lower middle class, both old and new, occupied the same geographical space in the town. Gregor Paulsson noticed that the income structure in the new quarters was rather homogeneous.[88]

The transformation of urban housing also changed the household structure particularly among shopkeepers and master artisans. In most Swedish towns the number of people living in the households of shopkeepers and master artisans declined. In Örebro the average number of people living in artisan households decreased from 5.7 in 1830 to 4.4 in 1890. The same process took place among shopkeepers' households. The average number of people living in the households of shopkeepers went down from 6.4 to 5.4 during the same period. The decrease in the number of people living in the households of small businessmen was first of all caused by a reduction in the number of employees living in the households of their employers. That is to say, the reduction was caused to a certain extent by the fact that other elements of the lower middle class, such as bookkeepers and shop assistants, stopped living in their employers' houses.[89] Instead they continued to live with their parents, or rented rooms in the town. Employees in the retail trade were also often unmarried.[90] Another reason for the decline in the households of small entrepreneurs was that it became much more common for the work place to become separated from the home. Instead many small shopkeepers and master artisans worked in rented premises in the town centre while living in the outskirts in small flats that had no room for anyone outside the family.

Urban population growth in late nineteenth-century Sweden also started a process where the lower middle class, especially shopkeepers and master artisans, became involved in financing the building of new houses. Especially among the minor house owners there were a lot of artisans and shopkeepers, but many people with white-collar occupations were also house-owners. In the town of Malmö in southern Sweden, the lower middle class owned about 50 per cent of all flats at the end of the nineteenth century, and in 1924 30 per cent of all flats were still owned by the lower middle class. White-collar workers also seem to have increased their ownership more than the traditional groups of small businessmen did.[91] The Swedish historian Hans Wallengren has characterised the house-ownership of the lower middle class as 'the social heart of the property structure'.[92] They functioned both as house owners and landlords, and in this capacity they came into close contact with the working-class population, who made up the majority of the tenants.[93] However, there were also many new houses owned by artisans and shopkeepers that lodged people from a rather broad social background. One of the buildings in the Söder quarter of Örebro clearly shows the occupational structure. In 1880 the following people lived in the house: two female servants, two widows, one bandmaster and his wife, one dressmaker with four children and a female servant, one copper-smith journeyman and his wife and three children, one baker with a wife and a female servant and one bookkeeper.[94] The changes in urban housing indicate a separation within the lower middle class, and in particular many shopkeepers disappeared from the traditional artisan quarters. The master artisans seem to have continued to maintain close social relations with the working class, both in the old and new artisan quarters, while shopkeepers more often settled down in the town centres. In many of the new quarters, there was hardly any mercantile business at all. In 1886 for example, in the earlier mentioned *Denmark* quarter of Helsingborg, out of a total population of 516 inhabitants, there was only one shop owned by a hawker. The hawker had a very limited range of goods, and the only things people could buy from him were groceries and salted victuals.[95] If the inhabitants of the quarter wanted to have something else they had to go to the market in the town centre, where the food was also cheaper, especially vegetables and meat.

The family relations of the lower middle class has so far been considered from a spatial point of view, but there were also the demographic aspects of marriages and baptisms. However, the demography of the lower middle class has received little attention from historians. The results that emerge are few, and they concern first of all the small businessmen. In northern Sweden, in the three small towns of Piteå, Haparanda and Härnösand, the marriage patterns varied, but marriages were common both in the group of small entrepreneurs and other parts of the lower middle class and the working class.[96] In the town of Örebro in the centre of Sweden, master artisans seldom married daughters of master artisans, and instead many artisans' wives were daughters with a rural background, either daughters of farmers or daughters of crofters. The same picture emerges when we look at the shopkeepers in Örebro.[97] The towns mentioned were small, but the marriage pattern in Stockholm between 1860 and 1890 was very similar. It is possible to distinguish three groups as the most important in the marriage pattern, namely small businessmen, white-collars workers and the working-class.[98]

The family was the core of the social world of the lower middle class, and particularly for the small businessmen who were characterised by the close links that existed between the spheres of production and reproduction. But there was also a world outside the close world of the family. In order to discern the social relations of the lower middle class family to other classes in society, one way is to study marriage patterns. It is also necessary to look more closely at other issues such as sociability. Who were their friends and with whom did they mingle? Questions like these are often difficult to answer because they concern daily life and few sources are available for the historian to study. We therefore have to look at special occasions in life, when daily routines changed and people came together to celebrate something important and spectacular in their lives. The records of baptisms have been used to reveal such family links. When parents baptised their children they invited a lot of people, who functioned as witnesses and godparents at the baptismal ceremony. The social patterns that existed within the Swedish lower middle class tell us a lot about the existing social relations, and indicate that different occupational groups within the old middle class had very different social relations. The social relations of the shopkeepers were very distinct. A majority of the witnesses at baptisms were shopkeepers (from groups above themselves within the upper bourgeoisie) and white-collar workers, while social relations with the working class seem to be missing.[99] Historians have argued that the close links to the upper bourgeoisie reflected a common mentality among shopkeepers that retailing was a specific step on the social ladder.[100] In France, for example, many of the founders of Parisian department stores had their social origins within the working class, which made people believe that retailing was open to all underprivileged groups.[101] In the small Swedish town of Piteå in northern Sweden, shopkeepers often invited people from the stratum above them when they baptised their children, a particularly common practice when the children were boys.[102] The latter observation is interesting because it tells us something about economic strategy. Boys represented continuity in the family business. The ideal situation was that the son would inherit the shop and therefore it was important to establish strong links with groups in local society able to support the family business in times of economic depression. The shopkeeper family's dependence on small businesses could be one reason for a rapprochement between the families and the social groups above them. To have close friends among the bourgeoisie or the wider community of business was one way of securing necessary capital, and to construct social and economic network relations outside close family relations was strategic for a family business.[103]

There is also significant evidence from other parts of Sweden that economic ties existed between retailers and the bourgeoisie. A number of rural retailers continued their businesses after bankruptcy thanks to the support of large sawmill owners. It was in the interest of the sawmill owners to have a shop close to the factory.[104] The great number of white-collar workers invited to the baptisms of shopkeepers' children seems to have a rather simple explanation. The lower white-collar workers were often employed in the business of the shopkeeper as bookkeepers or shop-assistants. It reflects the social conditions that existed in the retail business in the middle of the nineteenth century. They were characterised by paternal relations or as a wholesaler in Stockholm described these relations: 'Then, during the good old days the employee was regarded almost as a member of the shopkeeper's family, he lived in his house, he sat at his table, he mingled in his circles, married the shopkeeper's daughter, became his partner, and sometimes succeeded him in the business.'[105]

The presence of witnesses at the baptisms of master artisans' children indicates a totally different pattern from what we have seen so far. Master artisans dominate, but the picture reveals that their social relations to other social groups in local society were extensive. Between 10 and 15 per cent of the witnesses belonged to social groups above themselves, 30 per cent of the witnesses were either shopkeepers or lower white-collar workers, and 20 per cent of the witnesses were workers.[106] However, those registered as workers were actually to a large extent journeymen or apprentices, which means that representation from the handicrafts was much stronger than the results seem at first to indicate. Traditionally, as stated earlier, the handicrafts had developed a strong and paternal culture within the guilds, where journeymen and apprentices were seen as a part of the master artisan's household during the time they educated themselves to become masters. It seems as if master artisans did not have any distinct social barriers between themselves and other groups in local society. One reason for that might be the fact that for generations they had held a strong social and political position in urban areas, and before industrialisation began in Sweden in the early nineteenth century they also played an important economic role. The life experience, the life cycle of independent masters, also favoured close social relations with the working class. As former apprentices and journeymen they had experienced the life of the working class, and becoming a master artisan was a form of social mobility, but they still were working with their own hands.

In the middle of the century the number of white-collar workers was small. Most of them were employed either in the retail or wholesale trade as bookkeepers and shop assistants, or they were employed in local public services or by the state in the customs service or the Post Office. Lower white-collar workers seem to have had a similar social pattern among the witnesses to that of master artisans. Witnesses from their own social group dominated, but there existed no firm barriers against other social groups. However, a closer look at specific baptisms shows that the witnesses were often linked to the specific work place of the father of the baptised child, which meant that fellow white-collar workers both above and below themselves were invited to the baptismal ceremony. But there also existed strong social links within the same trade, and between different trades. This was often the case when a shop assistant was the father of the baptised child, or when customs officers were invited to the baptism. For example, the customs officer Nils Winberg and his wife Helena baptised their new born child on the 12th of December 1854. Among the witnesses were Nils Winberg's colleague, a customs officer, his superior the customs collector, a shipping-agent, a clerk and a bookkeeper probably also employed in the customs service, and finally a sheriff. These different occupations indicate the close social and work relations that had emerged within the customs service, but also those social relations that had grown from close work relations, the daily personal co-operation and contacts between the customs service, the police, and the shipping trade.[107]

Conclusion

During the hundred years from the middle of the nineteenth century to the outbreak of the Second World War, Swedish society experienced a major change from an agrarian to an industrial society. The major processes behind this change, the growth of industry, the bureaucratisation of the state administration and local administration, population changes and urbanisation also favoured a growth of these social groups that we associate with the concept of the middle class. However, these groups never formed a significant social class nationally, and only to a minor extent at the local level. They were a part of the foundation of modern Swedish society, but they were silent, and other social groups, the bourgeoisie and, later in the first half of the nineteenth century, the working class and industrialists, played the leading roles. Large segments of the emerging social class of white-collar workers joined the working class and the Social Democratic Party at a relatively early stage, and Sweden never experienced a political mobilisation of the lower middle class of the kind that took place in many other European countries.

Notes

[1] *Les Prix Nobel en 1923*, Stockholm 1924, pp. 11-12.
[2] Tom Söderberg, *Den namnlösa medelklassen. Socialgrupp två i det gamla svenska samhället intill 1770-talet*, Stockholm 1956, p. 7. See also August Strindberg, *The*

Son of a Servant (trans. Claud Field), London 1913. It is worth mentioning that the English translation of the book title neglects the fact that the original Swedish word *tjänstekvinna* means female servant.

[3] Söderberg, *Den namnlösa*. According to Söderberg, the term 'middle class' appeared in Britain in 1812. Söderberg's reference was probably the quotation from the *Examiner* of 31st August 1812, which appeared in the 1933 edition of *The Oxford English Dictionary*. However, the second edition from 1989 has a reference dateing the term 'middle class' back to 1766. *The Oxford English Dictionary*, 2nd ed., vol. IX., Oxford 1989. The 1812 reference is also mentioned in Geoffrey Crossick, 'From gentlemen to residuum: languages of social description in Victorian Britain', in Penelope J. Corfield (ed.), *Language, History and Class*, Oxford 1991, at p. 151.

[4] Söderberg, *Den namnlösa*, p. 7.

[5] Pontus Fahlbeck, *Stånd och klasser. En socialpolitisk öfverblick*, Lund 1892, p. 51.

[6] E.H. Thörnberg, *Samhällsklasser och politiska partier i Sverige. Studier och iakttagelser*, Stockholm 1917.

[7] Thörnberg, *Samhällsklasser*, pp. 22-3.

[8] Thörnberg, *Samhällsklasser*, p. 24.

[9] Carl J.F. Ljunggren, 'Medelståndspolitik', *Det Nya Sverige*, 1908, pp. 163-64.

[10] *Meddelanden från Sveriges minuthandlares riksförbund*, no. 12, 1909. This identification of the middle class as two principal groups is similar to the German perception at the end of the eighteenth century. See David Blackbourn, 'The German bourgeoisie: an introduction', in David Blackbourn and Richard J.Evans (eds), *The German Bourgeoisie. Essays on the social history of the German middle class from the late eighteenth to the early twentieth century*, London 1991, at p. 2.

[11] About Swedish schoolteachers see Christina Florin, *Kampen om katedern. Feminiserings- och professionaliseringsprocessen inom den svenska folkskolans lärarkår 1860-1906* (Acta Universitatis Umensis 82), Umeå 1987. Also Tom Ericsson, *Den andra fackföreningsrörelsen. Tjänstemän och tjänstemannaorganisationer i Sverige före första världskriget*, (Forskningsrapporter från historiska institutionen vid Umeå universitet), Umeå 1983; Mats Greiff, *Kontoristen. Från chefens högra hand till proletär*, Södra Sandby 1992; Bengt Nilsson, *Kvinnor i statens tjänst - från biträden till tjänstemän. En aktörsinriktad undersökning av kvinnliga statstjänstemäns organisering, strategier och kamp under 1900-talets första hälft* (Studia Historica Upsaliensia 179), Uppsala 1996.

[12] Ericsson, *Den andra fackföreningsrörelsen*, pp. 95-114.

[13] Tom Ericsson, *Mellan kapital och arbete. Småborgerligheten i Sverige 1850-1914* (Umeå Studies in the Humanities 86), Umeå 1988, pp. 139-40.

[14] Tom Ericsson, 'Cults, Myths and the Swedish Petite Bourgeoisie, 1870-1914', *European History Quarterly* vol. 23, no. 2, 1993, pp. 233-251.

[15] Ericsson, *Mellan kapital och arbete*, p. 141.

[16] Erland Hofsten and Hans Lundström, *Swedish Population History. Main Trends from 1750 to 1970* (Urval. Skriftserie utgiven av statistiska centralbyrån, nummer 8), Stockholm 1976.

[17] Eli F. Heckscher, *An economic history of Sweden* (Harvard economic studies, vol. XCV), Cambridge, Mass. 1954, pp. 209-266; Kurt Samuelsson, *From Great Power to Welfare State. 300 years of Swedish social development*, London 1968, pp. 145-164; Lars Kvarnström, *Män i staten. Stationskarlar och brevbärare i statens tjänst 1897-1937*, Stockholm 1998.

[18] Ericsson, *Mellan kapital och arbete*, pp. 60-68; Samuelsson, *From Great Power*.
[19] Ericsson, *Mellan kapital och arbete*, pp.72-3.
[20] Ericsson, *Mellan kapital och arbeite;* Samuelsson *From Great Power*.
[21] Ericsson, *Den andra fackföreningsrörelsen*, pp. 24-5.
[22] Ericsson, *Den andra fackföreningsrörelsen*, p. 26.
[23] Söderberg, *Den namnlösa*, 342.
[24] Tom Ericsson, 'Social mobility and the urban petite bourgeoisie: Sweden in a European perspective', in Anthony Miles & David Vincent (eds), *Building European Society*, Manchester 1994, p. 165. See specific studies by Heinz-Gerhard Haupt, 'Kleinhändler und Arbeiter in Bremen zwischen 1890 und 1914', *Archive für Sozialgeschichte*, 22, 1982; Alain Faure, 'The grocery trade in nineteenth-century Paris: a fragmented corporation', in *Shopkeepers and Master Artisans in Nineteenth-Century Europe*, Geoffrey Crossick and Heinz-Gerhard Haupt (eds), London 1984; David Crew, *Town in the Ruhr: A Social History of Bochum 1860-1914*, New York 1979; William. H. Sewell, *The Men and Women of Marseille*, 1820-1870, Cambridge 1985; Jean Le Yaouanq, 'La mobilité sociale dans le milieu boutiquer parisien au XIXe siècle', *Le mouvement social*, 108, 1979; Henrik Fode, 'Industrialization and the small-scale businessman: the self-employed craftsman and retailer', in *Commission internationale d'histoire des mouvements sociaux et des structures sociales. Petite entreprise et croissance industrielle dans le monde aux XIXe et XXe siècles*, 1, Paris 1981.
[25] 'Konkursdiarier 1864-1885', Rådstuvurättens arkiv, Härnösands stadsarkiv, Landsarkivet i Härnösand.
[26] Bo Öhngren, *Folk i rörelse. Samhällsutveckling, flyttningsmönster och folkrörelser i Eskilstuna 1870-1900* (Studia Historica Upsaliensia 55), Uppsala 1974, p. 232.
[27] Elsa Lunander, *Borgaren blir företagare. Studier kring ekonomiska, sociala och politiska förhållanden i förändringens Örebro under 1800-talet* (Studia Historica Upsaliensia 155), Uppsala 1988, pp. 100-1.
[28] Ericsson, *Social mobility*, 168. Tom Ericsson, 'Women, family, and small business in late nineteenth century Sweden', *The History of the Family*, vol. 6, 2001.
[29] Lunander, *Borgaren*, p. 100.
[30] Jean-Claude Martin, 'Le commerçant, la faillité et l'historien', *Annales*, 35, 1980.
[31] Anders Brändström & Tom Ericsson, 'Social mobility and social networks. The lower middle class in late nineteenth century Sundsvall', in Anders Brändström & Lars-Göran Tedebrand (eds), *Swedish Urban Demography during Industrialization*, (Report no 10 from the Demographic Database, Umeå University), Umeå 1995.
[32] Ericsson, *Mellan kapital och arbete*, p. 159.
[33] Brändström & Ericsson, *Social mobility and social networks*, p. 266.
[34] Ibid., p. 267.
[35] Samuelsson, *From Great Power*, pp. 138-9.
[36] Öhngren, *Folk i rörelse*, p. 166.
[37] Gregor Paulsson, *Svensk stad. Liv och stil i svenska städer under 1800-talet*, Del 1, Lund 1981, p. 571; Cf. Bertil Johansson, *Social differentiering och kommunalpolitik. Enköping 1863-1919*, (Studia Historica Upsaliensia 59), Uppsala 1974, pp. 32-39; Sven Hedenskog, *Folkrörelserna i Nyköping 1880-1915* (Studia Historica Upsaliensia 59), Uppsala 1973, pp. 20-23.

[38] See for example *Norrköpings historia. Del 5. Tiden 1870-1914*, Bengt Helmfrid & Salomon Kraft (eds), Stockholm 1972, p. 8; *Linköpings historia. Del 4. Tiden 1863-1910*, Linköping 1978, p. 243.

[39] *Östersunds historia. Del 2. 1863-1936*, Janerik Bromé (ed.), Östersund 1936, 33-4; Erik Gullberg & Lennart Ameen (eds), *Jönköpings stads historia, Del 3, Efter kommunalreformen 1863*, Värnamo 1971, pp. 29-30; Uno Westerlund, *Borgarsamhällets upplösning och självstyrelsens utveckling i Nyköping 1810-1880* (Studia Historica Upsaliensia 48), Uppsala 1973, p. 162.

[40] Artur Attman, *Göteborgs stadsfullmäktige 1863-1962, Del 1:1, Göteborg 1863-1913*, Göteborg 1963, pp. 370-373.

[41] Bromé, *Östersunds historia*, pp. 40-1; Johansson, *Social differentiering*, p. 72; Ingrid Åberg, *Förening och politik* (Studia Historica Upsaliensia 69), Uppsala 1975, pp. 78-80; Öhngren, *Folk i rörelse*, p. 231.

[42] Åberg, *Förening och politik;* Öhngren, *Folk i rörelse.*

[43] Åberg, *Förening och politik*, p. 79.

[44] Öhngren, *Folk i rörelse*, p. 166.

[45] Ericsson, *Mellan kapital och arbete*, p. 136.

[46] Pär-Erik Back, *Sammanslutningarnas roll i politiken 1870-1910*, Skellefteå 1967.

[47] Åberg, *Förening och politik*, p. 33; Johansson, *Social differentiering*, p. 24.

[48] Back, *Sammanslutningarnas roll,* p. 105.

[49] Back, *Sammanslutningarnas roll,* p. 107. For the city of Malmö see Hans Wallengren, *Hyresvärlden. Maktrelationer på hyresmarknaden i Malmö ca. 1880-1925*, Ystad 1994, pp. 38-58.

[50] Back, *Sammanslutningarnas roll*, pp. 113-115.

[51] Ibid., pp. 114-116. Compare with Lars Edgren, 'Craftsmen and political consciousness in Sweden 1850-1900', in Tom Ericsson, Jørgen Fink and Jan Eivind Myhre (eds), *The Scandinavian Middle Classes, 1840-1940*, Oslo 2004.

[52] See for example David Blackbourn, 'The Mittelstand in German Society and Politics, 1871-1914', *Social History*, 4, 1977; Philip Nord, 'The Small Shopkeepers' Movement and Politics in France, 1888-1914', in Crossick & Haupt 1984.

[53] Gullberg & Améen, *Jönköpings stads historia*, p. 33.

[54] 'Protokollsbilagor. Bilaga 9. 1910', Umeå fabriks- och hantverksförening, Folkrörelsearkivet i Umeå.

[55] *Hantverks- och Industritidning* 8, 1910.

[56] Ericsson, *Den andra fackföreningsrörelsen.*

[57] See for example David Blackbourn, *Class, Religion and Local Politics in Wilhelmine Germany*, Wiesbaden, 1980, Blackbourn 1977; Geoffrey Crossick and Heinz Gerhard Haupt (eds), *Shopkeepers and Master Artisans*; Geoffrey Crossick and Heinz Gerhard Haupt, *The Petite Bourgeoisie in Europe 1780-1914: Enterprise, Family and Independence*, London 1996.

[58] *Sveriges allmänna handelsförenings månadsskrift*, no 8, 1910.

[59] *Svensk hantverkskalender*, Stockholm 1912, p. 56.

[60] Tom Ericsson, 'Cults, Myths and the Swedish Petite Bourgeoisie, 1870-1914', *European History Quarterly*, vol. 23, 1993, pp. 233-251.

[61] Tom Ericsson, 'The Mittelstand in Swedish Class Society, 1870-1914', *Scandinavian Journal of History*, no. 9, 1984, p. 318.

[62] *Svensk hantverkstidning*, 12, 1914.

[63] *Hantverks- och Industritidning*, 30, 1906.

[64] Tom Ericsson, 'Mellan kapital och arbete', *Scandia*, 48, 1982; Ericsson, *Mellan kapital och arbete*, pp. 142-3; Tomas Hammar, *Sverige åt svenskarna*, Stockholm 1964; Stig Hadenius, *Fosterländsk unionspolitik. Majoritetspartiet, regeringen och unionsfrågan 1888-1889* (Studia Historica Upsaliensia 13), Uppsala 1964; Mats Tydén, *Svensk antisemitism*, Uppsala 1986.

[65] Ericsson 1982, pp. 265-268.

[66] See Svenbjörn Kilander, 'Staten byter ansikte - om statsuppfattning och samhällssyn i sekelskiftets Sverige', in *Vägen till Planrike. Om stat, sektor och sammanhang*, Kenneth Abrahamsson and Dick Ramström (eds), Lund 1984, pp. 185-6; Per. E. Lithander, *Återblick över tjugofem riksdagar i första kammaren 1886-1908*, Göteborg 1908.

[67] Ericsson 1982, pp. 265-268.

[68] Cf. David. R. Watson, 'The Nationalist Movement in Paris, 1900-1906', in Daniel Shapiro (ed.), *The Right in France 1890-1919*, (St. Antony's Papers, no 13), London 1962.

[69] *Meddelanden från Sveriges minuthandlares riksförbund*, 3, 1908. Similar statements in *Hantverks- och Industritidning*, 48, 1906; *Sveriges allmänna handelsförenings månadsskrift*, 8, 1901.

[70] *Meddelanden från Sveriges minuthandlares riksförbund*, 10, 1908 and 12, 1909.

[71] Tom Ericsson, 'Shopkeepers and the Swedish Model: The Petty Bourgeoisie and the State during the Interwar Period', *Contemporary European History*, vol. 5, no. 3, 1996, pp. 358-9.

[72] The literature on the Swedish model is quite extensive, and therefore only some major works in English are listed here. Klaus Misgeld et al (eds), *Creating Social Democracy: A Century of the Social Democratic Labor Party in Sweden*, University Park, Pa. 1992; Timothy Tilton, *The political theory of the Swedish Social Democracy*, Oxford 1991; Peter Baldwin, *The Politics of Social Solidarity*, Cambridge 1990; Hugh Heclo, *Modern Social Politics in Britain and Sweden*, (Yale studies in political science 25), New Haven 1974; Gösta Esping Andersen, *Politics against markets. The Social Democratic road to power*, Princeton 1985.

[73] Complaints about their weak parliamentary representation can be seen at the annual meetings of small business organisations. Cf. *Handlingar förelagda Sveriges köpmannaförbunds årsmöte 1934*.

[74] Nilsson, *Kvinnor i statens tjänst*; Ericsson, *Föreningen*.

[75] Quoted in Söderberg, *Den namnlösa medelklassen*, at p. 336.

[76] Ibid., p. 336.

[77] Ibid., p. 336.

[78] Ibid., p. 337.

[79] Göran Therborn, 'A Unique Chapter in the History of Democracy: The Social Democrats in Sweden', in Misgeld et al, *Creating Social Democracy*.

[80] The best summary of the history of the popular movements in Sweden is still Sven Lundkvist, *Folkrörelserna i det svenska samhället 1850-1920* (Studia Historica Upsaliensia 85), Uppsala 1976; Björn Olsson, *Den bildade borgaren. Bildningssträvanden och folkbildning i en norrländsk småstad*, Stockholm 1994. Compare older associations involving the lower middle class in Anders Simonsson, *Bland hederligt folk. Organiserat sällskapsliv och borgerlig formering i Göteborg 1755-1820*, (Avhandlingar från Historiska institutionen i Göteborg, 27), Göteborg 2001.

[81] Lundkvist, *Folkrörelserna*, p. 110.

[82] Ibid., p. 106.
[83] Ibid,. pp. 118-9.
[84] Öhngren, *Folk i rörelse*, p. 11.
[85] Lundkvist, *Folkrörelserna*, pp. 175-180.
[86] Paulsson, *Svensk stad*, p. 569.
[87] Ibid., pp. 570-1.
[88] Ibid., pp. 571; Öhngren, *Folk i rörelse*, p. 155 gives a similar example for the town of Örebro.
[89] Cf. Hans Norman & John Rogers, 'Familj och hushåll i förändrade produktionsmiljöer', in *Familien i förändring i 18- og 19-talett & mödesbeskrivning*, Erling Ladewig Pedersen (ed.), (Rapporter till den XIX. Nordiske historikerkongress. Bind III), Odense 1984, pp. 74-75.
[90] Lunander, *Borgaren*, p. 154.
[91] Wallengren, *Hyresvärden*, p. 50; Hans Forsell, *Hus och hyra. Fastighetsägande och stadstillväxt i Berlin och Stockholm 1860-1920*, Stockholm 2003.
[92] Ibid., p. 45.
[93] Back, *Sammanslutningarnas roll*, pp. 102-103; Paulsson, *Svensk stad*, 597.
[94] Paulsson, *Svensk stad*, p. 599.
[95] Ibid., pp. 572-3.
[96] Ericsson, *Mellan kapital och arbete*, p. 160.
[97] Norman & Rogers, *Familien*, p. 70-1.
[98] Margareta Matovic, *Stockholmsäktenskap. Familjebildning och partnerval i Stockholm 1850-1890*, Stockholm 1984, pp. 124-140.
[99] Tom Ericsson, 'Kinship and sociability: Urban shopkeepers in nineteenth-century Sweden', *Journal of Family History*, 14, number 3, 1989, p. 235; Mikael Svanberg, *Företagsamhet föder framgång. Yrkeskarriärer och sociala nätverk bland företagarna i Sundsvall 1850-1900* (Forskningsrapporter från Institutionen för historiska studier vid Umeå universitet nr 13), Umeå 1999. Compare Eva Helen Ulvros, *Kvinnor inom sydsvensk borgerlighet 1790-1870*, Lund 1996; Martin Åberg, *En fråga om klass? Borgarklass och industriellt företagande i Göteborg 1850-1914* (Avhandlingar från Historiska institutionen vid Göteborgs universitet. 3), Göteborg 1991.
[100] David Blackbourn, 'Between resignation and volatility', in Crossick & Haupt, *Shopkeepers*, p. 44; Theodore Zeldin, *France 1848-1945. Ambition, love and politics*, Oxford 1973.
[101] Zeldin, *France*, 108. Compare for Sweden David Tjeder, *The Power of Character: Middle Class Masculinities, 1800-1900*, Stockholm 2003.
[102] Alfhild Axelsson, *Så var det en gång i Piteå*, Piteå 1967, p. 72.
[103] Adeline Daumard, *Les bourgeois de Paris au XIXe siècles*, Paris 1970, pp. 129-133.
[104] Ericsson, *Mellan kapital och arbete*.
[105] *Sveriges allmänna handelsförenings månadsskrift* 1909.
[106] Tom Ericsson, 'Godparents, Witnesses and Social Class in Mid-nineteenth-Century Sweden', *The History of the Family*, vol. 5, no. 3, 2000.
[107] Ibid.

JØRGEN FINK

The Middle Class in Denmark 1840-1940

A portrait of a nation

Denmark is a small country, although in 1840 it was bigger than today and in 1870 smaller. The 100 years treated here transformed Denmark into a nation state, which in 1840 it was not. The King of Denmark ruled not only the kingdom of Denmark but also the old Danish duchy of Slesvig and the old German duchy of Holstein. After the Treaty of Vienna in 1815, the German principality of Lauenburg had belonged to him too, but no one ever cared about that. The population of Holstein had always been German. The population of Slesvig was mixed, but most people were Danish-speaking until 1800. In the first half of the nineteenth century, however, a considerable part of the population gave up Danish and began to speak German. Only the northern half of the duchy retained its Danish language and identity. The efforts of the Danish government to win back the national loyalty of the population of the southern part of the duchy only worsened the situation, and in 1848 the German populations of the two duchies made a revolutionary attempt to create an independent united German state. This led to the so-called Three Years War of 1848-50. Denmark subdued the revolutionary movement of the duchies, and they duly stayed with Denmark. Denmark won the war, but only because the great powers, Russia in particular, forced Prussia to withdraw from it. This outcome satisfied neither Danes nor Germans. Consequently in 1864 another war broke out, and due to the eminent skill of Bismarck and the considerable lack of skill of the Danish government, Denmark was completely isolated and lost both duchies. The loss of Holstein was a great relief, the loss of Slesvig a tragedy. So after the peace treaty of October 1864, Denmark was a nation state in the sense that there were no national minorities within the kingdom. However, it did not remain

57

unchanged as a nation state, because a group of Danes now lived under German rule. The 1920 referendum restored the northern half of Slesvig to Denmark, and since then it has been a true nation state with only tiny national minorities on either side of the border.

The importance of the nation's evolutionary history to the fate of the Danish middle class is that since 1864 Denmark has had no significant national minority within its borders so that national tensions and diversities have had no influence on the development of a class society. There was no 'national question' to cause either any divisions within the middle class or the unification of it against a common foe. Since 1864 the population of Denmark has been homogeneous from a national point of view.

Denmark was a young democracy. The absolutist monarchy quietly gave in to the polite and peaceful revolution of 1848. The outcome was the democratic constitution of 1849. It never worked satisfactorily due to the problems in the duchies, so after the loss of the duchies a new constitution had to be created. While the modified constitution of 1866 was still in principle a democratic one, it was less democratic than its predecessor as it was not based on equal, universal suffrage. Instead it greatly favoured the rich, in particular the landowners, who became the dominant political force for the rest of the century.

Denmark was an agrarian country and 80 per cent of the population lived in the countryside. Here the manors were traditionally the pioneers of agricultural progress. They prospered until the middle of the 1870s through the export of grain, but some of them had established dairies on their estates, and they produced butter of high quality. The greater part of the acreage, however, belonged to the farmers. Most of them were freeholders, but some still lived in a kind of tenancy. The number and size of the farms had been stable for many years. It was not permitted to divide or split up a farm. The farmers like the landowners made money from the export of grain, but they were too small to establish dairies on each farm, and the quality of their butter was very low. The number of crofters/agricultural labourers was small but growing. The surplus population would automatically drift into this lower class of the countryside unless they managed to escape through either education or migration.

The urban system consisted of three parts. First the capital, Copenhagen with 140,000 inhabitants in the middle of the century; second, about 65 provincial towns of almost the same (small) size, that is with between 1,000 and 5,000 inhabitants each; and third, approximately 5,000 tiny villages. The provincial towns had trading relations with the capital, and some of them also engaged in foreign trade but the provincial towns had almost no economic dealings with each other.

The building of the primary railway lines between 1844 and 1875 changed this pattern of trade and made commercial relations between the provincial towns possible. The old corporate guild system was abolished by a general trades Act of 1857 that introduced the liberalisation of trade from January 1862. This together with the foundation of a private banking system between 1857 and 1873 created some of the preconditions for a capitalist economy.

The urban social structure comprised a very tiny urban upper class, an *haute bourgeoisie* of merchants and ship owners. Industry was in its infancy and there were not very many factory-owners. In the capital there was an academic elite of professors and higher civil servants. The middle class was made up of a large number of artisans. In the capital there were shopkeepers too, but outside Copenhagen they were not numerous. In the provincial towns, trade was in the hands of the merchants who sold wholesale as well as retail. To the urban middle class belonged other small groups, teachers, innkeepers, carters and people belonging to the professions, but by far the most important group was the artisans. At the bottom of the urban society lay an unorganised lower class of day labourers, sailors, journeymen, servants and maids. A number of these belonged to the households of the middle or upper classes. Others were taken into public care in asylums, prisons or poorhouses. There were not many beggars, but street vendors wore the pavements smooth, poor women and children selling cheap and small items of all kinds, like *The Match Girl* of Hans Christian Andersen's story.

Danish people were comparatively well educated. The common school system had been established by the government in 1814 making seven years of education compulsory, and although for some years it was more of a dream than a reality, it had been efficiently working since the 1840s. Illiteracy was not completely eradicated but by far the greater part of the population had been taught to read, write and do arithmetic.

The dominant political force in the peaceful revolution of 1848 and the first decade of democracy were the national liberals. Theirs was a policy of a union between Denmark and Slesvig cutting all ties with Holstein. Slesvig should be fully integrated into the Danish monarchy, which should go on as a constitutional monarchy under democratic rule. As this political programme broke down completely and both duchies were lost, the national liberals broke down too. After an interlude a two-party system was established. The liberal party, *Venstre* (literally 'The Left') was the party of the farmers and the lower classes of the towns. The conservative party, *Højre* (literally 'The Right') was the party of the upper class both in the countryside and in the towns as well as of a portion of the middle class of the towns. The two-party system reflected the old antagonism between the commons and the lords. As the commons were represented mainly by farmers, to some degree this was an antagonism between countryside and town. The dominant group in the conservative party were the landowners and they furnished the prime ministers until the end of the century.

The transition to a capitalist economy 1870-95

Population growth

The demographic transition from high birth and death rates to low ones took place in the nineteenth century. The death rate began to decline around 1800. The birth rate followed suit but only from 1890. This delay caused a huge increase in the size of the population. The 924,000 Danes of 1800 had multiplied to 2.2 million 90 years later. The growth of the population in a way was even greater but was reduced by emigration, with 172,000 people leaving the country before the end of the century.[1] In the first half of the century the growing population mainly augmented the lower class in the countryside. About 80 per cent of the population lived in rural areas until 1860. But after 1860 the urbanisation process gathered speed and the towns increased their share of the population from 23 to 38 per cent in 40 years.[2]

Urbanisation changed the urban system. An urban hierarchy now emerged. The capital was still dominant containing half the urban population, but some of the provincial towns now developed into regional centres or shire centres while the rest of them lingered on as local centres. In the countryside the beginnings of a new type of urban development, the railway town, could be faintly seen.

Socio-economic development

Agriculture kept its place as the leading economic sector and underwent a remarkable transformation. Farmers were hit hard by an agricultural crisis in the 1870s, but changed their production in the next decade from grain to bacon and butter and in this way were able to overcome the crisis without customs or other protective measures. Through this the farmers became fully integrated into the international market economy. However, they were suspicious of the merchants (and urban trades and life for that matter) and preferred to organise the handling and distribution of agricultural products themselves. They joined together in a widespread co-operative movement to organise the agrarian market. In particular they created a dense network of co-operative dairies, and this improved the quality of the farmers' butter to a remarkable degree. They were now able, despite a very decentralised structure, to produce an homogeneous mass product of high quality for the world market. The outcome of this change of production was that the farmers took over the leading agricultural position from the manors, and in 1901 they took over the government. The power of the landowners was broken economically as well as politically.

The new widespread and farmer-controlled butter production had enormous consequences for the economic development of Denmark. The decentralised character of this industry that literally covered the whole of the country created a lot of small local market centres (partly concentrated in the railway towns) and this gave rise to a number of middle-class shops and workshops in the countryside.[3] The full effects of this change were seen in the years between 1895 and 1920.

Part of the process of urbanisation was the emergence of new urban markets. They were mainly local, but regional and national markets sprang up as well. This was part of the new hierarchical urban structure, and it made retailing possible on a grand scale. Shops (until 1870 rather rare outside Copenhagen) were now spreading rapidly.

Industry was a tiny and slowly growing economic sector. Copenhagen was by far the most important industrial city in Denmark, but the last quarter of the century saw the beginning of more widespread industrial activity in the larger provincial towns. Around 1880 a trade union movement was refounded on the ruins of an earlier revolutionary movement. It did not break with the earlier movement and kept close connections with the Social Democratic Party (in parliament since 1884), but the emphasis of the trade unions was on practical work rather than ideological discussions. The 1880s brought a sharp division between capital and labour.

These years marked a breakthrough for the class society. The old aristocratic upper class was transformed into a new mixed upper class of aristocracy, capitalists and the academic elite. This transformation took place as the old antagonism between peers and commoners gradually gave way to a stronger tension between capitalists and the working class. The 1880s saw the emergence of class conflict as the dominant social tension.[4]

This by no means implies that it became the only social tension. In the countryside the old pattern of division that entailed some antagonism between landowners, farmers and the lower group of small farmers and crofters continued, and one has to bear in mind that at the turn of the century more than half the population still lived in the countryside. However, while the tensions there are not to be ignored, class conflict between employers and employed became the dominant social conflict in the 1890s, and the capitalist economy made urban life and urban ways the model for the rest of society.

Class formation was still in its infancy and compared to the next period social differentiation had not gone very far. In the towns there was no clear division between upper class and upper middle class, nor between the upper middle class and the rest of the middle class. The middle class proper, the trading urban middle class of artisans and shopkeepers, was growing. This was due to the rapid urbanisation and the expansion of the market economy, which gave retailing and service greatly enhanced opportunities. The shopkeepers now became a numerous social group. The working class became a disciplined and very well organised social group. This was probably the most outstanding feature of the social development of Denmark in these years compared with what was happening in other countries. Some tension existed between skilled and unskilled workers, but the unskilled workers imitated the skilled and started to build their own solid organisational structure.

The middle class

The dominant position of agriculture in Danish economic life, and the dominant position inside agriculture that the farmers attained in these years was of immense importance to the overall position of the middle class in Denmark. In an economic sense the farmers belonged to the middle class, but they were suspicious of the towns and there was a sharp division between agriculture and the urban trades. The agrarian and the urban middle classes were separated and did not act in concert, but the existence of a great agrarian middle class made the position of the urban middle class secure in a political sense and made the influence of the whole middle class decisive in the shaping of Danish society. Denmark became a middle-class society, dominated by middle-class values. This became clear in the years between 1895 and 1920, but the foundations for this were laid in the years of the great depression.

The master artisans were the greatest and traditional part of the old middle class. They numbered 70,000 in 1870, 4,000 of whom were women. In this number is not included the rather large group of seamstresses: statistics counted them as master artisans, reality did not.[5]

Table 1 Independent businessmen 1870-1901

	Number of people	
	1870	1901
Agriculture	164,782	155,302
Industry	70,681	81,016
Commerce	19,734	40,837
Business total	266,349	289,427
Seamstresses	17,894	22,996

By far the greatest number of independent businessmen belonged to agriculture. Their number was almost double the number of businessmen in industry/handicrafts and four times the number in commerce. The number of master artisans/managers was slowly growing between 1870 and 1901 while the number of shopkeepers and wholesalers more than doubled. But despite this outstanding growth the number of shopkeepers was still low in 1901 compared with the number of master artisans. The table makes it perfectly clear that the old middle class was not in decline measured numerically in terms of the numbers of independent businessmen.

The overwhelming proportion of the master artisans lived in the countryside, about 70 per cent in 1870 and 60 per cent in 1901. They belonged mainly to eleven old handicrafts that had been permitted outside the cities since 1683.[6] Together with millers and clog makers (two handicrafts that did not belong to the guild structure), those eleven handicrafts in the countryside numbered 55 per cent of all Danish master artisans in 1870 and still 39 nine per cent in 1901. The master artisans of the countryside never belonged to the guilds. The urban masters generally despised their colleagues in the countryside and there was mutual suspicion between the two groups. The country masters did not normally pass any examinations as journeymen and for many of them handicrafts was only part of their occupation; they also had small plots of land they cultivated. The urban masters did not recognise the country artisans as masters, whatever scale they operated on, but only as artisans, if that.

The shopkeepers belonged to the cities, in particular the capital. Here in 1901 the number of shopkeepers exceeded that of master artisans. Outside the capital the number of shopkeepers was still below that of master artisans. The geographical distribution of master artisans and shopkeepers corresponded roughly to the distribution of the population. There were comparatively many master artisans in the provincial towns and comparatively few shopkeepers in the countryside. But apart from that the distribution was fairly even.

The growth in the number of masters and shopkeepers was accompanied by a rapid decline in their relative position. Their share of the total number of people in the trades was weakened, their absolute number was not. Copenhagen was of course far ahead of the rest of the country in this respect. The new middle class of employees was not registered separately in 1870, and in 1901 they were only a very small group in industry although a substantial group in the commercial trades.

The artisans were closely connected to local markets. Their ideal was the well-known, the traditional, the familiar, where economic conduct was closely bound up with the moral and where the foundation of business was a personal acquaintance with the customers who were co-parishioners of the master artisan. These local ties were clearly reflected in their pattern of organisation.

When the old guild system ceased to exist in 1862, dissolved by Act of parliament, artisans were almost left in a void in terms of associations. Some of the guilds lingered on in the new form of free trade associations, but they had lost their power, and their self-respect had been shaken. The artisans asked the Ministry of the Interior (Home Office) what to do and were told they could form free handicraft (cross-trade, not single trade) associations on a local basis. So that was what they did. And quite soon each Danish town had its handicraft association. They had some influence on local politics, often nominating candidates for the municipal councils in local elections, but other than that their main importance was in the social field. They arranged balls, Christmas parties for members' families, summer picnics, musical evenings and so on. But in economic matters they were of little help and they abstained totally from involvement in the labour market. In technical matters their greatest achievement was that they introduced technical education to their communities. Normally it was at their initiative that a technical school was founded in the towns. In this way the whole of Denmark had technical schools by the turn of the century. The schools provided technical education to supplement on-the-job training and due to the high level of literacy this education was a success (see below).

Like their members (who were definitely not all master artisans), the handicraft organisations were very closely tied to their home towns. But now and then attempts were made to unite them on a regional or a national level. Those associations established prior to the liberalisation of trade had tried to prevent that liberalisation by common action, but they failed and later attempts did not succeed either. But when the great depression had reached

Denmark in the middle of the 1870s, and hard times really were experienced, a national union of master artisans was finally created. The economic crisis meant that many needed assistance, but since 1872 the farmers (the liberal party) had had a solid majority in the lower chamber of Parliament, and they effectively blocked any help to the urban trades. As a reaction against this agrarian dominance a national union of master artisans was created in 1879. According to its name it was an organisation of both handicrafts and industry, but industry was almost wholly unrepresented in the association. It became a national union of master artisans only.

It was totally dominated by the local cross-trade associations of the small towns. To create a national union as early as 1879 was rather extraordinary, and it became difficult for this national organisation to act at the national level. The local handicraft organisations who were the constituent associations of the national union were gathered into three regional sections, and it was at the regional level that decisions were made. The national committee was often paralysed in its efforts as it was unable to overcome disagreements between regional sections. It was usually a case of Copenhagen against Jutland, which was dominated by the small towns. Their position was only strengthened when master artisans of the countryside began to join the national union through their own local associations in 1894.

The shopkeepers were a rather new old middle class. The shop seriously emerged as a commercial outlet in the last quarter of the nineteenth century and only then did shopkeepers become a social group of importance. Other groups also belonged to the old middle class: carters, innkeepers and so on, but they were small in number and continued to be so.

Politics and Culture

The Danish political system in these years was a two-party one. The two-party system was constituted by a political struggle concerning parliamentarian democracy. The constitution of 1866 introduced a partly democratic parliament with a democratic lower chamber and a plutocratic upper chamber dominated by the landowners, but the constitution laid down no rules for what should happen if a struggle arose between the two chambers. And this was exactly what happened. After 1872 the two chambers had opposing majorities. In the lower chamber the liberal party, *Venstre*, dominated by the farmers, had a solid majority, whereas the conservatives (since 1883 organised into the *Højre* party) constituted the majority of the upper chamber. The King did not trust the liberal party and between 1870 and 1901 there were only conservative governments. This provoked a bitter political struggle over the principle of parliamentary democracy, and this struggle almost totally paralysed the legislative process.

The political struggle between the liberal *Venstre* and the conservative *Højre* was one between countryside and town, but was fundamentally between commoners and peers. Both parties then became alliances of different groups. *Venstre* was an alliance of the majority of the countryside (farmers and crofters) and the lower classes from the towns. *Højre* became an alliance of the middle and upper classes of the towns with upper class landowners from the countryside. The constitutional struggle was the only glue keeping each of these two alliances together, and this became ever more difficult as the great depression deepened and economic interests gained political importance.

In 1879 the artisans had established their national union in despair at agrarian dominance in the parliament, and in 1883 the commercial world had followed suit by establishing a national union of wholesale and retail traders. But none of these unions achieved very much, and they disagreed on the most important economic debate of the 1880s, the tariff issue. The artisans wanted protection through customs duties, the tradesmen were free traders. The tariff debate concerned a matter of general economic importance. Customs were not a problem that particularly concerned the middle class. But another issue was put on the political agenda, and this was a middle-class one. For several years, actually from the very start, the national union of master artisans had advocated the abolition of freedom of trade.[7] This demand was raised by the master artisans of the provincial towns. But in 1886 the shoemakers of the capital supported the demand, and the next year the shopkeepers of Copenhagen raised the same question. Although the wholesalers of Copenhagen tried hard to stop it, in the end the national union of master artisans and the national union of tradesmen handed in a joint demand for a revision of the general trades Act that had introduced freedom of trade in 1857. In 1890 a parliamentary commission was established to deliberate on the matter. Both unions were represented in the commission.

Between 1890 and 1893 the commission worked on its report. These years became the formative years for the middle class as a political concept. When the report was released in the summer of 1893 it coincided with three other incidents that all contributed to making the idea of a middle class a political reality. Most important was the worsening of economic conditions, and 1893 was a year of economic crisis. This provoked the establishment of an agrarian union which demanded an end to the parliamentary deadlock, so that parliament could enact measures of relief for the agricultural sector. This in turn provoked the urban trades to strengthen their demands. These were the fundamental positions (the different economic sectors made irreconcilable demands on the political establishment) and the fundamental cause (an economic crisis), but what really brought the idea of a middle class to the fore and helped create a kind of (middle) class consciousness was one single event, the so-called Stores-project.

The Stores project was a somewhat megalomaniac idea of creating an immense commercial undertaking that would tie consumers and producers to each other thus making the traditional commercial activity of wholesalers and retailers superfluous. It was a grandiose scheme that incidentally would take care of all trade between Denmark and Great Britain (by far the most important market for Danish exports). When the plans became known all hell was let loose. The shopkeepers and master artisans of the capital almost took to the streets in rage. Infuriation was a mild word to describe the atmosphere. Anger was directed not so much at the relatively unknown architects of the plan as at their supporters, many of whom belonged to the land-owning wing of the ruling conservative party (*Højre*) and at the chairman of the national union of tradesmen, who had been rather lukewarm in his condemnation of the plan. When the Stores project (which had to be abandoned in the summer of 1893) was reintroduced under another name the next year, the shopkeepers of Copenhagen, who in 1890 had created a regional union of shopkeepers, used this as a pretext for breaking away from the national union of tradesmen (established in 1883) and created a new national union of shopkeepers. The Stores incident had made it clear to them that shopkeepers could not expect wholesalers (who dominated the national union of tradesmen) to take care of their interests. The shopkeepers belonged to the middle class and the middle class had interests of its own.

The Stores incident and the economic crisis of 1893 showed the frailty of the political alliance of the upper and urban middle classes who had supported the conservative party. The general election of 1895 demonstrated this clearly. It was a victory for the liberal opposition and further strengthened the agrarian element in parliament. This was the end of any chance of enactment of the 1893 report of the commission on the general trades Act. The conservative party, which was mainly in favour of the anti-liberal recommendations of the report, did not dare to challenge the agricultural sector and was left with very little freedom of movement.

In other respects 1895 was a turning point. The economic crisis had come to an end and was followed by prosperous times. This greatly eased tension among shopkeepers and master artisans. For the time being they lost interest in the possible revision of the general trades Act. A new question now captured the public attention. It was the problem of class relations between employers and workers and the regulation of the labour market.

So the outcome of the parliamentarian commission on the general trades Act and the crisis of 1893 and the Stores incident was threefold. The middle class had become a political concept for good, the traditional political two-party system was beginning to break down, and a rupture beyond repair between wholesalers and shopkeepers had split the national union of tradesmen. The class society was dawning.

It was a civil obligation that every child should have at least seven years of education. There was no obligation to send a child to school. If parents could undertake the education themselves or pay for a teacher in the home, education might be undertaken there. However, most children were sent to school and as the greater part of the population lived in the countryside, school for most children was the village school. The pupils there were between seven and fourteen years old and were normally divided into two groups, the younger and the older. The two groups went to school on alternate days. They were taught reading, writing and arithmetic and religion, national history and perhaps some geography.

In the towns there were three kinds of schools, the free school, the bourgeois school (a secondary school) and private schools. From 1881 the pupils at the bourgeois schools could finish school by passing a so-called preliminary examination. The idea was that this examination would be a qualification for further studies, but this did not happen. The municipal authorities then created a new kind of public school, *realskolen*, a name that cannot be translated, but it signifies that the school will concentrate on useful facts and knowledge, not on philosophy, spirituality or theory. The *realskolen* gave both primary and secondary education. These schools became a tremendous success and were the preferred schools of the upper part of the old middle class. The pupils would finish school by passing *realeksamen*, and this became the ticket to commercial and secondary technical education. To pass *realeksamen* pupils had to go to school for ten years, and in 1895 this was not the normal pattern. Most pupils left school after seven years, so the main effect of *realskolen* (being public and free of charge) was to improve fundamental education but only in the towns. There were some grammar schools too, but middle-class pupils were a minority here and their share of the pupils was falling. The grammar school prepared the pupils for an academic education and was mainly attended by children of academically educated parents. The different kinds of schools were not bound together into a common system. This made the overall educational system of Denmark somewhat inefficient and inflexible.

On top of the elementary educational system there were other kinds of education for young people (from 16 to 19).[8] The most common was the traditional apprenticeship. Since the liberalisation of trade in 1857 this had been without public regulation. In the time of the guilds an apprentice had had to demonstrate his skill by finishing some piece of work to be approved by the guild. Having passed this test he was accepted as a journeyman. This test disappeared as an obligation when trade was liberalised. The tests might actually continue but they were totally voluntary. In the years after 1857 the number of tests declined. This caused great anxiety among the master artisans who by tradition were responsible for the practical education of apprentices. When the national union of master artisans was established in 1879 it brought the problem of the apprentices' education to the attention of the government. The outcome was an official decree of 1884 that established public tests for journeymen-to-be. In a way public tests already existed due to a decree of 1862, but they had been boycotted by the master artisans. The new decree put the practical administration of the tests into the hands of commissions for each trade, and the master artisans were invited to provide the membership of those committees. Thus they were commissioned to undertake acts of public administration, and this became the model for further co-operation between the middle class and the public authorities: that delegates of the middle class were invited to partake in the administration of public decrees and acts. The middle class in this way was integrated into the socio-political web. This is not to say that the middle class always got its way, and the fate of the commission for the revision of the general trades Act is proof of that. But the middle class could not claim that it was totally neglected by the public authorities. The decree of 1884 was followed in 1889 by an apprentices Act. It contained only few stipulations but the importance of the Act was not its content (or lack of it), but the very fact that apprenticeship was once again recognised as a matter of public concern.

The traditional apprenticeship was supplemented by formal education at technical schools. There had been some moves in this direction in around 1800 but the first real technical school was established in 1843. As so often, the capital was the pioneer, and this school became a kind of model for the local technical schools of the provincial towns. They were normally established at the initiative of the local handicrafts' organisation and by 1880 almost all Danish towns had a technical school. In 1872 the first technical school in the countryside was established and although new technical schools were being set up in the countryside as late as the 1930s, most of the country was reasonably well provided for by 1895.

It was not a mandatory part of an apprentice's education that he/she had to attend a technical school. There had been some hope that the apprentices Act of 1889 would require that, but this hope was disappointed. As a consequence, participation was voluntary and lessons took place in the autumn and winter evenings after a long working day, so the desire for technical wisdom often had to give way to the need for sleep. The efficiency of the system was therefore not as good as timetables and official statistics might make it appear, but nevertheless the master artisans had created a home-grown countrywide educational system which in the years after 1895 became one of the foundations of the industrial breakthrough in Denmark. The master artisans also helped the industrial sector in another way. The number of apprentices in the workshops of the master artisans was far higher than the number of apprentices in the factories. An important part of the workforce of industry was thus purveyed by the master artisans.

The commercial trades were far behind the handicrafts in this respect. They used apprenticeship as their fundamental education but as in the handicrafts it was supplemented with formal education. The number of commercial schools however was low compared to the number of technical schools. The first commercial school was established in 1865 in the city of Århus and in 1895 only the bigger towns had such institutions.[9]

The Danish people were rather secularised. Certainly the overwhelming proportion of the population (98.5 per cent in 1903) belonged to the Danish Protestant Church, but they made little use of it.[10] It was for the solemn moments of family life. Although there were different and opposing movements within the church, on the whole religion played only a minor part in Danish social life, and the Danish people was rather homogeneous in this respect. Compared to other countries religious identification was of minor importance and was not in serious competition with class identification. Attempts to create a system of business and social associations on a religious basis were not successful.

Middle class ways of life

Traditionally the household was the framework of everyday life in the handicrafts. There was no separation of work place and living place, and journeymen and apprentices stayed in the house of the master and belonged to his household. This pattern gradually gave way. By the middle of the nineteenth century it was not uncommon for a journeyman to have a household of his own, and by the turn of the century apprentices did not necessarily live in the house of the master any longer. In the traditional household family, business had been the responsibility of the man and the household the responsibility of his wife. In a way this division of labour between the two genders continued, but as the size of the household decreased, the tasks of the wife changed. Caring for the family assumed a greater role in the daily life of the married woman. When the housewife became less needed in the house, she had more opportunity to earn a living for herself. In 1857 unmarried women achieved legal independence, married women did not get it until 1899. In 1857 women even got the right to run independent businesses, and in 1880 married women were granted the right to keep and dispose of their own earnings. But despite these legal rights only very few women actually ran businesses, a few in the handicrafts, a few more in retailing.

In the second half of the nineteenth century it had become more common to separate workshops and living spaces. At the same time the towns became more segregated. Gradually working-class districts emerged on the outskirts of the towns, and later bourgeois districts were to be seen too. In 1899 one of the first town plans in Denmark introduced a clear division between an upper-class, a middle-class and a working-class district.

Newspapers became the most important source of information in the later half of the nineteenth century. Danish newspapers had clear political affiliations. This was not a particular feature of the middle class. Newspaper reading became widespread throughout the Danish population. Membership of associations was probably the most common form of affiliation. This was not peculiar to the middle class either, but as mentioned the middle class established its own associations and they became instrumental in shaping a (somewhat fragmented) middle class identity.

The good old days 1895-1920

Economic Background

This was a golden age. The 25 years prior to 1920 brought prosperity to Denmark as never before. Agriculture now reaped the fruits of its change of production. Denmark catered for the British breakfast table by exporting ever-increasing amounts of butter, bacon and eggs. Agricultural prosperity laid the foundations for economic growth in all sectors of the economy, thus confirming the old saying that when the farmer is well-off, everyone is well-off. The First World War did not destroy this picture. The early years of war gave Denmark the full advantage of neutrality. Only 1917 and 1918 created economic difficulties, but they soon gave way to a bubble of wild speculation in 1919 and 1920. In the autumn of 1920 times changed, and this marked the onset of the depression of the inter-war years.

At the turn of the century the demographic transition had come to an end. Death and birth rates had both settled at a much lower level. The population was still growing, but the pace was reduced.

The secondary railway lines were erected between 1890 and 1920. This meant that the whole of Denmark was linked by railways. The distance to the nearest station rarely exceeded ten miles, which was within the range of horse-drawn carriages. This was of great significance in integrating all parts of the country into the market economy. The outcome was a very evenly distributed growth. All parts of the country experienced growth of population: the capital, the larger provincial towns, the smaller ones, the railway towns (which in 20 years established a wholly new urban system in the countryside), and the countryside itself. No single sector was left behind. Evenness was probably the most outstanding feature of Denmark's socio-economic development in this period.

Socio-economic development

As mentioned before, agriculture prospered and in particular Danish farmers had their finest hour, the manors lingered on, but crofters now came in too as many of them developed into smallholders [*husmænd*]. A smallholders' movement influenced Danish land-legislation and made it possible to establish many smallholdings big enough for a family to earn their living. The group of crofters who had earlier combined agriculture with some kind of handicraft was now divided. Some of them expanded their acreage and become full-time smallholders, others gave up their part-time agriculture and earned their living as full-time artisans. This growing specialisation of work was part of the high economic activity of the countryside. The increased division of labour became physically visible as a number of railway towns sprang up like mushrooms in fields all around the country. They were small concentrations of urban trades in the countryside. Agricultural production was very decentralised with more than 1,000 dairies all over the country. It was a very dense network due to inefficient local transport (carriages), but as soon as the product (butter) reached the railways, the world market was open. The export rate was very high. Farmers had established the dairies themselves on a co-operative basis, and they kept control over the sale of their products. The co-operative organisation of the trade was democratic in form, and the smallholders were invited in, but control of the trade rested solidly in the hands of the farmers whether the smallholders were in a majority or not. The system was advantageous to the farmers and the smallholders, and although they would rather die than admit it, the agrarian population was quite satisfied. There were moments when even the staunchest of farmers found difficulties in sustaining pessimism. This caused some admiration abroad and the English novelist H. Rider Haggard wrote a whole book about the phenomenon in 1911, *Rural Denmark and its Lesson*.

An industrial breakthrough occurred in the 1890s, and the next 25 years changed the role of industry in Danish economic life. In 1903 industry was for the first time able to make a contribution to the gross national product of the same size as the contribution from the handicrafts. In 1916 the contribution of industry surpassed the contribution of the handicrafts by 50 per cent.[11] In only 13 years industry had left the handicrafts behind for good. It was dominated by small scale factories catering for the agrarian market, and there was no mining or other heavy industry, but breweries, shipbuilding, factories that made machinery, cement works, sugar and paper had some sizeable companies, and although industry mainly sold its goods in the home market some 10 per cent were exported.

Skilled workers dominated the trade union movement, but unskilled workers were quite well organised too, and in 1898 a national trade union council was established with both groups of the working class as members. The Danish T.U.C. had a baptism of fire in the great lockout of 1899, the outcome of which was a mutual recognition of workers and employers. The so-called September agreement that ended the conflict was for more than 60 years the constitution of the labour market. The workers explicitly accepted that the right to manage belonged to the employers, and the employers recognised that the workers had a voice too. The decade from 1899 to 1910 was a formative one giving body and content to the September agreement and creating a fairly satisfactory system of industrial relations. Collective wage bargaining was introduced and so was a judicial system (including a labour court) to regulate workplace disputes.

The triumph of agriculture and the dominant position of middle class farmers meant that the old middle class of the urban trades was as secure as ever in its social position. It took part in the general economic progress and its numbers did not diminish, but its relative social position was reduced as industry took the lead in the urban trades.

The middle class

The middle class was still dominated by the old middle class. The new middle class was only in its infancy. The number of independent businessmen continued to grow. This was mainly due to the growing number of crofters, but shopkeepers too continued their growth. Master artisans apparently experienced a small decline in numbers, but on closer inspection they did not. The loss was due to a declining number of sweated occupations (washerwomen and so on) and a declining number of combined occupations in the countryside (artisans who were part-time crofters). The number of professional full-time master artisans was stable. The numbers can be seen in Table 2.

Table 2 Independent businessmen 1901-21

	Number of people	
	1901	1921
Agriculture	155,302	186,582
Industry	81,016	76,841
Commerce	40,837	54,463
Business total	289,427	343,231
Seamstresses	22,996	10,156

The number of master artisans was growing in Copenhagen but falling in the countryside. This created problems for the union of master artisans as the growing importance of the capital was not matched by a growing importance in the structure and politics of the union (see below). The number of shopkeepers was growing in all parts of the country and now even gained a solid foothold in the countryside. The overall tendency was an ever more even distribution of master artisans and shopkeepers in proportion to the Danish population.

Already in 1901 the shopkeepers had become the largest group of the old middle class in Copenhagen and they continued to progress with higher growth rates than the master artisans. Now they almost caught up with them in the provincial towns too. Only in the countryside were they still far behind although the growth rate here was by far the strongest. *Landhøkeren* [the country-huckster] now became a recognised and well-known figure.

The expansion of shops into the countryside meant that the middle class element of the population was strengthened here as the number of shopkeepers grew not only in absolute terms but proportionally too. Even in the smaller provincial towns this tendency prevailed, but in the larger provincial towns and the capital the opposite tendency was observed. Here the growth rate of workers and employees surpassed that of masters and shopkeepers.

Patterns of organisation in industry and handicrafts

When at the end of the 1890s the master artisans realised that it would not be possible to get a revision of the general trades Act through parliament, they decided that in future they would rely on the help they could provide themselves. This included the work of the trade associations and an endeavour to improve credit.

Of course, the supply of money was a problem for artisans and shopkeepers as it was for everyone else, but it was not a problem that aroused great anger among them. There was no great hostility towards the big banks. Nevertheless, as part of their intensified self-help efforts the years between 1895 and 1918 saw 20 new banks established that all had either 'handicrafts' or 'merchant' in their name. All these banks were local. There was no attempt to unite them or create regional or national banks for the middle class, and not a single bank mentioned the middle class in its name. The rather narrowly local horizon of the old middle class influenced its financial behaviour. The outcome was that 40 per cent of the handicrafts or merchant banks had to close down after a rather short life. The new banks were therefore only partly successful.

More important to the middle class was its activity in associations. It became instrumental in efforts to improve the market position of small enterprises and reduce competition or even better abolish it. At the same time this activity became an expression of a growing social differentiation. If the great depression (1875-95) had created an upper class and a lower class and in between a middle class, *la belle epoque* (1895-1914) created an upper middle, middle middle and lower middle class. And not only did the middle class become fragmented, it also turned into an old middle class as a new middle class (of employees) began to enter the arena. So increasingly the middle class became a patchwork of social subgroups.

The industrial breakthrough left its mark on the pattern of organisations creating a split between handicrafts and industry. Although the national union of master artisans (established 1879) continued to claim that it was an organisation of both industry and handicrafts, this had never corresponded to reality. In 1910 industrialists at last created their own national organisation, the Industrial Council, thereby indicating beyond dispute that they did not regard the national union of master artisans as their organisation. The Industrial Council, thanks to the energy and vision of one Danish industrialist, Alexander Foss, soon acquired a solid position in public life, whereas the national union of master artisans, which had never been a strong organisation, gradually lost what little influence it had been able to retain. In 1894 a split between wholesalers and retailers had developed in the commercial world separating upper and middle classes; in 1910 the same happened with industry and handicrafts.

The difficulties of the national union of master artisans were caused by the dominant position of the local handicraft organisations of the small provincial towns and the countryside. Theirs was a negative influence as they could block any positive suggestion and so paralyse an organisation, but it was difficult for them to bring about any positive measures. They clung to this power as their relative social influence decreased by the day.

This prompted some despair among some of the master artisans in the larger towns and, in particular, in the capital, but they were unable to find remedies for it. The problems of the national union of master artisans were exacerbated by the growing importance of industrial relations. Since the 1880s a deep split had developed between journeymen and masters. Former organisations that had been common to the two groups were divided. The journeymen formed trade unions of their own, and the master artisans did the same.

This introduced a new principle of organisation or rather reintroduced an old one: the single trade association. In a way this type of association recreated the old guilds although now in the shape of voluntary associations, but the new trade associations of master artisans fulfilled the same purposes the guilds had. They regulated relations with journeymen and workers and they made price agreements thus achieving discretely that very restriction of competition that the master artisans in vain had tried to bring about through the revision of the general trades Act in the 1890s. These single trade associations of the master artisans were far more efficient than the cross-trade handicrafts associations. But the new single trade organisations did not amalgamate into a separate national union, instead they joined the national union of master artisans of 1879. There they drowned in a sea of local cross-trade organisations and all they managed to do was intensify the inner troubles of the national union. This means that although the rate of organisation among the master artisans was very high the organisational structure of the master artisans was rather weak.

The situation became even worse when a separate employers' organisation was created. At the beginning of the 1890s the national union of master artisans began to consider how to cope with this problem. Committees were established, studies abroad undertaken, reports written and meetings held. Nothing happened. Meanwhile the trade unions of the workers gathered strength year by year at an amazing pace. Then in 1896 the great master artisans of the building trades of the capital lost patience. They joined forces with the association of the great construction companies and established the Employers' Association of 1896. This was not the first attempt at creating an employers' union on a multi-trade basis, but it was the first successful one. A year later the iron industry joined the Employers' Association of 1896, and at the beginning of 1898 some handicraft trades in the capital that did not belong to the building trades joined too. Now a split was emerging in the commodity-producing trades, not between industry and handicrafts but right through the middle of the handicrafts, as those handicraft trades of the capital that were dominated by the greater master artisans (bricklayers, carpenters, blacksmiths and so on) sided with the construction firms and the iron industry, whereas the handicrafts of the provincial towns and the countryside and those handicrafts of the capital that were dominated by smaller master artisans stuck to the national union of master artisans, which continued its effort to establish an employers' union of its own. This division that was somewhat antagonistic was one in the ranks of the master artisans that made itself felt more than once and that prevented the master artisans from maintaining a united front against industry.

However, early in 1898 the workers established their Trade Union Congress, and faced with this unity among their adversaries the employers came under pressure to unite too. In November 1898 the Federation of Danish Employers was established. It was an amalgamation of the Employers' Association of 1896 with the employers' union established by the national union of master artisans. The problem was that the last mentioned union was never actually established. So the members of the old Employers' Association of 1896 later teased the members of the national union of master artisans that they had simply joined the 1896 association. This caused an astonishing amount of anger among the members of the national union of master artisans and almost put the unity of the new association at risk. They asserted vehemently that what had occurred in November 1898 was an amalgamation of two associations and that people should not be misled by the tiny fact that one of the two associations did not exist. This question about what *really* happened in November 1898 might *sub specie aeternitatis* be judged as a minor one, but the sentiments it provoked showed that the new Employers' Union was an uneasy alliance and this potential split between the minor master artisans and the rest of the employers has been a reality ever since. Even today it demands some skill and tact to avoid a split. At any rate, the fact that the national union of master artisans chose to give up plans for an employers' association of its own further undermined its position.

The growing importance of class relations and the consequent increasing importance of employers' interests weakened the position of the handicrafts. When the industrial breakthrough occurred and large-scale capital entered the scene of production, the handicrafts did not unite in opposition to this threat to their future, but on the contrary were divided into three parts. The trades dominated by greater master artisans such as the building trades of Copenhagen joined the Employers' Union in an alliance with industry that was offensive as well as defensive. The middle group of master artisans entered into an alliance with industry that was exclusively defensive, that is they joined the Employers' Union when the trade unions were offensive but left it again when the trade unions adopted a defensive line. The small master artisans and in particular the master artisans of the countryside did not make any alliance with industry or join the Employers' Union, but they did not form an anti-capitalist union either nor did they pursue an anti-capitalist policy.

This last group of small master artisans of course contained the group of master artisans who had neither journeymen nor apprentices. They could regard themselves either as journeymen working at their own risk or as small master artisans. The loyalty of this group was demonstrated in 1920 during and after the so-called Easter crisis, a political crisis in which the Danish T.U.C. called a general strike. Tensions in the capital ran high but a political compromise was found before the general strike began, so it was called off. However, some trade unions were dissatisfied with this outcome and held strikes of their own, among them the baker journeymen of the capital. In this situation the master artisans who worked alone without any employees could have sided with the journeymen (who were actually their work colleagues), but they sided with the master artisans. The small masters closed their shops not to join the strike but on the contrary to volunteer as journeymen at those great bakers' shops that were kept going in order to prevent a lack of bread in the capital.

This pattern of associations testifies to the existence of three subgroups of the middle class inside the handicrafts. The three subgroups of master artisans were constituted by their different positions in the world of work. The upper middle class of master artisans were employers who only now and then physically took part in production. They were mainly occupied in management and administration. The middle middle class of master artisans were employers too, but most of the time physically worked alongside their journeymen and apprentices, thus being colleagues and employers at the same time. The lower middle class among the master artisans worked alone and had neither journeymen nor apprentices; they were not employers. These three social subgroups emerged amongst artisans, not in the sense that they necessarily gave rise to separate associations or acted as consolidated groups, but nevertheless the existence of these three subgroups was mirrored in the organisational development.[12]

When the Employers' Association of 1896 was established this signified a split between trades that were dominated by the greater master artisans belonging to the upper middle class. To them the relative importance of their interests as employers weighed so heavily that they preferred to ally with big business instead of waiting for the national union of master artisans to finish its attempt to create an employers' union. There was no clear division between them and the middle middle class of master artisans, but when a master artisan had three or four journeymen in his workshop, his interests as employer began to determine his choice of association. This of course is not to say that whenever the number of journeymen reached three or four the employer's interests gained the upper hand in the head of the master, but only that trade associations of master artisans in trades where the greater masters were numerous showed different patterns of organisation from organisations dominated by masters belonging to the middle masters.

The greater masters were most prominent in the capital, the middle masters in the provincial towns and the small masters in the countryside. To some degree then the difference between the three social subgroups was reinforced by differences between capital, provincial towns and countryside. This can further complicate the analysis of the social subgroups among the master artisans. But in the long run the pattern of organisation showed that social differences were more important than geographical ones. In the inter-war years some of the trade associations of master artisans in the countryside turned into specific associations of small master artisans with members not only in the countryside but in the provincial towns and the capital too.

Now, if the three social subgroups had never materialised in practice there would be no need to discuss the social differentiation of the artisans. But they did, and the creation of the Employers' Association of 1896 was not the only instance where the difference of interests between the three groups influenced the course of events. In 1905 the social differences within the master artisans again came to the fore. This was the beginning of a phenomenon that was later labelled 'the new guild movement'.[13] Master carpenters and master painters of the capital initiated a very tight system of control of competition. The initiative came from a group of young master artisans. Earlier in life as journeymen they had belonged to the trade unions and were well acquainted with collective action. They belonged to the group of smaller or middle master artisans. They easily won a majority for their proposals in the trade association of master carpenters and master painters, but needed further help if their system of controlled competition were to succeed. This help they sought in the Employers' Union. A paragraph in the statutes of the union stated that it was an obligation of honour for the members of the union to prefer other members in the choice of business partners. This was quite innocent, but after a very insistent campaign the painters and carpenters of the new guild movement managed to convince a majority of the members of the Employers' Union that this obligation should no longer be a question of honour but a mandatory duty for all members. This decision was taken late in 1908 despite vehement opposition from industrialists. They stated that they were against the proposition and that they would not be satisfied before the decision had been revoked. The showdown came half a year later at a meeting in June 1909. Here was industry against the handicrafts, the upper class against the middle, capitalism against a revived guild movement. But it is worth noticing that the clash took place within a common union, that it was a wish of both parties to continue their co-operation inside this union and that the stance of the middle class in this showdown was not an attack on capitalism as a destroyer of free competition, but an attempt to reduce and control competition themselves. The industrialists on their side did not demand that the new guild movement give up its regulation of competition. They only said that restriction of competition was not the business of the Employers' Union and that the union should not be drawn into the guild movement's efforts. And it is further worth noticing that the confrontation was not between capitalism as such and the middle class as such, but that the middle class was represented by a social subgroup, the middle masters. The new guild movement was an attempt by the middle masters to cater for the interests of this group in particular, and the movement miscarried not because of opposition from industrialists (heavy as it was) but because of the opposition from the greater master artisans. The bricklayers and carpenters of the capital turned against the new guild movement siding on this issue with industry and so repeating the pattern of alliances that had first been manifested when the Employers' Association of 1896 was established. Shortly afterwards the greater carpenter masters who had promised to support the guild movement withdrew their promise and that was the end of it. The disagreement between masters of the upper middle class and masters of the middle middle class overturned the guild movement, and the master carpenters and master painters of the capital had to give up their control of competition. After this failure however the masters of the former guild movement did not try to establish an alternative association of their own. Some of them left the Employers' Unions in disappointment but most of them entered it again when the growing strength of the trade unions in the wake of the First World War made the advantages of employer co-operation more obvious.

The new guild movement was not the last occation where the difference between the greater and the middle masters influenced the course of events. As late as the 1940s it caused a split in the national union of master artisans when the greater masters of the capital broke away and formed a competing national union of master artisans.

This difference prevented the master artisans from acting as a united middle-class organisation. The greater masters stuck to their alliance with big business inside the Employers' Union and would not support any measure that would endanger this alliance. The middle masters were less stable in their position. They would join the Employers' Union when the workers were on the move and they would leave when the employers took the offensive, but they were not antagonistic towards big business nor did they form associations to protect the middle class from the onslaught of capitalism. Even the small masters who were not employers sided with the employers in times of crisis. Since the middle of the 1890s class conflict had been the dominant social antagonism and this caused a split in the middle class. The greater master artisans sided with industry and the middle masters were thus prevented from any concerted action against industry, if they had any desire to take it in the first place. This in itself is doubtful. The attempt in the 1890s to reverse freedom of trade by changing the general trades Act could probably be seen as such an attempt but after all this did not entail far-reaching proposals, and after 1895 no serious attempt of that kind was undertaken. It is easy to find anticapitalism in middle class writing, but it is hardly to be seen when it comes to middle class action.

Pattern of organisation in the commercial trades

As previously mentioned the retailers belonged to the old middle class, but they were a brand new part of it and not much older than the new middle class of employees and white-collar workers. The rather late arrival of the retailers and shopkeepers meant that they had no long tradition either of trade or associations. Blacksmiths, carpenters and chimney sweeps are age old trades of a distinct character with established traditions, but grocers, haberdashers and ironmongers were not, at least not outside the capital. The shopkeepers of Copenhagen had longer traditions, and retailing in Copenhagen was different from retailing in the rest of the country in ways that did not change in the years treated here.[14]

This had consequences for the pattern of organisations. As mentioned above the retailers of Copenhagen had established a regional organisation in 1890. Members of the organisation were not individual shopkeepers but shopkeeper associations of the capital. After an unsuccessful attempt at creating a national union of shopkeepers in the wake of the Stores incident (1894-97), the Copenhagen shopkeepers' union tried to become the principal organisation of all shopkeepers in Denmark. The shopkeepers of the provinces however did not accept the Copenhagen union as their organisation. They created their own regional organisations for different parts of the country, and in 1907 these regional organisations were amalgamated into a national union. The only problem with this union was that it was actually a grocers' union, not a union of all retailing trades. It too tried to become the principal organisation of the shopkeepers of Denmark, but the shopkeepers of Copenhagen would not recognise it in that capacity, nor would the other national trade associations of Danish shopkeepers (textiles, tobacconists, and so on). They were however of minor importance. The two most significant shopkeepers' unions were the Copenhagen union that was multi-trade but only regional, and the union of grocers that was nationwide but single trade. Between those two an intense rivalry developed, but under the pressure of the war years an attempt was made at unifying them. This however became mixed up with the creation of the Business Party (see below) and was a very complicated affair but the outcome was abortive. This was due to a fundamental difference between the interests of the two unions. Here again social subgroups within the middle class prevented it from acting unanimously.

As with the handicrafts, three social subgroups emerged among the retailers too, but they were constituted by different criteria from those among the artisans where it had been the class struggle and the employers' interests that had been decisive. Among the retailers it was the relation to wholesale trade. There was a limit to how small consignments a wholesaler was allowed to deliver. If a shopkeeper wanted to buy canned meat for instance a consignment of say 144 (12 times 12) would be the minimum. The bigger shopkeepers (upper middle class) found no problems in trading directly with the wholesalers and often combined wholesaling and retailing themselves. The middle shopkeepers (middle middle class) were often able to buy directly from the wholesaler but they had no strong negotiating position. The small shopkeepers (lower middle class) were not able to buy directly from the wholesalers and bought their goods from the bigger shopkeepers.

The economic interests of these three subgroups did not coincide. The middle shopkeepers were eager to establish their own co-operative wholesale societies, the bigger shopkeepers were against that. The small shopkeepers did not care because they knew they had different interests from the other two and would receive no help from either.

The national grocers' union was dominated by middle shopkeepers and it was this union that took the initiative in 1919 uniting with the regional Copenhagen union. The middle shopkeepers wanted a strong union of all shopkeepers who could stand united against the wholesalers. The Copenhagen union was not against the establishment of a national union of shopkeepers, but wanted a rather weak union and definitely not a union that could be used as a platform against the wholesalers. The Copenhagen union was dominated by the bigger shopkeepers. In a very cunning manner they managed to welcome the invitation to amalgamate but also to further extend it to another association of provincial wholesalers so that in the end the grocers had to say no to closer co-operation. The relation to capital caused a split among the shopkeepers as it had done among the master artisans. In 1920 shopkeepers comprised the only major economic sector lacking a national union that could attend to its economic interests. The Copenhagen union would have agreed to the formation of a weak national union, the grocers did not want that. The master artisans actually had a national union but it was a weak one. Neither shopkeepers nor master artisans were able to create strong unions at the national level.

The new middle class became a common concept in these years. In 1915 a party programme particularly mentioned employees as a social group. But the new middle class only gained real importance in the inter-war years, which will be considered in the next section.

Political and cultural development

The growing importance of economic interests undermined the two-party system. In the 1890s the Labour Party had its breakthrough. It sided with the liberal party, *Venstre* in the struggle over parliament. This struggle ended in 1901. The King at last asked *Venstre* to form a government. After a few years of governmental responsibility *Venstre* split in 1905. The left wing of the party broke away and created a party of its own, The Radical Left. So a four-party system was born and ever since 1905 these four parties (known as the four old parties) have formed the core of Danish political life although the number of parties is much greater today.

After the split of the liberal party (*Venstre*) the main divide in Danish politics ran between the Labour Party and The Radical Left on one hand and The Left (*Venstre*) and The Right (*Højre*) on the other. That is to say that from 1905 The Left belonged to the right, and The Radical Left pursued a policy of excessive centrist moderation. Names can be misleading. The division between capital and labour had now become the dominant social and political conflict. The middle class had to adapt to that. This was to create great problems for the conservative party. The old party of The Right was transformed in 1915 and renamed the Conservative Democratic Party (literally the Conservative People's Party) and a new programme was adopted that stressed that it should be a party of the middle class. However, the party was still the party of the upper class too, and there was bitter strife between the capitalist and middle-class wings of the party between 1918 and 1920. The story of this struggle is told elsewhere in this book. The outcome was a complete defeat of the middle-class wing which nevertheless in the long run became the dominant wing of the party. But in the political upheaval that followed the end of the First World War the middle-class wing had to give in. It had isolated itself completely, and no representatives of the middle class even tried to come to its rescue.

On the contrary. Distressed middle-class groups had created a political party of their own, *Erhvervspartiet* [the Business Party], which won representation in the Danish parliament between 1918 and 1924.[15] The idea of a new party came from the national union of master artisans. The Copenhagen section led by former members of the new guild movement was dissatisfied with the union and found that too little attention had been given to the economic difficulties of the master artisans in the war years. It then suggested that the associations of the middle class should constitute themselves as a political party. In 1917 it invited the retailers, innkeepers and carters to participate, and they accepted. To many master artisans, however, the only important concern was that more master artisans should be elected to parliament, but they did not care whether this happened inside or outside one of the old parties. The master artisans managed to get one master baker elected as a conservative MP in 1918 and after that the national union of master artisans would not get involved in a new party. So the initiative passed to the retailers. They took it and in the spring of 1918 had established a non-party list in the capital for the general election and they won one seat. In the summer of 1918 this non-party list was constituted as the Business Party. A year later some of the master artisans of the capital joined the party on their own behalf.

This was mainly a party of the capital, Copenhagen. Although it was transformed into a national party, its main strength lay in the capital. It was joined by some middle-class associations that had been established in the greater provincial towns since 1911, and who had gained two seats in one town at the municipal elections of 1917. However they did so only reluctantly because they had wanted a true political party whereas the Business Party was a narrow party of middle-class business interests and had no ideas as to foreign policy, church policy, educational policy, cultural policy and so on. The ideological foundation of the party was a firm belief that profits in general were too low. In 1922 the party split. The master artisans of the capital continued with the Business Party on a narrow economic platform, but the shopkeepers joined with groups outside the party, among them the former middle-class associations of the provincial towns and members of the defeated middle-class wing of the conservative party, and started a new party with a more general political programme, *Det frisindede Landsparti* (The Broad-minded National Party: the name is as strange in Danish as in English), but very soon this broke down too. Both the Business Party and The Broad-minded National Party were dissolved in 1924.

Thus in the years from 1918 to 1924 attempts to create a middle-class based political party failed and in a strange way this is proof of the strength of the middle class in Danish society, because society was saturated with middle-class values and middle-class ideas, but they were conceived as 'Danish' or 'normal' or 'natural' and not particularly 'middle-class'. The middle class was in no danger and those groups behind the Business Party who tried to speak for the middle class actually misused the name for very narrowly restricted trade purposes.

New educational acts of 1899 and 1903 combined the different kinds of schools into a uniform school system.[16] The public school would take all pupils through five years of basic schooling and then give them the choice between two further years of basic schooling or entry into the so-called middle school. This was a creation of the 1903 Act, and it provided four years of secondary schooling. Pupils would finish the middle school by passing the middle school examination. Pupils could continue in the public school for one more year and then pass the *realeksamen* mentioned earlier. This examination was now integrated into the public school system. The former grammar schools were now changed into gymnasia, upper schools. They normally started with a middle school of their own of four years, and pupils who passed the middle school examination satisfactorily could continue in the gymnasium for three years and then take the *studentereksamen* which is equivalent to the general certificate of education in England. The point of the new system was that the middle school became common ground for the public and the upper schools. The curriculum was the same and so was the validity of the middle school examination irrespective of where it was taken. Bright pupils of the public schools would thus automatically qualify for entry into the gymnasium if they wanted to (and if their parents allowed them to do so). The intention of the new school Acts was democratic. The idea was to pave the way to education for the gifted whatever their social background. But at the same time the new Acts were geared to fulfil middle class needs in so far as the new middle school examination and the *realeksamen* became the logical goal for many pupils of the public schools, and the curriculum contained knowledge that was useful to a business career. The *realeksamen* continued to be the preferred examination for the middle class. In the long run the intention of the 1903 Act was fulfilled, and it became instrumental in a greater social mobility, but only after the Second World War was this clearly seen.

In the gymnasium new programmes of study in modern languages were introduced. Together with the mathematical-scientific programmes that had been introduced in 1871 this quickly made the traditional study of classical languages an obsolete part of the gymnasium, mostly used by clergymen *in spe*. But in the first years after the new Act the gymnasium was still dominated by pupils of upper class (academic) background.

The middle class ways of life

The old idea of the household as the basic entity in social life gave way in this period. Although you could still find journeymen and apprentices who lived in the master's house this was no longer the rule. The nuclear family, perhaps augmented by one or two housemaids, now became the dominant form. The separation between public and private spheres became more pronounced as was also seen in the growing separation of living place and working place. Tenement houses were the most common kind of habitation in the towns, and most people lived in flats. There were garden cities in the suburbs, but they were far from dominant.

The growing social differentiation also had implications as regards family life. The ideal was that the husband earned the money and the wife took care of the family physically and emotionally. The upper middle class had far better opportunities of establishing this kind of family than the lower social groups. In the middle middle class the pattern was less clear, but to a greater degree the wife took part in business life. She might do the bookkeeping as was often the case in the handicrafts or do the selling in the retail shops. In the lower middle class the involvement of the wife was even more prominent. Lower middle class families could only engage in economic undertakings if the whole family took part in the work.

The association was still important as an instrument for participation in public life. There were associations of all kinds. Most common were the economic associations with some kind of connection to trade, business or work, but other platforms could do the same job. Especially in newly erected or fast growing towns, religious congregations or temperance lodges could fulfil the same functions trade associations or political parties did elsewhere, but when the communities became more established, they lost this position. Summer picnics, song evenings and Christmas trees were still an important part of the work of most associations. After the First World War this changed.

The inter-war years 1920-1940

Economic background

The inter-war years were years of crisis and depression in Denmark as everywhere else. For the urban trades the twenties was the worst decade, for agriculture it was the thirties, but none of them experienced really good times, and whenever there were signs of a possible economic recovery a new crisis struck. In the inter-war years there was a considerable marginalisation of many social groups. The growth rate of the population was affected and fell to almost stagnation point in the thirties. The geographical distribution of the population changed too. To some degree this was caused by a new transport revolution.

The railways had completely changed the Danish transport system since the 1870s, but from the 1920s lorries instigated a revolution in local transport, quickly replacing horse-drawn carriages. This undermined the position of the secondary railways, and the population became increasingly concentrated in the capital and the larger provincial cities. This was the youth of suburbia. However, the spread of the suburbs was restricted by the still comparatively small number of private cars. Doctors, architects and salesmen whose work entailed a lot of travel bought cars but in general they were luxury goods bought mainly by the upper class. Only a few middle-class families could afford private cars in the inter-war years.

In the countryside, especially in the marginal areas, the population declined. This was a new trend. Until 1920 the countryside had participated in the general growth of the population and progress of the economy, but now some areas experienced the beginning of depopulation. This was not only an effect of the economic crisis but also a contribution to it as part of a vicious spiral..

Socio-economic development

The economic difficulties of the inter-war years affected all sectors of the economy. The urban trades were the first to get into difficulties. Danish industry experienced a harsh crisis in 1921 and 1922 when international competition returned, and it tried to overcome the problems by rapidly modernising production and reducing wages. The workers tried to prevent a pay cut and there were massive strikes in the years from 1921 to 1925. Nevertheless wages were gradually reduced, and productivity improved during the 1920s, but it was not enough. Danish industry lost competitive power in these years.

Agriculture, which had a high export rate, got into difficulties in its two main markets: Great Britain and Germany. When normal international trade broke down at the beginning of the 1930s both agriculture and industry were affected, but the problems were most difficult to solve for agriculture, which no longer had free access to the world market, whereas industry benefited from new opportunities, because for the first time ever the home market was protected (not by customs but by import regulations due to the permanent lack of foreign currency). This gave industry a new status and the sector grew, but due to the lack of foreign competition productivity did not improve much during these years. The protection of the home market gave handicrafts a breathing space too, and except for the very harsh years of 1932 and 1933 the urban trades were not too badly affected.

The middle class

The economic problems of the inter-war years changed the composition of the middle class. The old middle class was affected by the problems of agriculture, and that part of the old middle class that catered for the local market in the countryside got into trouble. A number of smaller businesses with little economic strength had to give up. Those artisans and retailers of the countryside who managed to continue were increasingly concentrated in the bigger railway towns. The growing suburbs created some new possibilities but it was not easy to establish a viable shop or workshop in these newly built surroundings, and an increasing number of businesses failed. This meant that a growing number of middle-class businesses belonged to the marginalised group whose economic conditions were rather precarious. The differences between the stable core of the class and the marginal groups became greater.[17]

The rationalisation of Danish industry in the 1920s created more employees and the expansion of Danish industry at that level of productivity in the 1930s continued this process. The new middle class now became generally acknowledged as a new social group.

The old middle class

The artisans still formed the greatest part of the old middle class, but shopkeepers almost caught up with them. The number of private businesses continued to grow in the inter-war years. More so in the 1930s, where the protection of the Danish market offered them better opportunities than in the 1920s when competition was rather fierce. New smallholdings were still established by public initiative so the number of independent agrarians grew too.

Table 3 Independent businessmen 1921-40

	Number of people	
	1921	1940
Agriculture	186,582	207,872
Industry	76,841	85,793
Commerce	54,463	78,241
Business total	343,231	393,914
Seamstresses	10,156	7,181

Increasingly handicrafts and retailing became urban trades. If the typical man of the old middle class in 1890 had been a master artisan in the countryside, in 1940 he would be a shopkeeper in a provincial town. The shop replaced the workshop as the main outlet of the middle class. In the towns not only were master artisans overtaken by shopkeepers in numbers, but many artisans had opened shops themselves, butchers, bakers and shoemakers for instance.

The inter-war years witnessed an increased decline in the relative position of independent businessmen compared with employees and workers. The growth in number of the independents was now accompanied by a clear decline in their relative importance. There were no opposing trends any longer. It was the same in all parts of the country, and master artisans as well as shopkeepers were caught up in the trend.

The number of employees continued to grow in the commercial trades, but only slowly in industry. The growth of the new middle class however was not sufficient to offset the decline of the old, and the number of workers grew in the urban trades.

Table 4 Employees 1901-40

	1901	1921	1940
Agriculture	14,090	16,162	14,130
Industry	8,222	29,401	53,607
Commerce	26,568	60,143	130,603
Business total	77,372	125,644	231,808
Public service	...	44,318	52,589

Public service does not include the church, education, the military or health care.

Table 4 shows the number of employees 1901-40 but has to be read with some reservation; it is difficult to find exact numbers and Danish statistics did not define employees in the same way from year to year.[18] Commerce was by far the most important economic sector for employees with industry far behind. The number of public employees was greater than the table shows, but the exact definition of this group is particularly difficult. The most outstanding feature however is the very rapid growth of privately employed people in the inter-war years.

Pattern of organisation

The new middle class did not unite in one single national union of employees. The inner divisions of the group were more important than their position as employees. The first group to form trade associations were the technical employees, *maskinmestre* [engineers tending machines], *værkførere* [foremen] and so on. The first association of this group had been established as early as 1873. They were the trusted employees representing the interests of the employer against the workers. When the constitution of the Danish labour market was adopted by the September agreement of 1899, the employers laid great stress on the point that trusted employees were not to be members of the Danish T.U.C. The distinction between trusted and common employees thus became part of the basic conditions of the labour market. In 1910 the technical employees joined together in a national union. It was a middle class union excluding the common employees on the one side and the academically educated civil engineers on the other.

By the time the trusted technical employees established a union, the common employees had already established a union of their own. It happened in 1900 and was an association of typewriters, shop assistants, storekeepers and so on. After several attempts, this union joined the Danish T.U.C. in 1932 (see below).

In the 1930s the employees of the financial sector at last began to form associations. Bank clerks, insurance company clerks and savings bank clerks formed associations but did not unite into a common one for the financial sector. This only happened rather recently.

Quite a number of employees were public servants. They made associations of their own maintaining the distinction between common and trusted employees. These two groups formed separate national unions. The distinction between public and private employment was only rarely overcome at the association level in the years treated here. After the Second World War this distinction has gradually lost importance.

The middle-class identity was strong enough to prevent the establishment of a single union comprising both trusted and common employees, but the identity was not so strong that all trusted employees united in one single association that crossed the boundaries of the economic sectors. The economic sector, or an even narrower platform of branch or trade, became the foundation of the associations of the trusted employees.

Political and cultural development

As mentioned before, the front line of Danish politics separated The Radical Left who sided with the Social Democratic Party and The Left who sided with the Conservative Democratic Party. However, the political situation was complicated because the political right wing consisted of two former enemies, The Left and the successor of The Right. Their old hostility had not disappeared. There were tensions between agriculture represented by The Left, and the more greater urban trades, industry, shipping and wholesaling represented by The Conservative Democratic Party, and these tensions created a split between the two parties of the right. This provoked a general election in 1929 which initiated more than 50 years of Social Democratic dominance in Danish politics.

The economic crisis of the inter-war years saw 'The Establishment' under pressure. (*Systemet* was the Danish name used by the many opposition groups that came into existence.) There were new radical political formations left and right and a number of new radical business associations too,[19] and there was definitely much ado, but, seen in a comparative perspective and seen from the safe distance of posterity, about almost nothing. The outstanding feature of the inter-war years was the strength of the core. 'The Establishment' was beleaguered but not in danger. Danish agriculture probably suffered worst

The most important political issue of the inter-war years was the battle over the political loyalty of employees. Employees had been recognised as a new, distinct social group. In 1915 the Conservative Democratic Party was the first to identify the employees as a social group in need of special political attention. This was part of the attempt of the reformed party to establish itself as *the* party of the middle class. Only in the 1930s were employees mentioned in another party programme, that of The Radical Left. The Left did the same in a political statement of 1938 but only in the negative sense that employees were to be denied the right to strike. The Conservative Democratic Party and The Radical Left were the two parties that most vehemently courted the favour of the employees, but the real ideological battle for the political loyalty of employees was not fought between these two parties but between The Conservative Democratic Party and the labour movement. In 1900 a trade union of lower employees had been established and it had tried several times to join the Danish T.U.C. This was met with vehement resistance not only from elements of the membership but much more so from forces outside the trade association. The employers warned the employees against taking this step. However, finally in 1932 a large majority of the delegates of the association voted for entry into the Danish T.U.C. This caused an outcry among the anti-socialist forces in Denmark, and the conservative youth movement (which at that time was under the influence of fascism and Nazism) tried to establish an alternative on a non-socialist basis for the lower employees.[20] The youth movement had to give up this idea. Instead it brought pressure on the

Conservative Democratic Party to do something for employees. The mother party yielded to the pressure of the youth movement and in the spring of 1937 presented employees legislation to parliament. The governing Social Democratic Party originally rejected the idea but its coalition partner The Radical Left was more positive. The outcome was that the government of the Social Democratic Party and The Radical Left involved itself in the issue, and in April 1938 an employees Act was passed with a large majority. Only the Conservative Democratic Party was divided on the issue and the rightist business wing of the party voted against it. The purpose of the Act was quite different from what had been the intention of the Conservative Democratic Party when they opened the question in parliament, and the Act caused tensions between the old and the new middle classes. In particular the shopkeepers tried hard to be exempted from the obligations that the new Act placed on employers towards their employees.

Beside the employees Act another Act caused some tension between the new and old middle classes. It was the apprentices Act of 1937. This was met with fierce opposition from the retailers and the master artisans and they actually boycotted the Act by almost completely avoiding the use of apprentices for some years. The employees however, and in particular the lower level of employees, welcomed the new Act.

The coalition between the old and new middle classes was in no way simple or obvious. The Conservative Democratic Party encountered great difficulties in its attempt to reconcile the conflicting interests of the two groups and in the end failed.

Middle class ways of life

Public life changed its character during the inter-war years. The different kinds of trade associations retained their importance in economic life but gradually lost their importance in social life. The eight-hour day had been introduced by law in 1919 marking an end to long workdays. As late as 1914 the journeymen of the barbershops had managed to negotiate the working week down (!) to 71 hours. Only 5 years later it was limited by law to 48 hours a week. In the inter-war years leisure took on a new meaning. New kinds of leisure activity emerged, such as the cinema, sport, cycling, and so on. Public entertainment even entered the home by way of the radio. A public broadcasting service was established in 1926. This influenced the everyday life of the middle class as it influenced the everyday life of the working class, but it did not contribute to a clearer middle-class identity. On the contrary. If anything, the distinction between working class and middle class in the cultural and private spheres of life shrank in the inter-war years. This was principally caused by the cultural policy of the labour movement. Attempts at creating a working class culture admittedly did not abandon the idea of creating an alternative to the bourgeois culture, but soon the main effort was concentrated on establishing equal rights for the workers to cultural and educational provision.[21] The Danish labour movement was dominated by a reformist and petit bourgeois outlook; the middle class did not have to defend a particular middle-class way of life.

So despite the still far-reaching social differentiation and despite the great differences between rich and poor, the manners of the upper class became, transformed and emulated by the middle class, the model for the lower class too. The size of the working-class family that in 1880 had been well above that of other families had come fairly near to the average by 1940. And the working class did not demand that bourgeois theatres be closed, but asked for cheaper tickets.

100 years of the middle class

The problem with the Danish middle class is the problem of being able to see the wood for the trees. Danish society was permeated by middle-class values and middle-class manners and the middle-class way of life, but it was not conceived as particularly middle-class. The Danish national identity was a middle-class identity. National songs bear witness to that. One famous song is known by its opening line: *Langt højere bjerge..* ('Far higher mountains are found abroad...'; actually there are no mountains at all in Denmark). A much quoted line of that song contains the national ideal: 'That day in richness we have come far, when few are too wealthy yet fewer too poor.' Another song has the title 'A plain, merry and industrious life.' Neither too much nor too little. Moderation and modesty had become the pride and boast of the Danish nation. Not a word is mentioned in these songs about the middle class or any other class for that matter. They are songs for the Danish people about the Danish people.

Four words were used for the middle class: *middelklassen*, *middelstanden*, *mellemklassen* and *mellemstanden*. *Klasse* means 'class', *stand* 'estate', *middel* means middle (with connotations of a central position), and *mellem* means 'in between' (without connotations of any central position). These four words were used totally interchangeably. There was no distinction between them. No one cared to give a more precise definition of the middle class. It was a term used only under certain circumstances.

If you start looking for phenomena that are explicitly conceived as middle-class ones you will find only tiny unimportant fragments of many kinds. Because the overall position of the middle class was secure, narrow economic interests were given an attention they did not merit. The establishment or thwarting of wholesale societies, the restriction of competition among the painter masters in Copenhagen, and so on. The most ambitious attempt at creating a distinctive anti-socialist and anti-capitalist society was undertaken by the co-operative movement of the agricultural sector [*andelsbevægelsen*], but it was conceived as a specifically agricultural endeavour, not as a specifically middle-class one, and even less so as it contained clear anti-urban elements.

A particular middle class identity was only evoked when times were difficult in some way. The Stores incident was one example, the difficulties of public economic regulation in the First World War another.

The Danish middle class is there all over the place, but if you start to look for it, it vanishes through your hands.

Notes

[1] P.C. Matthiessen, *Some Aspects of the Demographic Transition in Denmark*, Copenhagen 1970; 'Folketal, areal og klima 1901-60', *Statistiske Undersøgelser* 10 [Population, Area and Climate Statistical Analysis] København 1964, pp. 14; Kristian Hvidt, 'Det folkelige gennembrud og dets mænd 1850-1900', [The Democratic Breakthrough and its Men 1850-1900] *Gyldendal og Politikens Danmarkshistorie* [A History of Denmark, published by Gyldendal and Politiken] vol. 11, København 1990, p. 264.

[2] Hans Chr. Johansen, 'En samfundsorganisation i opbrud 1700-1870' [A society in transition 1700-1870], *Dansk Socialhistorie* [A Social History of Denmark] vol. 4, København 1979, p. 56; Hans Chr. Johansen, 'Dansk økonomisk statistik

1814-1980', [Danish Economic Statistics 1814-1980] *Gyldendals Danmarkshistorie* [A History of Denmark, published by Gyldendal], vol. 9. Copenhagen 1985, p. 22.
[3] Niels Peter Stilling, *De nye byer.Stationsbyernes befolkningsforhold og funktion 1840-1940* [The New Towns. Demography and function of the new railway towns 1840-1940], 1987; Jørgen Fink, *Butik og værksted. Erhvervslivet i stationsbyerne 1840-1940* [Shop and Workshop. Business in the railway towns 1840-1940], 1992.
[4] Jørgen Elklit, *Fra åben til hemmelig afstemning* [From Open to Secret Ballot], 1988.
[5] Jørgen Fink, *Middelstand i klemme? Studier i danske håndværksmestres økonomiske, sociale og organisatoriske udvikling 1895-1920* [Middle Class in Agony? Studies in the economic, social and organisational development of the Danish master artisans 1895-1920], 1988. The tables are compiled by use of official Danish statistics found in Statistisk Tabelværk III,18; V A 4; V A 16 and V A 23.
[6] Jørgen Fink, *Middelstand i klemme?*, 1988, p. 195.
[7] Vagn Dybdahl, *Partier og erhverv. Studier i partiorganisation og byerhvervenes politiske aktivitet 1880-1913* [Political Parties and Occupation. Studies in the organisation of political parties and the political activity of the urban trades 1880-1913], 1969, pp 1-2.
[8] Per Boje og Jørgen Fink, *Technical education and the industrial development in Denmark 1850-1950* (17th International Congress of Historical Sciences, vol. I, pp. 271-290), Madrid 1992.
[9] Jørgen Fink, *Butik og værksted*, 1992, pp. 254.
[10] Lorenz Rerup, 'Tiden 1864-1914' [The Years 1864-1914], *Gyldendals Danmarkshistorie*, Søren Mørch (ed.), 1989, p. 269.
[11] Per Boje and Jørgen Fink, *Technical education and the industrial development in Denmark 1850-1950*, 1992, p. 279.
[12] Jørgen Fink, *Middelstand i klemme?*, 1988.
[13] Jørgen Fink, 'Den nye lavsbevægelse. Ærlig pris for ærligt arbejde' [The new guild movement. Honest pay for honest work], *Erhvervshistorisk Årbog* [Danish Yearbook of History], 1986; Jørgen Fink, 'Den nye lavsbevægelse II. Sociale grupperinger inden for byggefagene i København' [The new guild movement II. The formation of social groups in the building trades], *Erhvervshistorisk Årbog*, 1988.
[14] Jørgen Fink, 'En hovedorganisation som aldrig blev til. Danmarks Butikshandlendes Hovedudvalg' [A top organisation that was never established. The Committee of the Shopkeepers of Denmark], *Erhvervshistorisk Årbog* [Danish Yearbook of Business History], 1991.
[15] Erik Nordholt, 'Erhvervspartiets historie og dets samfundsopfattelse' [The Business Party and its ideology], *Erhvervshsitorisk årbog*, 1972.
[16] Vagn Skovgaard-Petersen, *Dannelse og demokrati. Fra latin- til almenskole, Lov om højere almenskoler 24 April 1903* [Education and Democracy. From grammar school to common school. The law on higher public schools of April 24th 1903], 1976.
[17] Jørgen Fink, 'Håndværksmestrene i stationsbyen' [The master artisans of the railway towns], *Nyt fra stationsbyen* [Railway town newsletter], no. 11, 1987.
[18] There is no general history of employees in Denmark. An overview with further literature can be found in Birgit Andreasen, 'Kontoret og kontoristen' [The office and the clerk], in Flemmeing Mikkelsen (ed.) *Produktion og arbejdskraft gennem 200 år* [200 Years of Production and Workforce], 1992.

101

[19] Niels Finn Christiansen and Karl Christian Lammers, 'Democracy and the lower middle classes: interwar Denmark', in Rudy Koshar (ed.), *Splintered Classes*, 1990.
[20] Carl Gustav Johannsen, 'Funktionærlovens forhistorie inden for Det konservative Folkeparti' [The origin of the law on employees and The Conservative Democratic Party], *Historie* [History] vol. XI, 1976. The subject is treated in a forthcoming book, Jørgen Fink: *Den nye middelstand* [The New Middle Class].
[21] Ib Bondebjerg og Olav Harsløf (eds), *Arbejderkultur* II *1924-48* [Workers' Culture II, 1924-1928], 1979, pp. 56 ff.

JAN EIVIND MYHRE

The Middle Classes of Norway, 1840-1940

The middle class in history and historiography

In 1973, Sverre Steen, the grand old man of Norwegian history, observed that the middle class was the 'forgotten class' of Norwegian historiography. The three decades that have passed since that statement was made have seen relatively little work appear to remedy this situation, although the thrust of social history has alleviated it to some extent.[1] However, Norwegian society in the nineteenth and twentieth centuries in many ways followed a well-known path of Western modernisation, economically, socially and politically.

So how are we to interpret this neglect on the part of Norwegian historians? I would like to put forward two propositions, both implying that historiography has been part of the development of the Norwegian middle classes. The first is that the neglect to a certain extent reflects reality; from certain points of view the middle classes have not been very important. The second is that historiographical development reflects contemporary society; the historians of the 1920s to the 1940s were more absorbed with the rise of the middle classes than their colleagues some decades earlier or later.

To say that neglect reflects reality does not mean, of course, the absence of middle classes (or layers, strata, ranks) in Norwegian society, only that the existence and role of the Norwegian middle classes between 1840 and 1940 is a particularly awkward one. Although the terms 'middle class(es)' [*middelklasse(r), mellomklasse(r)*] or 'middle rank' [*middelstand*] were in frequent use during that period, they were seldom very potent concepts, either politically or economically, socially or culturally. To Steen, the middle class seemed rather 'nameless' in the nineteenth century, whether this was due to the class not daring to speak its name or not.[2]

The fact that historians used the term 'middle class' or closely related concepts relatively rarely therefore only *partly* reflects the social reality of late nineteenth and early twentieth-century Norwegian society. Different concepts from those describing the social middle were usually in the forefront when people wanted to make sense of social configurations, as we shall see below. I say 'partly' because the historian's task, of course, is also to get behind verbal usage. Were there important traits in Norwegian society during the century in question that take on more meaning when we see them in the light of some middling social structure? I think so, but few historians have dedicated themselves to such questions.

The reason for this reluctance on the part of the historians may be sought in the times of the historians themselves. Between the world wars, and particularly in the 1930s, 'the thrust of the middle class', as one commentator called it,[3] became obvious to all contemporary observers, both in terminology and in the social landscape. The historians' sense of the social middle became more acute, as is evident in the historical scholarship of Wilhelm Keilhau (1931 and 1935), Knut Greve (1942) and Sverre Steen (1942 and 1948).[4] Greve's contribution to the five-volume Norwegian cultural history, published around 1940, is noticeable for the fact that the rise of the middle classes was thematised at all, something that did not happen in its eight-volume successor from 1980[5], or for that matter in any comparable publications from the subsequent four or five decades. This was also the age when novelists began to wonder what was going on in *the office*, as opposed to the factory or the home.[6]

It is also quite noticeable that of all the five major multi-volumed histories of Norway published since the 1930s, the oldest (by Keilhau) is the one with the bulkiest treatment of the rise of the middle classes, however defined, in the nineteenth and early twentieth centuries.[7] Another reason for this may be that Keilhau, being educated as an economist rather than an historian, stood outside the two main trends of Norwegian scholarship. There was on the one hand the national, rurally oriented tradition, where the middle classes had little or no conceptual place. To rural society, 'middle class' was an alien term; the concept did not fit very well into the domestic-foreign dichotomy. On the other hand, there was the radical, more or less Marxist, tradition, much more interested in the working class or the bourgeoisie than the middle class.

These two traditions, either in their pure forms or in combination, have dominated Norwegian historical scholarship for most of the twentieth century.[8]

In their social-historical studies from the 1950s, both Ingrid Semmingsen and Dagfinn Mannsåker touched upon the concept of middle class. 'Until the last decades of the last century it was mainly the middle class in town and country that influenced social development in Norway,' writes Semmingsen in an article about 'the dissolution of estate society in Norway'. 'Social development' meant introducing political democracy and economic liberalism.[9] The statement is somewhat misleading however, since she includes peasants and farmers in the middle class, since the higher public officials, an unequivocal elite in nineteenth-century Norwegian society, were the main proponents of economic liberalism, and since her middle class concept is rather vague anyway. Interestingly however, Semmingsen, sensibly, comes close to rejecting the problem confronting her about the dissolution of estate society in nineteenth-century Norway. Historians from Sweden, Denmark and Finland setting out to perform the same task, were not faced with such a problem. In their countries, unlike Norway, there had been an estate society to dissolve, in the normal legal and political sense of the concept.

Semmingsen's contemporary Dagfinn Mannsåker found the concept of middle class of no use in his study of the social recruitment of the Norwegian clergy in the nineteenth century. He identified some middle layers, but ended his stratification analysis by identifying four different strata, avoiding conceptual problems by simply naming the strata I to IV.[10]

The question of where to place the peasants (later to be farmers) in the social structure, was a particularly awkward one. Steen put them in the middle ranks of the Norwegian social structure (as *mellomklasse*) in the late nineteenth century, due to their being economically independent, having the vote and being culturally quite self-confident.[11] However, in the views of several historians, the term 'middle class' refers to a structure of which the farmers were not fully a part.

The rise of the middle class(es) has not been much more than a footnote in the major works on Norwegian history that have appeared since the Second World War. Some of the processes one normally associates with the middle classes, such as urbanisation, the emergence of organisational society and the development of political democracy, are treated without much explicit reference to the middle class. The most valuable literature in the field are books and articles about individual professions or trades, written as theses or for the anniversaries of organisations.[12] It seems easier, however, to apply a middle class perspective to the twentieth than to the nineteenth century. Mannsåker writes that 'in a country with a social structure like Norway's in the nineteenth century, it would no doubt be beneficial to social historical research to dispose of the concept of middle class totally, although without resorting to the simplistic dualism of upper class and lower class.' A terminology with a middle class, Mannsåker says, is rooted in a very different kind of society, namely one with nobility.[13] However, most textbooks or syntheses of Norwegian history from the mid-nineteenth to the mid-twentieth centuries do address the rise of the middle classes, albeit within the space of only a few pages. Most of the historians, incidentally, prefer to refer to this phenomenon in the singular form, the middle class.[14]

For most authors, the lack of nobility did not pose a problem because there was still clearly an upper class. In the twentieth century, the nobility's role as the upper stratum, the leading class, declined in Europe. The bourgeoisie, or the haute bourgeoisie, stepped forward as the new upper class, leaving space for a middle class between the bourgeoisie and the working class. In the latest synthesis of Norwegian history in the first half of the twentieth century, Knut Kjeldstadli places the middle class in two settings. In terms of social, economic and political conflict lines, Norwegian society is perceived as a triangle, showing the farmers, the working class and 'the bourgeois with the urban middle class' in the three corners. In a different setting 'a new middle class emerges' as a new way of life, which was partly a pale imitation or variation of that of the haute bourgeoisie, and partly its own.[15]

Norway in Europe: mainstream and periphery

What, then, was so peculiar about Norwegian society? A few basic observations need to be made about the *population* and *settlement*, the *economy*, the *politics* and the *social structure*.[16]

From a European perspective Norway was a territorially large, but thinly settled country throughout the century between 1840 and 1940. The censuses showed a population of 1.33 million in 1845, 2.24 million at the turn of the century and 3.16 million in 1946, concentrated along the coast. South-eastern Norway was the only area with a substantial inland population. By the mid-nineteenth century roughly 12 per cent of Norwegians were town dwellers (15 per cent if we include unincorporated suburbs and other densely populated places). There were no villages in Norway. In 1900 about 28 per cent (35 per cent) lived in towns, 28 per cent (46 per cent) in 1930 and 28 per cent (49 per cent) in 1946. The urbanisation process in the first half of the twentieth century therefore mainly took place outside the formally incorporated towns.[17]

The Norwegian economy in the nineteenth century must be described as an economy of parts.[18] One the one hand there was the foreign sector, conducted through the towns. Grain, colonial goods and industrial goods were imported, whereas the main export commodities were fish, wood products and metals. The domestic sector, diminishing over time, produced goods and services for internal consumption. Although foreign trade reached into every corner of the country, Norwegian agriculture is commonly described as quite subsistence-oriented. Industrialisation set in from the 1840s on, both within towns (machinery, textiles and other consumer industries) and outside (sawmills, planing mills, pulp and paper factories). Major industrial expansion took place in the 1870s, the 1890s and the decade following the break-up of the union with Sweden in 1905, notably in power-consuming metallurgical manufacturing. By the First World War, Norway was in many respects an industrialised country, somewhere in the middle rank of industrialising Western European states. In 1920, the number of people employed in industry reached 300,000, the same as in agriculture.[19]

Industrialisation had a great impact on the social landscape, creating not only an industrial working class and a new group of functionaries, but also a considerable group of middlemen. Norwegian industrialisation was accompanied by two important developments. First, the government pursued a policy of radical economic liberalism until late in the nineteenth century, doing away with the privileges of the crafts and the trades at an early stage (the two decades following 1839 being particularly important). The outcome of this was a comparatively weak petite bourgeoisie, the small master artisans and the shopkeepers and small merchants. Secondly, a strong state emerged as both cause and effect of the lack of an haute bourgeoisie in industry and finance, which, in turn, was partly a function of Norway being a small and relatively poor country.

As we have noted, there was no nobility. It was abolished by parliament in 1821 as a consequence of the democratic constitution of 1814, but it was already negligible by this time and had been for a century or two. Nevertheless, there was a clear awareness of an upper class in nineteenth-century Norway. In the first decades of the century, the lumber-, metal-, and fish-exporting bourgeoisie of the towns were sometimes referred to as 'lumber patricians', 'lumber nobility' or 'Christiania nobles'. Together with the senior civil servants [*embetsmennene*], they were frequently called *de kondisjonerte* [the cultural elite] or *den bedre stand* [the upper rank]. With the decline of this bourgeoisie in the wake of the Napoleonic wars, the civil servants reigned supreme as the upper class by the middle of the century. In the second half of the century, however, a strengthened *Wirtschaftbürgertum* arose, slowly matching the *Bildungsbürgertum* in social standing.

In Norway in the nineteenth century, therefore, one tended to divide the society into the haves and have-nots in relation to what constituted the two Bürgertums: education and wealth, or in the terminology of the time, *Intelligents og Formue* [intelligence and fortune]. There were few people with middle-range education, although there were, of course, quite a few medium or moderately wealthy merchants, shopkeepers or artisans, sometimes referred to as *middelklasse* or *middelstand*. However, the crucial dividing line, running through a number of social institutions, separated the propertied classes from the property-less ones, and even the smallest yeoman, master artisan, tradesman or urban house-owner fell on the privileged side, for example by having the vote. The main point, of course, was economic independence. Although constituting the bulk of the Norwegian population until well into the twentieth century, the agrarian population cannot easily be fitted into a social structure containing a middle-class, as already noted.

A pivotal variable in Norwegian nineteenth-century society was the question of nationality, another dimension that does not lend itself easily to identifying a social middle. True enough, the political opposition from the 1870s on, a coalition of rural and radical urban forces, sometimes used the term 'middle class' to describe its social basis, but the term carried little analytical value.

There were consequently only a few variables that could define some middle classes or strata of importance in nineteenth-century Norway. The twentieth century was to experience a change in this. A number of changes, institutional or non-institutional, took place around the turn of the century. We may therefore speak of two fairly distinct periods in the rise of the Norwegian middle class, the nineteenth and the twentieth centuries.

The vote, originally (1814) based on property and education only, was extended by a census system in 1884, and universal suffrage (for men) was introduced in 1898 (for women in 1913). Landed property (capital) meant less than before, movable property more, as industrialisation proceeded towards the end of the century, and particularly after 1905. Education between elementary school and university graduation virtually exploded from the last decades in the nineteenth century on. The question of national identity and attitudes after 1905 operated in the background as a social and political demarcation line.

The middle classes became easier to spot because new terms arose and older terms changed their meanings, terms denoting classes, professions, occupations, industries or larger groups of employees. A major reason for this was the rise around the turn of the century of middle-class organisations along the lines indicated: teachers' associations, unions of bank clerks, organisations of municipal functionaries and the like.

Last but not least, the general social and economic development headed in a direction that made room for a definable and visible middle class. A more definable economic *haute bourgeoisie* developed, albeit a smaller and less visible group than the upper middle classes or *Wirtschaftbürgertum* of, say, England, Germany or Sweden. A wide group of small and medium-sized producers and distributors came to constitute the new old middle class. It has been argued that this group, which was not dominated by artisans and shopkeepers, set the pace and tone of the Norwegian economy and society, the Norwegian *Sonderweg*, or 'special way', in the first decades of the twentieth century.[20]

The senior civil servants [*embetsmennene*], the Norwegian mandarins, had relatively declined by the First World War, but their 'successors', academically educated professionals in the public or private fields, had a strong position, partly due to the strong Norwegian state. They may be said to belong to the elite rather than to the middle classes treated in this essay. In terms of numbers, the new horde of public and private clerks, white-collar functionaries, came to dominate the middle class. They had no common name in Norwegian, but were called *bestillingsmenn* (which until around the time of the First World War denoted middle or lower public officials), *tjenestemenn* (which has the same meaning, but sometimes including trusted workers), *funksjonærer* [functionaries, officials], *betjenter* [attendants], *kontorister* [office clerks] and *bestyrere* [managers]. Above all, they were the ones who came to be associated with the middle class. The representatives of small business so noticeable in other countries, the shopkeepers and artisans, played a comparatively small role in Norwegian society, both in terms of numbers and in terms of social and political influence.

The language of the middle

Three different terms were more important than any others when people wanted to describe the middle layers of Norwegian society in the nineteenth and twentieth centuries; *middelklasse* [middle class], *middelstand* [middle rank] and *borgerskap* [bourgeoisie or burghers]. The term *mellomklasse* is sometimes used synonymously with *middelklasse*, '*mellom*' meaning in-between rather than middle.

What was the social meaning of the three terms? How were they related to each other? Knut Greve, one of the few authors who has focused on the Norwegian social middle, called his 1942 essay, covering the period from the early nineteenth century to the Second World War, '*Fra* [from] *borgerskap til* [to] *middelstand*'. With this title, he meant to focus on both the changes in the way people of that period talked about the social middle and what that social middle consisted of. By '*borgerskap*' he did not mean the bourgeoisie in the modern capitalist sense, but the privileged burghers of pre-industrial Norway. It was merchants, some shopkeepers, master artisans and sea captains who constituted the great majority of the social middle between the elite of the *kondisjonerte* and the *allmue* [the mob or the common people].

The *middelstand* was a quite different entity, whose main component was the large new wage-earning groups. To use the term *middelklasse* would have been perfectly possible by 1942, and Greve in fact changed between the two in his article. It is from certain perspectives noticeable that the term '*stand*' [rank] held sway in daily use in the twentieth century, and in fact was used interchangeably with 'class'. Even the labour movement well into the twentieth century sometimes used the term *arbeiderstanden* [the labouring ranks] to denote the class-conscious collective of workers.

In the nineteenth century '*stand*' was normally used to describe larger segments of society. These segments could either be vertical or horizontal. The most important vertical segments or columns were *embetsstanden* [senior civil servants], *kjøpmannsstanden* or *handelsstanden* [merchants, businessmen] and *håndverkerstanden* [artisans]. For most of the nineteenth century, elections provide good examples of social thinking in terms of rank. In both local and national elections in a town like Christiania (Oslo) the electors could only choose between slates of candidates for each *stand*, which had fixed quotas of representatives when for example electing the tax commission or the town council.[21]

'*Stand*' might also represent horizontal strata, like *den bedre stand* [the better ranks], *borgerstanden* and *den ringere stand* [the humbler ranks], terms employed in early nineteenth-century Trondheim, Norway's third largest town.[22] In the twentieth century this comprehensive usage was mainly transferred to the rising middle class, to lines of business or industry (*handelsstanden* [the commercial profession]), and to an indefinite number of small social groups, mainly occupational groups (for example *kelnerstanden* [waiters]).

Contemporary terminology in the nineteenth and early twentieth century therefore employed '*stand*' for a variety of purposes, often without taking notice of the original meaning, which was the ordering of society into vertical legal ranks or estates in early modern society. What Norwegian social historians did from the

1970s on was to employ this verticality, without its legal aspect, to characterise pre-industrial society. *Standssamfunnet* [rank or estate society] was in their terms synonymous with this pre-industrial society, whose main social characteristic was the prevalence of vertical social bonds of loyalty and dominance, responsibility and dependence. They ran from master to servant, from master artisan to journeyman and apprentice, from merchant to *handelsbetjent*, from senior civil servant to lower civil servant to trusted workers wearing a uniform (guards, non-commissioned officers and the like),[23] from husband and father to wife and children. These vertical and personal social ties dominated Norwegian society, vividly depicted in the parliamentary debates from the 1860s to the 1880s about a possible extension of the suffrage.[24] Its counterpart and historical successor was *klassesamfunnet* [class society] in which bonds of loyalty (or rather, solidarity) were horizontal, between masters (capitalists), between workers, and, perhaps, between people of the middle classes.[25]

As a matter of fact, the terminology used in the nineteenth century as well as in the twentieth was not very consistent.[26] An extreme example would be the romantic nationalist poet, and sometime historian, Henrik Wergeland (1808-1845), who frequently changed between '*middelklasse*', '*middelstand*' and '*mellomklasse*' (in the plural as well as the singular), '*borgerskap*', even '*borgerstand*'.[27] Was there any kind of system in this terminology of the middle? To my mind, one may single out three tendencies.

First, vertical social thinking, the concentration on social differences, was less widespread in Norway (and even in the other Scandinavian countries) than elsewhere in Europe. The evidence is admittedly not very strong, but most sources point in the same direction. The results from searching through thousands of pages in a database covering the writings of many prominent Norwegian novelists and essayists in the nineteenth and early twentieth centuries was surprisingly meagre. That is to say, their social vocabulary was not highly developed.[28] Major encyclopaedias between 1860 and 1940 do not mention the words '*middelklasse*' or '*middelstand*', not even '*klasse*' in the social sense of the word.[29] In the major Norwegian dictionary (1947), the word '*middelklasse*' referred to '*middelstand*', which was the main entry: 'Middelstand, en, (after German *Mittelstand*) ... mainly a literary term, part of a society that economically and socially takes a middle position between the upper class and the lower class (in our country especially smaller businessmen, lower public officials, functionaries).'[30]

Relatively speaking, the prevailing view of social differences and social conflicts seems to have been a rather harmonious one. In parliament, several speakers in the 1870s and 80s pointed to the Norwegian egalitarian tradition. Classifying people into classes is old-fashioned, a representative of the radical-liberal opposition said in 1881. It does not fit Norway, he claimed.[31] Preliminary results from a study of the frequency with which words containing 'class' were used in the USA, Great Britain, and Norway at that time seem to say that there was little class thinking in Norway reflected in class-language.[32]

Secondly, the use of the terms of the middle seems to increase in the second half of the century we are dealing with (i.e. roughly 1890 to 1940). From being vague sociological-cultural terms, *'middelstanden'* and *'middelklassen'* seem to take on rather more potent social and political meanings from near the end of the nineteenth century onwards. In the struggle against the old *embetsmann* regime and its successor (the Conservative party, *Høyre*), the farmer-urban liberal-radical opposition sometimes invoked the term *'middelklasse'* to describe itself. By this they meant the solid, hard-working population, the economic and social backbone of the nation, thereby implying the parasitic nature of their opponents,[33] but also decrying their opponents' ties to particular interests.

Thirdly, as already mentioned, there seemed to be little difference in the way *'middelstand'* and *'middelklasse'* were used throughout the whole period between the mid-nineteenth and mid-twentieth centuries. In England the story was different. The concept of class became more important as the nineteenth century moved on. The introduction of 'class' was usually connected with the breaking down of pre-industrial society, the destruction of older social bonds, and the confrontation of the new social groups, that is classes. It is debatable, however, whether the adoption of new concepts reflects social reality (Briggs), changes reality (Wahrman) or whether the new terms were an invention within that reality (Crossick).[34]

Interpreting the use of the term 'class' as a marker of the coming of modern Norwegian society does not make sense until, perhaps, the inter-war years, despite rapid modernisation and industrialisation from the 1840s on. One reason might be that the old society was not really a society of 'ranks', 'orders' or 'degrees'[35], not a *standssamfunn* that needed to be broken up or away from in the European sense.

The term '*borgerskap*', when it was not used in its formal sense of a burgher, partly overlapped with the 'middle' terms, in the sense that some parts of the *middelklasse* stood below the *borgerskap*, and the *middelklasse* did not reach into the higher parts of the *borgerskap*. Sometimes the French term *bourgeoisie* was used. In time, the designations containing 'middle' seem to have slipped slightly down the social scale, without any 'upper' terms taking their place. Whether one would call oneself 'upper class', or was considered to be so by others, was a question of emotions [*følelsessak*], Sverre Steen wrote.[36] The great ship-owners, for example, might call themselves 'upper middle class' in the inter-war years, paying tribute, perhaps, to the national quest for equality. If Norway had an upper class, these people were certainly at its core.

The closest one could get to an official version of the social structure, apart from the voting regulations, was the official statistics, particularly as they were presented in the censuses taken at ten-year intervals. The published census returns convincingly reveal contemporary views on social categorisations.[37] In the first half of the nineteenth century a social middle is hard to find. The statistics contain both vertical and horizontal dimensions, but seldom at the same time. Its categories were *embetsmenn*, merchants/shopkeepers and artisans with or without citizenship such as burghers, seamen, servants, day labourers and paupers. The rural areas had a separate classification. From 1845 on, the classification became more detailed, listing about 25 categories, with no apparent systematic classification, except within groups of categories, like master artisans-journeymen-apprentices. Three groups are of special interest to the historian of the social middle: *Bestillingsmenn* [lower public officials], *handelsbetjente* [shop assistants] and *kontorister* [office clerks], whose line of business is not given.

The establishment of the Central Bureau of Statistics in 1876 formalised the considerable change in official Norwegian statistics that had taken place from the 1860s onwards.[38] The census results of 1875/1876, and the official estimates made to establish the possible consequences of an extension of the vote to new social and economic categories of people, set statistics concerning the Norwegian social structure on a firm footing.[39] A number of factors were to decide the social standing of a certain job, the most decisive being the degree of independence [*selvstendighet*] of the job position, including the degree of responsibility or subordination. A tripartite division was made, consisting of independently working people at the top, private and public functionaries [*betjente*] in the middle, and workers and others in a similar subordinate position at the bottom. Of particular interest to us is the second group, meant to include employees who were not workers (except the senior civil servants, the *embetsmenn*, whose position was regarded as independent).

The censuses from 1890 to 1930 were to see an increasing diversification of these three social categories. The category of independents needed to vertically separate the woman selling fish at people's doors, or the poor shoemaker working on his own, from the large industrialist or big merchant, which was not done at first.[40] This category, as well as that of the workers, underwent only minor changes in the censuses up to the Second World War. Most significantly, the major alterations were made in the middle category. The bureau began to separate higher from lower functionaries, office managers [*kontorsjefer*] and operation managers from bookkeepers and other office clerks, office functionaries from professional functionaries (like engineers). The criteria seemed to be degree of responsibility, education and professional orientation. Over time, there was a marked tendency to move from thinking socially (who you are) to thinking economically (what you do).[41]

This development in social categorisation gives a striking impression of a society where change and innovation was mainly a phenomenon of the social middle. None of the three main categories is given a comprehensive name, however, they remain categories I, II, and III, showing acute awareness of social differences, yet remaining true to, perhaps, an ideology of social neutrality.

Criteria for the social middle

What were the main criteria for social classification in Norway from the mid-nineteenth to mid-twentieth century, and how do they relate to a social middle? As stated already, two stand out as particularly important in the nineteenth century, *property* and *education*. And as mentioned above, both were represented, as the only criteria, in the franchise rules of the 1814 constitution, which, except for some adjustments made in 1884, lasted until 1898, when all males got the right to vote. Women received the vote through a process stretching from 1901 to 1913.

Ownership of land, and in some cases other forms of property as well, was of the utmost importance in most formal situations in nineteenth-century Norwegian society. The national census of 1865, the first since 1801 to record names rather than just numbers, normally classified the rural population according to people's status as propertied (yeoman, farmer; *gårdbruker* in Norwegian) or property-less (crofter, cottar; *husmann*), rather than their actual occupation, which might be fisherman or carpenter. The census, for various reasons, divided the whole population into just two categories, the propertied and the non-propertied. The same dichotomy loomed large in the works of the brilliant social scientist and surveyor, Eilert Sundt, writing from the late 1840s to the late 1860s.[42] The tax system was heavily based on land ownership until the 1880s, and so were a number of other social rights and duties.

This separation of the propertied from the non-propertied, however, was of limited use in singling out some middle group in society. Rural society, with its dominance of farmers and crofters (peasants), constituted a different and parallel social structure to urban society. Property in itself did not distinguish middle classes from the elite, and to some degree even urban workers owned their house and piece of land. On the other hand, as we shall see, not all property-less people belonged to the labouring classes.

From the late 1860s, the Norwegian parliament [*Stortinget*] debated a possible extension of the franchise. Since most propertied people in late nineteenth-century Norway already had the vote much of the discussion concentrated on the new group of people who were often not propertied, but rather well educated, or at least had some breeding [*dannelse*] or knowledge [*kunnskap*]. These were the key words. The people in question belonged to *middelstanden*, was one argument put forward in parliament in favour of their having the vote.[43] Who were they? Some occupations were mentioned as examples: teachers[44], station masters, clerks [*kontorbetjente*], managers [*bruksfullmektige*], that is, lower civil servants and private functionaries. The privately employed or independents with an academic education (engineers, lawyers, architects, medical doctors) were probably too few to be mentioned, but their age was soon to come. The outcome of the debates on the vote was the introduction in 1884 of the census principle[45], partly as a result of the practical impossibility of extending the vote based on criteria concerning education.

The debate is significant to us in two ways. First, it signalled that income began to rival real property as a measure of economic independence.[46] Secondly, although the position of the senior civil servants [*embetsmenn*] in Norwegian society was waning, other groups who based their position on education and breeding, were on the rise: professionals and quasi-professionals. The small group of tycoons of industry, finance and shipping that emerged in twentieth-century Norwegian society need not concern us here, except perhaps as ideals or targets for middle-class groups. However, many people from the professional groups, private lawyers, hospital consultants, civil engineers, as well as managers in large companies, were really members of an elite in Norwegian society, although they might possibly call themselves (upper) middle class, a twentieth-century *Bildungsbürgertum*.

The power of education in Norwegian society and its social structure is illustrated by the case of the elementary school teachers. Their influence rested on two pillars. One was the democratisation of Norwegian education from the late nineteenth century on. Before then the (old) middle classes often sent their children to private schools, whereas both the elite of *embetsmenn* and the workers sent their offspring to public schools, although different ones. In the course of two generations a uniform school system developed. Whereas in Oslo only 58 per cent of children of elementary school age went to public schools in 1876, the corresponding figure was 97 per cent in 1935, and at this time we are speaking about the same kind of school, a public 'folk school' [*folkeskole*] system, founded in 1889.[47]

The second pillar was the prominent role of teachers in the successful nationalist democratic movement (the *Venstre* party). They were well represented in parliament and even in the cabinet.

117

However, they often saw themselves as representing rural interests (they usually lived in the countryside), and could therefore hardly acts as vanguards of the middle class. They generally saw themselves as representing the solid middle layers (including farmers) of Norwegian society at large, without actually representing the middle class.

Although far from all middle-class occupations demanded secondary or further education, most middle-class people valued education highly, not least for their sons and in time also for their daughters. The share of high school [*gymnasium*] graduates with functionary fathers grew immensely throughout the nineteenth and early twentieth centuries, from about 10 per cent around 1850 to about 40 per cent around 1930.[48] Education therefore served as a reasonably good marker of middle-class status, although it was of little use in distinguishing the elite from the middle class, especially in the twentieth century. Other markers also helped to signify middle-class status, such as working conditions (white collar, the employment relation) and cultural factors like consumption, which we will turn to later.

The rise of the middle classes

Who were the emerging middle classes in Norwegian society between the middles of the nineteenth and twentieth centuries? How much of the social structure did they occupy? What were the main social components of the middle classes? Where did the people of the middle come from? Providing a quantitative assessment of the Norwegian social middle is not an easy task, particularly in the first years of our period, and particularly when it comes to distinguishing the (lower) middle class from the higher echelons among independent working people in business, crafts, industry and so on. Table 1 gives a rough impression of the results obtained from processing the published censuses between 1845 and 1930.

In the course of 85 years the number of middle-class Norwegians thus increased between eight and nine times in the towns as well as in the country as a whole, while the total population only slightly more than doubled. We shall take a look at two crucial dimensions of the middle classes, namely the rural versus the urban middle class and the 'old' versus the 'new' middle class. After that, we shall inspect the latter two more closely; the petite bourgeoisie first, then the functionaries, with some subsequent comments on recruitment to the middle classes.

Can we talk about rural and urban middle classes? Estimates for the countryside, and therefore for the country as a whole, are difficult to make (Table 1). There were certainly middle-class people in suburbs and other unincorporated urban places. Their relative number increased with time, as suburbs changed from mainly working-class to mainly middle-class residential areas and as small town-like settlements (later to be called *tettsteder*) developed central functions. The countryside (Norway had no villages) contained a number of teachers and other public employees, together with private functionaries and smaller sawmill owners, artisans and the like. Although these middle-class occupations in the countryside became more important with time, they did not loom very large, even at the end of our period. Moreover, these people hardly considered themselves as part of a social middle the way their urban counterparts to a certain degree did. Teachers, as already noted, even acted as forceful spokesmen for rural interests.

Table 1. The size of the middle classes in Norway 1845-1930[49]

Gainfully occupied population

	1845	1875	1900	1930
The towns				
'Old' middle class	18%	17%	12%	8%
'New' middle class	6%	17%	22%	27%
Total for the towns	24%	33%	34%	35%
N=	15,000	41,000	85,000	130,000
The whole country (estimated)				
Excluding freeholders	5%	8-10%	15%	20%
Including freeholders	30%	30%	33%	40%

Farmers and fishermen are another matter. In one sense the Norwegian yeoman or freeholder, like his Danish counterpart, held an intermediate position in Norwegian society, ranking above labourers in town and country. In the countryside only a tiny class of landed proprietors, together with an equally tiny group of senior civil servants, were the freeholder's social superiors. The freeholders were the largest group having the vote in nineteenth-century Norway, and playing an important role in Norwegian politics, particularly after 1884, when a liberal urban/farmer coalition formed a cabinet. Up to the middle of the twentieth century, there were considerable rural-urban differences and antagonisms. However, from an economic (subsistence farming, many small or tiny farms) as well as a cultural (old folkways) point of view, the majority of Norwegian freeholders were 'peasants' rather than 'farmers' until well into the twentieth century.

As Table 1 shows, a considerable shift from the 'old' and the 'new' middle classes took place. Whereas around the middle of the nineteenth century the towns harboured a middle class dominated by craftsmen, shopkeepers and small merchants, in 1930 they were filled by a large group in the social middle consisting of functionaries of all kinds, but mainly people employed in three kinds of activities. They were handling information (like bureaucrats or teachers), selling (retail, wholesale, transport, banking, broker activities) or providing services (like nursing or counselling). An apt name for the group as a whole may be middlemen or mediators.

We know surprisingly little about the lower middle classes, and particularly the petite bourgeoisie, the smaller, less visible brother of the *Wirtschaftsbürgertum* in the period between the middles of the nineteenth and twentieth centuries. This is particularly surprising when one takes into account the fact that their forerunners, the burghers large and small, were the citizens *par excellence* of the Norwegian towns. They were the most permanent town dwellers, they provided much of the income of the towns (through the export of lumber, fish and metal), and they dominated the town councils (although the state officials [*embetsmenn*] in some respects stood above them). It must be noted, however, that it is not easy to draw a distinct line between the merchants (along with a few artisans) who belonged to the social elite and those who must be classified as belonging to the (lower) middle class. In the nineteenth century there are formal designations for small innkeepers [*vertshusholdere*] and small grocers or hucksters [*høkere, marketentere*], but the dividing line between the elite and the middle classes must surely be drawn higher up the social scale.

The petite bourgeoisie, small business (shopkeepers, modest tradesmen, artisans and other small producers), were most visible locally towards the end of the nineteenth century and at the beginning of the twentieth.[50] In limited arenas, in small towns and unincorporated urban places, they played an important role in the everyday life of the community. Apart from local histories, where they are often treated more as individuals than as members of groups, their historiography is meagre. One explanation is that the lower middle class of shopkeepers and artisans was simply not very important in Norwegian society. The artisans, although quite numerous (only around the turn of the century did the number of people in factories surpass the number of people in artisans' workshops), were partly on the defence against developing industrialisation. Some, though, managed to establish successful, albeit usually small, capitalist enterprises.[51] The shopkeepers were simply neither numerous nor influential, politically, socially or economically.

On the other hand, Norwegian capitalism, a thriving one to be sure, was strongly influenced by a broad class of relatively small to middle-sized businesses, whose representatives had considerable social and political influence, particularly in the second half of our period, the 50 years before 1940.[52] Although Norway had no Krupps or Thyssens, quite a few Norwegian capitalists definitely belonged to an elite or a *Wirtschaftsbürgertum*, but the line between these and the broader middle class of smaller industrialists or businessmen is, of course, difficult to draw.[53] In conclusion, the 'new old' middle classes became relatively less important over time, numerically speaking. The traditional lower middle class of self-employed people, so significant throughout Europe[54], was relatively unimportant in Norway. However, a sizeable and enterprising group of small capitalists exerted considerable influence in society, at the economic, the political and the social levels. This group should rightly be classified with the middle classes.

The hundred years covered by our study was, numerically, the century of the 'new' middle class, as Table 1 clearly shows. In the incorporated towns alone, its numbers grew from less than 4,000 in 1845 to more than 100,000 in 1930. According to the (admittedly rather primitive) 1845 census, this new middle class was made up of three groups, *handelsbetjente* [shop assistants, salesmen], *bestillingsmenn* [lower public servants] and *kontorister* [clerks], in diminishing numerical order. The 1875 census allows us to classify all private functionaries (whether clerks, assistants or managers) according to industries. The dominant industry was trade (retailing and wholesaling), followed by shipping, where a considerable class of shipmasters and mates are placed in the middle category. At this time there were still only a few functionaries in the manufacturing industry.

Table 2. *The different elements of the Norwegian middle class 1845-1930*[55]

The growth of middle class people within selected occupations.

	1875	1900	1910	1930
Municipal functionaries	5613	12778	14927	23973
Government functionaries	4819		14868	
Elementary school teachers	3372	5001	5681	8367
Functionaries in retailing and wholesale	8618			55624
Functionaries in banking and insurance	335			10404

At the turn of the century the same tendency prevailed. It must be noted that the relative size of the group of public employees within the new middle class declined throughout the century, even when we take into consideration the fact that an increasing portion of the *embetsmenn* has to be grouped with the middle class and not the elite. The category of middle class functionaries within manufacturing industry increased, but was still small compared to that of the trades.

From the last years of the nineteenth century we are entering the age of the shop assistant and the black-coated clerk, two of the occupations that filled the ranks of the new middle class. At a more structural level, the middle classes were to an increasing degree filled up with people belonging to that booming category of industrial society, namely *middlemen* of all sorts, not only in retailing or wholesaling, but also in banking, insurance, transport and communication, as well as brokers and agents, and employees in businesses dealing with hotels, restaurants and entertainment. And there were of course the swelling ranks of the public functionaries at four levels, the state, the counties [*fylker*], the *fogderier* and the municipalities [*kommuner*]. Municipal functionaries increased in number from 5600 in 1875 to 12,800 at the turn of the century and 24,000 in 1930.[56]

The lower public officials illustrate the many-sided and dynamic character of the new middle class exceptionally well. They formed an association in Christiania (Oslo) in 1890, *Bestillingsmændenes Forening* [Association of Lower Public Officials], with a list of about 50 titles or occupations permitted to enter the organisation. This list had to be constantly expanded in the years that followed.

Some groups among the public functionaries, such as the teachers and the nurses, are those best described in the literature, mainly due to their organisational strength which has resulted in commissioned histories.[57] There is also a literature on the organisation of private functionary groups, like bank clerks, and some dissertations on various groups, like shop assistants.[58]

Not even groups like teachers and shop assistants are easy to categorise as middle class when we consider the group as a whole. The majority of elementary school teachers were working in the countryside, where most of them had been born. Most of them were followers, and many indeed leaders, of the nationalist movement which became politically victorious in 1884. Their rural backgrounds and ideologies largely prevented them from associating themselves with the urban middle class, even though their social status was definitely well above that of the workers, and steadily rising throughout most of our period. (It should be mentioned that the fast-rising group of teachers in the urban areas conformed more to the general picture of a middle class.)

Teachers had a relatively uniform education, background and salary, that is, if we consider the genders separately. Shop assistants were a more disparate lot, even if we only consider the women.[59] The shops demonstrated a social hierarchy of customers and shop assistants. Many fashion shops (selling clothes) expected their assistants to be well-behaved, well-dressed and well-educated. For bookstores the last qualification was perhaps the most important of the three. For selling food, no particular qualifications were demanded. The occupation of shop assistant seems to have been divided into a middle-class section, with middle-class or upper class customers, assistants recruited from the middle-class (or even higher) and the job itself having a middle-class status, and a working-class section, with the jobs being working-class in status and assistants being recruited from the working class. Customers might also come from higher social strata, although they often had their servants buying milk and meat for them.

The growth of the middle classes meant that much of the social mobility was 'necessary', brought about by changes in the social structure. Social mobility was probably more common in the twentieth than in the nineteenth century. One author remarked that the 1912 generation experienced a more open society than its parents or grandparents. There was a low correlation between one's occupation and one's social background.[60] Of course the growing middle classes had to be recruited from below, as well as from 'within' (small businesses were traditionally handed down from father to son, although we know too little about this) or from 'behind' (the wide burgher class). We also know that quite a few were recruited from 'the side', that is from the freeholders. Some also came from above, notably unmarried women who from the 1850s filled the ranks of elementary school teachers and telegraphers. At school, these daughters of *embetsmenn* and wealthy *Wirtschaftsbürger* met young men from the countryside as their colleagues, an interesting social encounter. Women from an elite background working in a middle-class occupation are aptly described as *overgangskvinner* [women in passing], often tormented by the discrepancy in status. At the telegraph stations, they met men who were more of their own social standing, but not quite.[61]

For the young men of the countryside, two important routes led upwards socially: colleges for teachers (seminaries) and schools for petty officers [*underoffisersskole*]. The last might lead not only to a (modest) military career, but also to careers in public service, such as the railways.[62] At the upper level of administration in the Norwegian railways between 1860 and 1913, roughly one in six employees came from farms. One in five had fathers in private businesses, and more than half came from the families of *embetsmenn* or functionaries in the private or public sectors. Very few workers' sons made this considerable leap. When we turn to the lower levels of administration or at the stations, however, upward social mobility from the working class to the middle class becomes highly visible. Two in five were recruited from urban or rural workers, well over a fifth from the farmers. Internal recruitment became important in time, and at the turn of the century about one in four had fathers who were railway functionaries. The railway, in its turn, acted as a social springboard in the sense that the sons of functionaries usually got better jobs than their fathers did.

An exception to the rule that the new middle classes were recruited from *behind, below, the side*, or (in time, from) *within*, is the case of the *embetsmenn* being recruited to the middle classes from *above*. However, as already mentioned, parts of the class of senior civil servants can no longer be considered part of the elite in the early twentieth century.

As already indicated, the history of the female middle class is somewhat different from that of the men. It is, first, a double story, that of employed women and that of the housewives. The employed (unmarried) female middle class, teachers, telegraphers, clerks, and shop assistants in fashion shops or bookstores, were to begin with clearly recruited from the elite or from the well-to-do within the middle classes themselves. Only after the First World War did young women in larger numbers enter middle-class occupations from a more modest starting point. We know little about the wives, except for the spouses of railway functionaries. Interestingly enough, the wives seemed to be of a somewhat higher (and more urban) social extraction than their husbands, which goes to show that these socially rising men got socially superior spouses into the bargain.

So the middle classes were multifarious and constantly changing throughout the century between about 1840 and 1940, both in their composition and their origin. We will now turn to discussing their coherence or non-coherence as a social group, and reasons for and against treating them as a social entity. We shall look at the middle classes at work, in associations, in the family, and in politics.

Diverting experiences: the middle classes at work

In this section I shall first discuss the role of the middle classes in the economy, that is, as producers and consumers, sellers and buyers. After that I shall consider the attitudes towards work that one may find in the middle classes.

The position of the various middle social groups in the economy certainly did not contribute to uniting the middle class. Generally, it divided the class in two, the producing and distributing 'old' middle class on the one hand, and the consuming, wage-earning 'new' middle class on the other. It is not clear, however, whether this created any tangible conflict or animosity in our period.

The wage-earning character of the new middle class meant that, in principle, it had some interests in common with the working class. A considerable portion of Norwegian functionaries, mainly in the public sector, joined the labour movement, not mainly out of solidarity with the workers, but because they thought that the AFL [*Arbeidernes faglige landsorganisasjon*], later the LO [*Landsorganisasjonen*], the Norwegian Federation of Labour (founded in 1899), best served their interests. There were also other reasons why the new middle class did not form a strong organisation of their own, as they did in Sweden [*tjänestemannarörelsen*]. Quite a few solved the problem of an old age pension through a collective pension insurance scheme, funded by the employers and so binding them to them.[63]

This kind of pension was seldom offered to workers, a fact that highlights important differences between workers and functionaries. The people of the new middle class, in Norway as elsewhere, were expected to stay in one job and work their way up in the system, to 'wait and advance' as they said in German-speaking countries [*Warten und aufrücken*].[64] There was a possible contradiction in this. On the one hand, the promise of internal advancement motivated employees to be loyal to their employers, who in return, paid them monthly salaries instead of the daily or weekly wages offered to the workers. The salary was an important mark of the middle class, signalling solidity and trustworthiness. A good illustration would be that the main single criterion for admittance to the Association of Lower Public Officials [*Bestillingsmændenes forening*] in Christiania in 1890 was being paid by monthly salary, and not weekly or daily. On the other hand, while mobility was part of the ideology of the functionaries, in practice the possibilities of advancement within a firm were rather restricted, inducing functionaries to seek better opportunities elsewhere. Some insurance companies discovered at around the time of the First World War that they might make money out of the functionaries' struggle to combine security and the possibility of advancement by changing jobs. They offered collective pension schemes which they sold to the companies where pension rights were not dependent on staying with the company.[65]

Chances of advancement seem to have been particularly poor between the world wars. During some periods, especially in the first half of the twentieth century, public employment actually offered better opportunities for ambitious lower middle class men, for example in the state railways, which were also popular with men with a military education. Public servants, however, had to wait much longer than their private counterparts to acquire full rights to negotiate with their employers on matters such as pay, working hours, advancement and pensions.[66] As a matter of fact, many functionaries, public and private, often lagged behind workers in these respects. Interestingly enough, the Norwegian term *'tjenestemann'*, originally a (lower) official or public servant, came to replace the term *'bestillingsmann'* [public functionary] around the turn of the century, at least in formal matters. The *tjenestemann* concept in time included many workers as well, since the kind of contract with the employer rather than the work itself, was the crucial matter.[67]

The position of the 'old' middle class, the petite bourgeoisie, as independent producers rather than dependent employees, made their social situation different indeed. Their social position rested upon their economic performance, of course, but also on their relations with their customers. Prior to, or in the early stages of mass production, or mass retailing, the customers to a certain degree lent social status to the artisans or retailers they frequented. The butcher in a working-class area was socially inferior to the owner of a small but exclusive store selling men's clothes. In the period between 1912 and 1930, advertisements seeking women to work in food shops did not specify how they should look. When selling clothes, however, saleswomen were expected to be used to associating with a more refined clientele.[68]

The relations between the 'old' and 'new' middle classes in their roles as producers/sellers and consumers respectively also have interesting aspects stemming from the consumption patterns of the functionaries. The opinion of the time had it that they would be bad customers for food, that they would eat below their means. They would be modest, but 'normal' customers for clothes, for example, dressing according to their means. Finally, they would be good customers to producers of goods and services relating to housing, since they would be residing above their means. The 'old' and 'new' middle classes thus, through these different areas of buying and selling, related to each other in a complex fashion, although we are admittedly short of knowledge in this field.

Most functionaries, contrary to some views expressed since the Second World War, did not have shorter working hours than workers, particularly in the generation or two following the breakthrough of the labour movement in the late nineteenth century. Shop attendants in particular, were frequently expected to work very long and unregulated hours, often until nearly midnight. 'Demanding pay for extra work would be sinking to the level of workers,' some shop employers responded to their employees' demand in 1910.[69] The city of Christiania introduced closing regulations in 1913 and again in 1929, when normal opening hours were set from 7.30 a.m. to 6 p.m. on weekdays. On both occasions, the working hours were contrasted with the shorter hours of workers and office clerks.[70]

Although the work discipline in many white-collar jobs was as harsh as in a factory, and the hours were just as long (especially in the nineteenth century), the clerks might be expected to work overtime, if business demanded it.[71] But working overtime, making an individual effort for the good of the firm or to please the employer, was also a way of getting promoted, a very different attitude towards work than that normally taken by the workers. One may call it a career-oriented attitude, an attitude that might also make the ambitious middle-class man bring his work home with him into his spare time, thereby mixing work and leisure in a way unknown to a worker. In this way of living, education played an important (and indeed increasing) part over time. For municipal functionaries in Christiania, a fairly good general education (normally, *middelskole* or *realskole*, secondary school, lasting until approximately the age of 16) would do at the beginning of the twentieth century. In time however, both general and special schooling were increasingly in demand. In the early twentieth century, the national postal service demanded *middelskole* from their clerks and people behind the counters.[72] Where education was lacking, it might be provided by the municipal departments themselves.[73]

When the introduction of closing regulations was debated in 1912 and 1913, the owners of many small shop, notably fruiterers and tobacconists, strongly opposed such regulations. They argued that such shops were purely family businesses and so did not have to consider employees.[74] Mixing work and leisure was also a characteristic of the old middle class, with the artisan and the small shopkeeper being two examples. One might speak in these cases of a way of life where work and leisure cannot be separated. Small business were family affairs, and this put a stamp on the entire lives of those involved in them..

The long hours of the petite bourgeoisie were necessary for survival, but there was also an element of a strong work ethic involved. Among business people higher up the hierarchy, one could easily discern the Norwegian version of the protestant ethic and the spirit of capitalism, the *haugianismen*, for example in towns like Drammen, Trondheim, Stavanger and Bergen. One should also mention, however, that there were simultaneous currents in Norwegian society manifesting scepticism towards commerce in general.[75]

The middle classes in public and private

The middle class, while not organising itself as a class, nevertheless organised all aspects of the lives of its members. To describe the middle classes in their private and public settings involves a paradox. The middle classes have at the same time been described as cherishing privacy like no other classes while also being particularly publicly oriented in the sense of being especially prone to forming associations.[76] The contradiction is just an appearance, however, and vanishes if we say that the middle classes are characterised by a clear-cut separation of the private and public spheres. This, however, seems to raise further questions, even paradoxical ones. Were the middle classes collectively private? What was the nature of their associations; were they middle-class in nature? It may help to classify our ways of looking at social groups in terms of two dimensions, as in Figure 1. These are the subjective-objective dimension and the dimension from concepts of similarity to collective concepts.[77]

Figure 1. Ways of studying the middle classes

	Similarity concepts	Collective concepts
Subjective criteria	IV 'I am middle-class'	I The Association of Lower Public Officials
Objective criteria	III Classifying the middle class according to occupation, income, etc.	II Identifying a middle-class culture or mentality.

In historical studies of labour, an important task, perhaps *the* overriding one, has been to show under what circumstances workers have moved historically from quadrants IV and III to I and II. In middle-class studies the crucial question is whether II exists at all and whether I exists in a general form. The answer to the last question is no. As has been noted, the Norwegian middle class(es) did not organise as such. How then can we explain their high propensity to associate? In this section I shall first try to relate the middle classes to the contemporary 'spirit of association'. Then I shall look at consumption and lifestyles as possible middle-class characteristics, and finally I shall discuss family life and related values.

The 'spirit of association' [*assosiasjonsånden*] was the name that observers of the time gave to the enormous upsurge of organised activity in Norwegian society from about 1840 on. The first associations were mainly local, but from around 1880 the number of nationwide organisations took an upward swing, from fewer than 50 to around 650 at the eve of the Second World War. In a country with the highest propensity in the world to associate voluntarily, the middle classes stood out as the classes that organised all aspects of their lives.[78] The associations may be divided into four major types: occupational or professional organisations; philanthropy or charity organisations; associations tied to some world view (like temperance); and finally, purely social associations or clubs.

The first professional organisations were, in a sense, the guilds. With the liberalisation of the economy, particularly from 1839 on, the traditional guilds dissolved, but were later to be replaced by occupational organisations. In 1838, *Christiania Haandværkerforening*, an association of artisans in the capital was founded, later to incorporate manufacturers as well and become national.[79] Its members were to include modest middle-class producers as well as major ones belonging to a social elite, although at times its main role was to protect the interests of the common craftsman.

The merchants and shopkeepers of Christiania associated at about the same time, in 1841, and it is noticeable that the wealthiest merchants were not involved. The same is the case when we turn to the public employees. It was the professions and occupations a little way down the social scale who organised themselves around the middle of the nineteenth century or earlier, petty officers, elementary school teachers, doctors. Their social superiors, judges, university professors, priests and senior officers, did not organise, partly because they saw themselves as standing above particular interests.

While the elite did not have to associate, and while the workers were not yet ripe for association, the middle classes organised, partly to advance the status of their occupations (like the teachers), partly to defend their economic interests (like the artisans). Towards the end of the century middle-class employees began to organise across occupational borders. The office clerks and shop attendants of Trondheim formed an association in 1879.[80] Their female counterparts did so in the capital in 1890.[81] The bank clerks of Christiania did not get together in an association until 1904. They were latecomers compared to workers because of their closer personal relationships with their employers [82] Early associations such as these hardly challenged their superiors and to a certain degree acted mainly as social clubs.

In 1888 a number of subordinate state and municipal officials met in Christiania and two years later formed the first interest organisation covering a wide range of new middle class occupations, earlier referred to as *Christiania Bestillingsmannsforening*. The organisation soon became a national one, demanding better employment terms. At the beginning of the twentieth century, many of the older associations, together with a host of new ones, acted as trade unions very much in the manner of the labour movement, which quite a few of them actually joined. On the other hand, a number of functionaries' organisations were faithful to the employers, remaining 'yellow' in the eyes of the labour movement.

This means that a strong independent functionaries' movement akin to the *tjänestemannarörelsen* in Sweden never materialised in Norway. Apart from the success of the labour movement, some of the tameness of Norwegian functionaries may be explained by the pension question being solved by the employers through the purchase of collective pension schemes from insurance companies. This question, always high on the agenda of employees, might otherwise have acted as a cement for a functionaries' movement.[83]

In many occupations, comprising academically educated professions as well as semi-professions (for example teachers) and occupations further down the lower middle class, there was a strong *esprit de corps* until the beginning of the twentieth century, which meant loyalty towards the employer, whether public or private. With an emerging professionalisation from the late nineteenth century on, this loyalty was put to the test, and in many occupations loyalty to the profession, the trade, or the field turned out to be the stronger. Quite a few professions, lawyers, civil engineers, architects, and high school teachers, among others, organised shortly before the turn of the century. In any case, a potential common middle-class cause did not develop, even if we restrict it to the new middle class.

Philanthropic associations were abundant in Norwegian society in the century between the middle of the nineteenth and the middle of the twentieth century. It is however, difficult to claim that such organisations were more a domain for the middle-class than for the elite, whether we are thinking about housing the poor, clothing the children, protecting animals or helping released convicts. One gets the impression, however, that associations founded to promote certain major ideas or values were to a large degree filled with dedicated souls of the middle class. We are speaking for example of missionary associations or other religious organisations and temperance movements. In matters concerning religion or alcohol, the social elite in Norway played a role through political leadership or no role at all, simply because mission and temperance did not concern them.

The women's movement, experiencing its first heyday in the 1880s, has been characterised as 'probably the first openly interest-based middle-class movement in the country going beyond the individual occupational group or profession.'[84] What is socially interesting about this movement, however, is that it encompasses women from both the middle classes and the professional academic elite.

Not every organisational activity had a distinct social profile. Sports activities, taken as a whole, seem to cross class as well as rural urban boundaries, as did some particular forms of sport, like skiing and football (which started to become popular around 1900). Wrestling and boxing had mostly working-class followers, while tennis and sailing wore the stamp of a social elite. Were there middle-class sports? Gymnastics and athletics seem to have been peopled by the middle class around the turn of the century.[85] Many sports, however, seem to have spread rapidly through the classes or from town to country or vice versa. This is in itself a testimony to the relative absence of rigidity in the Norwegian class system.

Finally, did the middle classes associate for social as opposed to economic or political purposes, and to what extent was doing so part of what made them distinct? To the degree that neighbourhoods were relatively uniform socially, local welfare organisations [*velforeninger*], typical of the suburbs of the larger towns, might serve to reinforce middle-class unity. There is no doubt that, in general, membership patterns of social organisations followed class lines. In many small Norwegian one-company towns from the beginning of the twentieth century, workers and functionaries often lived separate organisational lives.

The lifestyles of the Norwegian middle class have been characterised by concepts such as 'modern' and 'conventional'. The concepts may appear somewhat contradictory, but are not. The opposite of modern is traditional, and of conventional unusual, independent or original. When the middle classes have been characterised as having a modern lifestyle, one is normally referring to the new middle classes. Being a (relatively) new social construction, they were as inhibited by tradition as the old middle classes or the peasants/farmers. This was visible in several ways. Because the new middle class was made up of wage earners, they had lengthier periods of spare time and, in the twentieth century, an increasing amount of leisure time. The 48-hour week was enforced through legislation in 1919, but was introduced locally before then. Already, in 1909, more than half of shop assistants had at least two weeks' vacation every year, although their employers normally decided when.[86] This meant that leisure activities, often organised, increased over time, and particularly among functionaries. Some were certainly modern, like cycling. During the interwar depression, the leisure industry was one of the few expanding and flourishing industries in Norway.[87]

Being modern, however, was an attitude, perhaps more than anything else. It entailed a positive attitude towards novelties in clothing, housing, eating and transport, above all innovations with a scientific air about them. Housework became almost a scientific enterprise with its new devices for storing food, cooking and cleaning.[88] This also meant an upgrading of the work of housewives, which from early in the twentieth century was regularly called an occupation, *husmoryrket*. There were schools for housewives, where young women of the social elite as well as the new middle class were expected to go, although the majority could not afford to. The first half of the twentieth century saw the breakthrough of the housewife, particularly among the new middle class, although the ideal also spread to the working class. The model was partly taken from bourgeois women, although their position from the late nineteenth century on was a bit different: they tended to be house managers rather than housewives, with maids or servants to perform the menial work. Having a maid was the ideal of many a middle class family as well. Many kept one, but the majority could not afford it.

The interest of the middle classes in modern styles and artefacts made them a favourite target for the new and rising advertising business. Although the concepts of fashionable [*moteriktig*] or modern [*moderne*] were no novelties, they spread to a vastly larger audience. In housing, the two were combined in the inter-war years. Specific colours or artefacts might be fashionable, but the whole style, rational, scientific, simple, functional, was thoroughly modern.

It is easy to overestimate the modernity of the new middle classes, both in general and in relation to other classes. The old middle class, the modest businessmen, shopkeepers and artisans were certainly not resistant to modern lifestyles, but their occupational heritage and their roles as employers and self-employers put them in a different situation from functionaries. At the same time, remnants of older ways of living and thinking survived alongside newer ones. As late as 1917, advertisements for shop assistants in the capital's newspapers were referring to 'moving day' [*flyttedag*], usually either April 14th or October 14th, the dates when servants and labourers in the countryside changed employers, being the transitions between the summer and winter working seasons.[89]

The conventionality of the middle classes consists in two traits. First, as we have already touched upon, much of their lifestyle was more or less an imitation of that of their social superiors, the educated and moneyed bourgeoisie. Second, the middle classes were known to take certain expressions of bourgeois life styles to extremes so as to create their own rigid, philistine [*spissborgerlig*] lifestyle out of social insecurity. This consisted in keeping up appearances, checking emotions and the like, often presented in novels and well known from folklore, but poorly researched. One of the more curious sides of it was that children spoke one, adult-like, formal, language at home, and another, more popular, language in the streets.[90]

The family pattern of the middle classes evolving from the late nineteenth century took the bourgeois family as a model;[91] the family had a housewife and one or more servants. This model could relatively easily find its way into the new middle class, at least for the families who could afford a servant. The lower part of the old middle class was different in the sense that the whole family was a firm, the family being a production as well as a consumption unit. However, in the twentieth century this kind of family also tried its best to conform to the bourgeois model, using maids as domestic servants rather than as assistants in the firm.

We actually have little systematic knowledge on the keeping of servants, except for an study of Christiania in 1875.[92] In that year the proportion of households keeping a servant was 24 per cent for all households in the city, 50 per cent for independent artisans, 22 per cent for shopkeepers [*småhandlere*], 73 per cent for 'ordinary merchants' [*vanlig handlende*], 76 per cent for middle functionaries, 28 per cent for lower functionaries, 4.5 per cent for workers. Keeping a servant was closely correlated with income. Workers and functionaries were in fact equally prone to keeping a maid given the same income except for one peculiarity; at really low incomes the servants disappear form working-class households but remain in many lower middle-class households, testifying to the importance to middle-class status of keeping a servant.

The relative number of servants declined with time, from about 9 per cent of the gainfully employed population of Christiania in 1875 to 4 per cent in 1910. It is likely that that lower middle classes were the first ones to stop keeping servants. Artisans and shopkeepers declined relatively in numbers and struggled economically in the face of competition from industrial capitalism. Functionaries of course became numerous, but lost ground in terms of wages to such as the working class. For the normal lower middle-class family in the inter-war years a servant was not only beyond their means but also beyond their dreams, and even out of fashion in an emerging welfare state. The servant as a mark of middle class was on the wane.

The rise of the modern housewife and the decline of the domestic servant took place simultaneously, in the last half century prior to the Second World War. As already mentioned, from the 1890s onwards the role of the housewife was upgraded, the work was gradually made more scientific, and being a housewife was called an occupation or a profession [*husmoryrket*]. Norwegian housewives were organised as early as 1898 in Christiania, nationally from 1915.[93] The movement was initiated by women of the social elite, but its effects in the first half of the twentieth century were strongest on the middle classes. There are indications that the housewife ideology, as well as its practice, was stronger in Norway than in most Western countries, except perhaps the USA.

The fall of the servant and the rise of the housewife also coincided with a remarkable fall in fertility from around the turn of the century. This profound social or demographic innovation went from the top of the social scale downwards and from urban to rural areas.[94] Because the elite was small, and the boundaries of the middle classes blurred, the decline in family size was first identified as a middle-class phenomenon. What is certain, is that the new attention to children and childhood, starting in the last two decades of the nineteenth century, was mainly a middle-class phenomenon (although some of this, too, began with the elite).[95]

In 1889, an elementary school law was passed requiring comprehensive schooling, compulsory until the age of fourteen. Three years later, work protection legislation forbade most paid work for children under twelve and reduced it substantially for those over that age. In 1896, the world's first child welfare law was passed, effective from 1900. Day-care for working-class pre-school children [*barneasyler*] had existed since 1838, as a practical solution for mothers who had to work outside the home. There was no middle-class equivalent to this before the second half of the twentieth century. However, pedagogical (Fröbelian) kindergartens had existed from about 1870, as a kind of supplementary education. With the next century, upbringing was gradually becoming a science, or at least a craft, a skill middle-class housewives and mothers were supposed to acquire, but could not fully obtain, hence the kindergartens.

Kindergartens were few and far between, however. When some housewives in Oslo in the 1930s took the initiative of creating more such short-term kindergartens, the reasons were mainly to keep children off the increasingly dangerous streets, and to have more time to themselves. A hallmark of a middle-class married woman with children in the 1930s was thus *not* having a maid.

The social middle as a political project

I would venture to suggest that the relations between classes and politics are more complicated in Norway than in most other Western countries. There are several complicating elements. First, there is the appeal of the labour parties beyond workers and radical intellectuals well into the ranks of countryside freeholders and functionaries. Secondly, there is the national dimension, dividing the urban elite and middle classes. Thirdly, there is the dimension of the so-called counter-cultures which to a certain extent coincides with the national issue, but has a more regional, urban-rural, and socially vertical aspect to it. Fourthly, the lack of an aristocracy gave the bourgeois elite, at least from about 1860, a conservative role in politics.

Politics in the nineteenth century were founded on urban-rural and nationalist dimensions, in addition to rank divisions (senior civil servants, merchants, artisans, peasants). The peasants, never in the majority but always to reckon with in parliament, pursued a policy of narrow occupational interests coupled with some democratic causes. The old middle classes, inside or outside of parliament, played important roles in building an economic infrastructure, like railways and a banking system. The *embetsmenn*, dominating the parliament as well as providing the bureaucracy, were a class of ardent modernisers, claiming with a certain justice to act on behalf of the common weal, although quite elitist in outlook. Nevertheless, the upper crusts of Norwegian society in the second quarter of the century would invoke the term 'middle ranks' [*middelstanden*] to describe themselves as a vanguard leading nation building.[96]

From the 1850s, though not clearly marked until the 1870s, a democratic nationalist opposition to the regime of the *embetsmenn* made itself felt. It was based on a coalition of peasants/farmers and urban radicals of all classes. It was in this context that the concept of 'middle class' was advanced in the late nineteenth century as the basis on which Norwegian democracy ought to be founded, and it was directed against the ruling elite of senior civil servants.[97] The movement, which found its organisational expression in the *Venstre* (left) party never saw itself as mainly a middle-class party, and mobilised many workers and wealthy businessmen. In the twentieth century, however, representatives of *Venstre*, among others, have from time to time expressed the view that the middle groups of society, the petit bourgeois (lower middle class) and the smaller farmers, represented society as a whole, while for example capitalists and workers represented special interests.[98] But of course, this was after the workers had started defecting to the Labour party and the business elite to the *Høyre* (right) party, who had changed from an *embetsmann* party to a business party in the generation following the fall of the old regime of the senior civil servants in 1884.

No political party in the twentieth century tried to represent the middle class. The Conservative Party (*Høyre*, founded 1884) represented business interests and to a certain degree appealed to the old middle class and private functionaries who resented socialism. The Agrarian Party (*Bondepartiet*, 1920) was a class party. The Christian People's Party (*Kristelig folkeparti*, 1932) represented national and traditional values, the counter-cultures, mainly in the countryside. In this, it competed with the Liberal Party (*Venstre*, 1883), which also contained an urban, more radical wing. In some ways, this party may be said to represent middle class voters. The Labour Party (*Arbeiderpartiet*, 1887) managed to appeal to quite a few functionaries in the public sector. In the Norwegian power triangle of the first half of the twentieth century[99], there was a bourgeois, a labour and an agrarian corner, which left no particular space for middle class interests.

Conclusion

Although the Norwegian middle classes in the century between 1840 and 1940 may be identified in many ways, they are still hard to pin down, economically, socially, politically and culturally. One may point to middle-class occupations, although they change with time. In the nineteenth century, when the senior civil servants were regarded as an upper class and functionaries were few, the term 'middle class' or 'middle ranks' tended to be given to business people, merchants, shopkeepers, artisans and the like. With the economic bourgeoisie taking the social lead in the twentieth century, a middle class man was mainly thought of as a functionary. Income as a criterion is not reliable either, particularly in distinguishing the social middle from the social lower classes. It is also difficult to identify the middle classes with political movements.

The model of early twentieth-century Norwegian society in terms of political and cultural influence as a triangle with the bourgeoisie, the farmers and the workers in the corners[100] shows the powerlessness of the middle classes, but also the limitations of the model as a picture of the Norwegian social formation (which it is not meant to be). A sizeable portion of the population was not to be found in any of the corners. The middle class shared many ideals and outlooks with the bourgeoisie, it was to a large degree recruited from the farmers, and it shared living conditions with the workers to a degree without wanting to admit it.

Being in the middle on various reckonings in a sense united these people in various ways. Some groups who considered themselves middle class, small business people, functionaries (and in some cases small farmers) saw themselves as standing above, or beside, the groups voicing special interests, capitalists and workers. But the main metaphor was the virtue of being middle in the sense of being social buffers or mediators, a strongly needed role in society.

This was one of the factors making the middle classes visible. Another was their role in the rise of civil society. In most organisations not representing narrow economic or political interests, the middle classes played a pivotal role. They never organised in the name of the middle class, however. This is one of the reasons why the 'middle classes' or 'middle ranks', terms quite common in our period, particularly in recent decades, were so hard to identify, and in some respects played only a modest role in the public debate.

Notes

[1] Sverre Steen, 'Den glemte samfunnsklassen og det nye system', *Drømmen om frihet*, Oslo 1973, pp. 132-143. For a short discussion of Norwegian middle-class historiography, see Jan Eivind Myhre, 'Finding the middle class. Norway in a comparative perspective, c. 1870-1940', *Scandinavian Journal of History* 3/1994, pp. 237-249.
[2] Sverre Steen, *Kristiansands historie. I fredens århundre 1814-1914*, Oslo 1948, p. 441.
[3] P.P. Sveistrup, 'Mellemklassens fremstød', *Sosialt Arbeid*, 1935, ss. 405-409.
[4] Wilhelm Keilhau, *Det norske folks liv og historie*, vols. IX (1840-1875) and X (1875-1920); Knut Greve, 'Fra borgerskap til middelstand', in Anders Bugge & Sverre Steen (eds), *Norsk kulturhistorie Vol. 5. Fra igår til idag*, Oslo 1942, pp. 33-99; Sverre Steen, 'Fra igår til idag', in Bugge & Steen (eds). pp. 1-32; Steen 1948.
[5] *Norsk kulturhistorie*, 8 vols., Oslo 1980. The three volumes and around. 50 articles covering the nineteenth and early twentieth century, do not thematize the rise of the middle classes or the bourgeoisie, but treat aspects of bourgeois and middle class culture without really saying so.
[6] See for instance Hans Geelmuyden, *Kontoret* [The office], Oslo 1940.
[7] Edvard Bull et al (eds), *Det norske folks liv og historie*, 10 vols., Oslo 1929-1935; Thorleif Dahl et al (eds), *Vårt folks historie*, 9 vols, Oslo 1961-1964; Knut Mykland (ed.), *Norges historie*, 15 vols., Oslo 1975-1979; Knut Helle (main ed.), *Norges historie*, 12 vols., Oslo 1994-1998.
[8] One of the exceptions in the last generation is Francis Sejersted. Being mainly an economic and political historian of conservative political persuasion, he takes an interest in the main actors of Norwegian capitalism, the small and medium sized middle class businessmen. See e.g. *Demokratisk kapitalisme*, Oslo 1993, chapters 4 and 5.

[9] Ingrid Semmingsen, 'The dissolution of estate society in Norway', *Scandinavian Economic History Review*, 1954, p. 203.
[10] Dagfinn Mannsåker, *Det norske presteskapet i det 19. hundreåret*, Oslo 1954, pp. 200-203.
[11] Steen 1973, p. 134.
[12] Best represented are teachers (elementary and high school), doctors, nurses, telegraphers, master artisans, saleswomen. We know little about e.g. shopkeepers and clerks and other functionaries.
[13] Mannsåker 1954, p. 162. All translations by J.E.M.
[14] The 15-volume *Norges historie*, published in the 1970s, gives some attention to the rise of the middle classes. Francis Sejersted, *Den vanskelige frihet 1814-1851* (vol. 10), Oslo 1978, placed them within the widening of bourgeois society. Hans Try, *To kulturer– en stat 1851-1884* (vol. 11), Oslo 1979, devotes a few pages to the new and growing 'groups in the middle' (*mellomgrupper*). Per Fuglum, *Norge i støpeskjeen. 1884-1920* (vol. 12), Oslo 1978, mentions the middle classes only indirectly, via a broad treatment of the numerous new associations. Edvard Bull, *Klassekamp og fellesskap 1920-1945* (vol. 13), Oslo 1979, is mainly preoccupied with workers, farmers and fishermen. The middle classes or bourgeois society is treated only indirectly or in passing The next three books were originally published in the 1970s and 1980s, but appeared in new editions in the late 1990s. Tore Pryser, *Norsk historie 1814-1860*, Oslo 1999; Jostein Nærbøvik, *Norsk historie 1860-1914*, Oslo 1999; Berge Furre, *Norsk historie 1914-2000*, Oslo 2000. Although parts of the same series, the three authors treat the middle classes quite differently: Pryser's takes a social-structural account, with the middle class as an, albeit modest, part of the story. To Nærbøvik, the middle classes are a number of concrete occupations. Furre is not occupied with the middle classes as a whole, focusing mainly on politics and economic history. More attentive to the issue than Furre is Anne-Lise Seip, *Nasjonen bygges 1830-1870. Norges historie, vol 8*, Oslo 1997; Gro Hagemann, *Det moderne gjennombrudd 1870-1905. Norges historie, vol 9*, Oslo 1997, and particularly Knut Kjeldstadli, *Et splittet samfunn 1905-1935. Norges historie, vol 10*, Oslo 1994.
[15] Kjeldstadli 1994, pp. 15, 110.
[16] The best general introduction in English is Rolf Danielsen et. al., *Norway: A History from the Vikings to Our Own Times*, Oslo 1995, pp. 230-333.
[17] Jan Eivind Myhre, 'The urbanization of Norway 1850-1980', in Thomas Hall (ed.), *Urban Planning in the Nordic Countries*, London 1991, pp. 122-129, 164-165; Finn-Einar Eliassen, Knut Helle, Jan Eivind Myhre and Ola Svein Stugu, *Norsk byhistorie 700-2000*, forthcoming, Oslo 2004.
[18] For a general survey of Norwegian economic development, see Fritz Hodne, *An Economic History of Norway 1815-1970*, Trondheim 1975; Trond Bergh et. al., *Growth and Development. The Norwegian Experience 1830-1980*, Norwegian Foreign Policy Studies No 37, Oslo 1981.
[19] Including craftsmen.
[20] Sejersted 1993. He includes farmers in his category of small bourgeois.
[21] Jan Eivind Myhre, *Hovedstaden Christiania 1814-1900. Oslo bys historie*, vol. 3, Oslo 1990, e.g. pp. 448-450.
[22] Knut Mykland, *Fra Søgaden til Strandgaten 1800-1880. Trondheims historie 997-1997*, vol. 3, Trondheim 1997, pp. 22ff.
[23] The novelist Alexander Kielland has a wonderful scene in *Arbeidsfolk* ['Labourers'] (1881) where entrusted workers from different public departments

and services have a party, drinking a toast by addressing each other with the highest titles in their hierarchies: general, minister etc. See also Sivert Langholm, *Elitenes valg*, Oslo 1984, pp. 196-7.

[24] Klaus Frode Solheim, *Oppfatningen av forholdet mellom samfunnsklassene slik det kom til uttrykk i stemmerettsdebattene på 1800-tallet*, unpublished history thesis, University of Oslo 1976, p. 45.

[25] In Norwegian history the foremost representative of this view is perhaps Tore Pryser, *Norsk historie 1800-1870. Fra standssamfunn til klassesamfunn*, Oslo 1985. A clear and well-founded statement, Pryser nevertheless introduces the Norwegian class society a little too early, a failing only made worse in the latest edition, which ends in 1860. One of the major international inspirations is Harold Perkin, *The Origins of Modern English Society 1780-1880*, London 1969.

[26] The inconsistent use of the terms 'class' and 'rank' is also found in many nineteenth century English writers. See Geoffrey Crossick, 'From gentlemen to the residuum: languages of social description in Victorian Britain', in Penelope J. Corfield (ed.), *Language, History and Class*, Oxford 1991, p. 154.

[27] In my search for terminological practice, I have able to use the archives of Leksikografisk institutt and the database in preparation by Dokumentasjonsprosjektet. The search words were *borgerskap(b), borgerstand, bourgeoisie, mellomklasse, middelklasse, middelstand, småborgerskap* in a number of authors from the late eighteenth to the early twentieth century. Thanks to Dag Gundersen and Christian Emil Ore.

[28] http:/www.dokpro.uio.no

[29] *Nordisk Conversations-Lexicon*, Copenhagen ca. 1860; *Salmonsens store illustrerede Konversationsleksikon for Norden* (Norwegian edition), Copenhagen ca. 1900; *Illustreret norsk konversationsleksikon*, Kristiania (Oslo) 1907-1913; *Svensk Uppslagsbok*, Malmø 1930s.

[30] *Norsk riksmålsordbok*, bd. II, første halvbind, Oslo 1947, p. 136-137. My translation. The original entry reads: '**middelstand**, en, (eft. tysk *mittelstand*) ... mest litt., del av et samfund som økonomisk og sosialt inntar en mellemstilling mellem overklasse og underklasse (i vårt land særl. mindre, selvstendige næringsdrivende, bestillingsmenn, funksjonærer).'

[31] Sivert Nielsen, according to Solheim 1976.

[32] Ulf Torgersen, 'Edb-arkiver for mediatekst', *Tidsskrift for samfunnsforskning* 2/1995.

[33] Jens Arup Seip, 'Flerpartistaten i perspektiv', *Nytt NorskTtidsskrift* 3-4/1994, pp. 203-220.

[34] Asa Briggs, 'The language of "Class" in early nineteenth-century England', *Collected Essays, Volume One*, 1985 (1961?), pp. 3-33; Dror Wahrman, *Imagining the Middle Class. The Political Representation of Class in Britain, c. 1780-1840*, Cambridge 1995; Crossick 1991, pp. 152, 156.

[35] Briggs 1985, p. 3.

[36] Steen 1973, p. 133.

[37] Jan Eivind Myhre, 'Om behovet for klasser. Middelklassens vekst og fall i Norges offisielle statistikk,' to be published by the Central Bureau of Statistics in 2004 in a book on Norwegian historical population statistics, edited by Kjartan Soltvedt and Espen Søbye.

[38] Einar Lie and Hege Roll-Hansen, *Faktisk talt. Statistikkens historie i Norge*, Oslo 2001.

[39] *NOS Ny Række C. No. 1. Bidrag til en norsk Befolkningsstatistikk. Inledning til Tabeller indeholdende Resultaterne af Folketællingen i Norge i Januar 1876*,

Kristiania 1882; *Statistiske Oplysninger om de Fremsatte stemmerettsforslags Virkning*, Kristiania 1877.

[40] Both in 1900 and 1930 a category of people working independently, but alone, was created, and named *selvstendig arbeidende*, in the French translation of the 1930 census: '*Travailleurs isolés, c'est a dire: petits patrons travaillant seuls*' (hefte 6, p. 53).

[41] Lie and Roll Hansen 2001.

[42] On Sundt (1817-1875), see Anne-Lise Seip, 'Eilert Sundt. A founding father of the social sciences in Norway', *Scandinavian Journal of History* 3/1986, p. 220-242; Michael Drake, *Population and Society in Norway, 1735-1865*, Cambridge 1969.

[43] Ole Jacob Broch 1868, according to Solheim 1976, p. 74.

[44] Jan Eivind Myhre, 'Lærerne som middelklasse og profesjon', in Reidun Høydal (ed.), *Nasjon - region - profesjon. Vestlandslæraren 1840-1940*, Oslo 1995.

[45] The vote was extended to men with a certain taxable income.

[46] At the same time, taxation was changing from property-based to income-based.

[47] Myhre 1990, p. 437; Alfred Oftedal Telhaug and Odd Asbjørn Mediås, *Grunnskolen som nasjonsbygger. Fra statspietisme til nyliberalisme*, Oslo 2003.

[48] Henrik Palmstrøm, 'Om en befolkningsgruppes utvikling gjennom de siste 100 år. Statistiske studer vedrørende norske akademikere', *Statsøkonomisk tidsskrift 1935*, p. 334. The increased share also naturally reflects the increasing number of functionaries.

[49] Source: national censuses. The figures for the towns refer to the incorporated towns. It is easier to estimate figures for the towns than for the countryside.

[50] In historiography, they are to be found mainly in town and parish histories, but there are also accounts of tradesmen's associations: Wilhelm Keilhau, *Handelens venner*, Oslo 1951; Fritz Hodne, *God handel. Norges handelsstands forbund gjennom hundre år*, Oslo 1989.

[51] See Tore Pryser, Artisans in Kristiania 1840-1885, *Commision internationale d'histoire des mouvement sociaux et des structures sociale. Petite entreprise et croissance industrielle dans le monde aux XIXe et Xxe siècles*, Paris 1981; Eirik Schibsted, *Skomakerborgerskapet i Christiania på 1800-tallet*, Main thesis in history, Univ. of Oslo 1983; August Schou, *Håndverk og industri i Oslo 1838-1938*, Oslo 1938; Grieg, *Norsk tekstil I-II*, Oslo 1948, 1950.

[52] Francis Sejersted, Den norske 'Sonderweg', in *Demokratisk kapitalisme*, Oslo 1993, pp. 163-20. Sejersted calls this group *småborgerskapet (petite bourgeoisie)*, perhaps somewhat misleadingly.

[53] In Table 1 the elite is not included in the middle class. At the other end of the social ladder, quite a few small independently working artisans and even shopkeepers and vendors, definitely fall below the middle class, notwithstanding their independent status. This group can in part be identified in the published censuses, but also leaves some room for a few qualified estimates.

[54] Geoffrey Crossick and Heinz-Gerhard Haupt (eds), *Shopkeepers and Master Artisans in Nineteenth-Century Europe*, 1984; Geoffrey Crossick and Heinz-Gerhard Haupt, *The Petite Bourgeoisie in Europe 1780-1914*, London 1995.

[55] Sources: Lars Thue, *Fra bestillingsmannsforening til moderne fagforbund. Kommunalansattes fellesorganisasjon 1936-1986*, Oslo 1986 (municipal functionaries); Palmstrøm 1935 (teachers), (both building upon the national censuses 1875-1930). National censuses 1875-1930.

[56] Thue 1986, p. 14.

[57] Kari Melby, Kall og kamp. *Norsk sykepleierforbunds historie*, Oslo 1990; Gro Hagemann, *Skolefolk Lærernes historie i Norge*, Oslo 1992; Åsmund Arup Seip, *Lektorene. Profesjon, organisasjon og politikk 1890-1980*, FAFO, Oslo 1990; Erling Strømberg, *Telegrafistene 1855-1890*. *En gruppe offentlige funksjonærer vokser fram*, Main thesis in history, University of Oslo 1977; Erling Kristiansen, *Fra fornem bønn til kamp for lønn. Filologenes og realistenes Landsforening/Norsk lektorlag/Norges Undervisningsforbund 1892-1992*, Oslo 1992.
[58] Anders Bergløff, *Norske Bankfunksjonærers Forbund 1922-1947*, Oslo 1947; Solveig Langstrand, *Ekspeditriser i Kristiania ca. 1907-1930*, Main thesis in history, University of Oslo 1991; Elin Gjertsen, 'Espeditriser i Trondheim 1918-1940', *Trondhjemske samlinger 1978*, pp. 189-305.
[59] Langstrand 1991.
[60] Tore Lindbekk, *Samfunnsendring og sosial mobilitet i Trøndelag*, Oslo 1983, pp. 161-164.
[61] Hagemann 1992; Strømberg 1977; Anne-Beate Hagen, *Overgangskvinner. Almueskolelærerinner i Christiania 1860-1890 - levestandard og sosial status*, Main thesis in history, University of Oslo 1999.
[62] Aage Lunde, *Det norske jernbanepersonale 1854-1914. Sosialhistoriske undersøkelser*, Oslo 1969, pp. 255ff. See also Inger Bjørnhaug, De offentlig ansatte som historisk forskningsfelt, *Arbeiderhistorie 1994*, pp. 149-175
[63] Elin Myhre, *Å selge en forretningsidé. Livsforsikringsselskapet Norske Folk og den kollektive pensjonsforsikring (1917-1940)*, unpublished manuscript 1999.
[64] Mario König, Hannes Siegrist, Rudolf Vetterli, *Warten und aufrücken. Die Angestellten in der Schweiz 1870-1950*, Zürich 1985.
[65] Elin Myhre 1999.
[66] Geelmuyden's book *Kontoret* [The Office] gives a picture of an advancement system that was both rigid and unfair. Åsmund Arup Seip, *Rett til å forhandle. En studie i statstjenestemennenes forhandlingsrett i Norge og Sverige 1910-1965*, Oslo 1997; Aslak Bøe, *Kommunale kontorfunksjonærers forening, Oslo. Beretning om virksomheten i 25-årsperioden 1906-1931*, Oslo 1931.
[67] Å. A. Seip 1997.
[68] Langstrand 1991, p. 58.
[69] Langstrand 1991, p. 96.
[70] Langstrand 1991, pp. 69ff.
[71] Rules at the district office in Drammen, Norwegian State Railroads, 1863-72, *Ny Giv* 1/1994, p. 13.
[72] Bjørnhaug 1994, p. 152.
[73] Bøe 1931.
[74] Langstrand 1991, pp. 69ff.
[75] After Hans Nielsen Hauge (1771-1824), lay preacher, religious reformer and economic entrepreneur. Francis Sejersted, 'Marked og moral', *Demokratisk kapitalisme*, Oslo 1993, pp. 30ff. The scepticism towards commerce does not originate with the ruling class in the nineteenth century, the senior civil servants, who took a favourable attitude towards business. It was more visible among the peasants/farmers and parts of the intellectual democratic opposition.
[76] Steen 1973.
[77] Developed for the study of social groups in general by Ottar Dahl, 'Noen teoretiske problemer i sosialhistorien', *Historisk tidsskrift 1955*, pp. 183-203.

[78] In the second half of the twentieth century, according to several studies. Abraham Hallenstvedt and Jan Trollvik (eds), *Norske organisasjoner*, Oslo 1993 and earlier editions; Sverre Steen, 'De friville organisasjoner og det norske demokrati', *Historisk tidsskrift* 1948, pp. 581-600; Johan Raaum, 'De frivillige organisasjonenes framvekst og utvikling i Norge', *NOU 1988:17 Frivillige organisasjoner*, Oslo 1988, pp. 239-355.

[79] August Schou, *Håndverk og industri i Oslo 1838-1938*, Oslo 1938.

[80] *Trondhjems Handels- og Kontorbetjenters Forening*, Gjertsen 1978.

[81] Langstrand 1991, p. 192.

[82] Bergløff 1972, p. 12.

[83] E. Myhre 1999.

[84] Gro Hagemann, 'De stummes leir? 1800-1900', in Ida Blom and Sølvi Sogner (eds), *Med kjønnsperspektiv på norsk historie*, Oslo 1999, p. 138.

[85] Helge Pharo, *Tjalve hundre år*, Oslo 1990; Finn Olstad, 'Idrett – en del av historien?', in Knut Kjeldstadli, Jan Eivind Myhre and Tore Pryser (eds) *Valg og vitenskap. Festskrift til Sivert Langholm*, Oslo 1997, pp. 164-187; Matti Goksøyr, *Idrettsliv i borgerskapets by. En historisk undersøkelse av idrettens utvikling og organisering i Bergen på 1800-tallet*, Oslo 1991; Finn Olstad, *Norsk idretts historie, bd. 1. Forsvar, sport, lassekamp 1861-1939*, Oslo 1987.

[86] Langstrand 1991, pp. 98-99.

[87] Francis Sejersted (ed.), *Vekst gjennom krise*, Oslo 1982.

[88] Kjeldstadli 1994, pp. 115ff.

[89] Langstrand 1991, p. 58.

[90] Merete Wishman, 'Stabilitet i en urolig tid. Middelklassekvinner i Trondheim 1900-1940', *Trondhjemske samlinger 1983*, pp. 89-112.

[91] Wishman 1983; Anna Jorunn Avdem and Kari Melby, *Oppe først og sist i seng. Husarbeid i Norge fra 1850 til i dag*, Oslo 1983.

[92] Brita Wiig, *Tjenestepikehold i Christiania i 1875*, Main thesis in history, Oslo 1980. Her figures are based on a statistically representative selection.

[93] Kari Melby, 'The housewife ideology in Norway between the two World Wars, *Scandinavian Journal of History* 2/1989, pp. 181-193.

[94] Sølvi Sogner et al, *Fra stua full til tobarnskull*, Oslo 1984.

[95] Jan Eivind Myhre, *Barndom i storbyen*, Oslo 1994; Monica Rudberg, *Dydige, sterke, lykkelige barn. Idéer om oppdragelse i borgerlig tradisjon*, Oslo 1983.

[96] A.-L. Seip 1997, p. 58.

[97] Jens Arup Seip, Flerpartistaten i perspektiv, *Nytt Norsk Tidsskrift* 3-4/1994, pp. 203-220.

[98] Kjeldstadli 1994, p. 37.

[99] Kjeldstadli 1994.

[100] Kjeldstadli 1994.

Part 2
Themes

LARS EDGREN

Craftsmen and Political Consciousness in Sweden 1850-1900

I

The petite bourgeoisie has often been considered as an important source of radicalism in early nineteenth-century Western Europe. On the other hand, craftsmen in Germany in particular are often seen as staunch supporters of conservative and anti-semitic parties, strongly opposing the advance of industrial capitalism.[1] The lively research on the European petite bourgeoisie in the last decades has delved deeply into such questions of consciousness and political alignments, and has attempted to carry out comparative studies to improve our knowledge.[2]

The purpose of this essay is to add some Swedish evidence to this developing fund of knowledge. Comparative studies often concentrate on the leading European countries, particularly England, France, and Germany. In order to advance the discussion of possible causes of differences between countries it is necessary to bring other countries into this framework.[3] This essay will attempt to do just that. The study is limited to master craftsmen in an urban setting; shopkeepers are a quite different group, and deserve their own studies. An attempt is made to assess the complex Swedish evidence, but also to put it in a comparative perspective. Swedish developments are discussed on a national level, but local evidence from the city of Malmö in southernmost Sweden is also used. By the turn of the nineteenth century Malmö was a major industrial city and the third largest city in the country.[4]

The first part of the essay will focus on the organised efforts of masters to argue for changes in the laws regulating crafts, what I will call the 'masters' movement' (which corresponds to what in German is called the *Handwerkerbewegung*). The second part deals with masters' participation in other organisations, and attempts to discuss what this might reveal about their political attitudes. It deals primarily with Malmö. The third part of the essay attempts to locate Sweden in the current discussion of the petite bourgeoisie in Western Europe.

But first a comment concerning the concepts of 'liberalism' and 'conservatism'. When discussing political attitudes in the nineteenth century these concepts are almost inescapable. Neither of them has a clear or definitive meaning, either in the scholarly literature or (even less) in the actual political practice of the past. Even if they capture important aspects of the political struggles of the nineteenth century, such as conflicts between corporatism and individualism, different views on authority and hierarchy, different attitudes to a free market economy, they were never realised in an ideal form in practice. Therefore individuals and groups could well hold views that from a theoretical, analytical viewpoint might appear contradictory. The ideologies were also changing over time. What was a radical proposal in 1850 might be commonly accepted 50 years later. In particular, many of the liberal causes would be common property even among 'conservatives' by the end of the century. From this we must conclude that it is not enough to label views as 'conservative' or 'liberal', but that it is necessary to delve deeper into the actual nature of political views held. It might even be tempting to try to write without using these concepts. However, this is hardly a satisfactory solution. They were very much part of the language in which the political struggles of the period were fought. There will be no attempt made here to do without them totally, but instead to try to clarify the meaning in each case. As a label for those craftsmen who in different ways were proposing legal changes to restrict freedom of trade I will use the term 'restrictionist' in preference to 'conservative', since the latter term implies certain wider views of society.

First of all we are going to investigate the craftsmen and their attitude to economic principles. Crucial here is of course their attitude to the guild system and freedom of trade. However, first it is necessary to give a short account of the relevant background legislation.

II

The guilds survived in Sweden up to the mid-nineteenth century. The independent exercise of a trade in the towns required an apprenticeship, a three-year period of work as a journeyman, and finally a proof of skill in the trade by making a 'masterpiece'. Membership of a guild was compulsory and all masters also had to become burghers of their town. As such they had political rights in local government and participated in elections to the Burghers' Estate in the Swedish parliament, organised on corporate principles with four Estates (nobles, clergy, burghers, and peasants). The state exercised a relatively firm control over the guilds. A general guild law of 1720 made the system nationally coherent and limitations were put on the ability of local guilds to harass competent applicants.[5] Through a law of 1846 the guilds were abolished, but full freedom of trade was not introduced. The right to become a master was still regulated and required a masterpiece, but control was taken out of the hands of the masters within the same trade. Compulsory associations of masters [*Hantverksföreningar*] replaced the guilds. The most crucial change was that anyone had the right to pursue a trade as long as no workers outside the family were employed. However, this system was short-lived and in 1864 full freedom of trade was introduced.

Criticism of the guilds was common in the late eighteenth century, and demands for freedom of trade were widespread in the early nineteenth. The craftsmen staunchly opposed such attempts and mobilised their representation in the Burghers Estate of the *Riksdag* (the Swedish parliament) in order to try to block any reform. Even though they were a clear minority in the Estate, a restrictive economic policy had a wide appeal to the Burghers. Only towards the middle of the nineteenth century would a majority in this Estate favour free trade principles.[6] The new legislation of 1846 resulted in a mobilisation of a national masters' movement, with the new compulsory *Hantverksföreningar* [Craft Associations] as centres of mobilisation. The result was a number of local petitions and two national petitions in 1850 and 1853 demanding changes in the law.[7] These provide an insight not only into the views of craftsmen on economic issues, but also into their general outlook on society. The petitions are strikingly similar. They repeat much the same arguments, often almost word for word. A dominant theme in these petitions is that the economic organisation of society had to serve other, non-economic purposes. Trade laws should serve the interests of the Burgher's Estate, support established masters in securing a livelihood, protect customers, and guarantee the moral supervision of young men. The craftsmen as an independent group in society had to be preserved. Capitalism threatened the independence of the masters who owned nothing but their skills, a resource that was insufficient to face an open competition with capital. The crafts therefore needed protection from the state.

While the attack on the guild system was argued in the language of natural rights, the inalienable right of everyone to earn their living in any way they chose, the masters' petitions implicitly argued that no such natural rights existed. Rights always existed in relation to duties to society, and could only be established in a social context. Young people had to be supervised until they could responsibly take up these duties and rights. In these ways limits on the freedom of trade were defended; only by being forced to work as apprentices and journeymen to established masters could the young men of the crafts become full members of society. Freedom to choose one's own trade would lure irresponsible young men away from dependent work before they had the maturity to bear this burden. They would marry early, have children, and being unable to support their families, would fall under the care of Poor Law authorities (as this sad story typically ended in the petitions). Liberal key words such as 'liberty' and 'freedom of trade' were used and considered desirable, but the masters added words like 'responsible' and 'ordered' to them to indicate that their understanding of these words was quite different from that of the proponents of free trade.

The masters thus certainly did not believe in the blessings of free competition, and neither did they put any faith in natural rights. The state had an obligation to create ordered conditions and support authority and moral responsibility in society. In this sense the ideology of the masters can certainly be claimed to be 'conservative'. This does not mean that they had read much of the current ideological literature. These ideas were most likely deeply rooted in the guild traditions, and had been used for a very long time to defend the prerogatives of the burghers. While the ideology had its basis in the guild tradition, the demands of the masters did not include the restoration of the guilds. Attempts were made to restrict the freedom to open a craft shops outside towns, but this age old demand from the urban masters was not a leading theme in the agitation. The criticism was primarily directed against one aspect of the new law, the unrestricted freedom to start a new workshop as long as no workers were employed.

The petitions registered support from masters (and some journeymen) in almost all Swedish towns of any consequence. However, outside the crafts, the masters hardly received any support at all. Their arguments seemed to be only a stubborn defence of a special interest at the expense of the rest of society. Attempts to use the *Riksdag* of 1853-54 to push for the masters' demands were easily defeated. Not even in the Burghers' Estate was there any support for the masters anymore, and the proponents of free trade could even refrain from debate and confront the masters with silence. The government also turned down all the petitions.[8]

It must have been quite clear to the masters that they had no hope of turning back the tide of economic reform. Fresh attempts were made after 1853, but a despondent mood spread among the masters. In the early 1860s the question of the trade laws was once again raised, but now the issue was the abolition of the last remnants of the old restrictions. Opposition from the masters was quite weak, but almost all *Hantverksföreningar* that were asked about their views declared against further reform, and wanted to maintain the restrictions on the independent establishment of workshops. The weakness of the response hardly meant that masters had changed their minds. The despondent mood can however be clearly seen from the reaction of the *Hantverksförening* in Stockholm, the old stronghold of the restrictive opinion. They declared that they were not opposed to the changes, even if they felt that it would not be too much to ask for some minor restrictions on new masters. This was not a change of mood; it was rather acceptance of defeat.[9]

There can hardly be any doubt that the majority opinion among masters on economic issues up to the 1860s was in favour of restrictions. The question is not quite so simple for the later period. Tom Ericsson, the leading Swedish historian of the petite bourgeoisie, claims that by the turn of the century craftsmen had developed a new, more positive view of state intervention in the economy. In the nineteenth century many small businessmen had a more liberal economic outlook. It is, however, unclear when and for how long this liberal mood identified by Ericsson was dominant.[10] Tom Söderberg on the other hand labels the period from 1870 to 1883 as the 'conservative period of the masters' movement' and suggests that the 1890s were marked by a more practical attitude.[11] The evidence therefore needs to be evaluated once more.

After the introduction of freedom of trade in 1864 the organisations declined. The *Hantverksföreningar* were no longer compulsory, but in some cities they were kept going as voluntary associations. In other cities they were wound up, but would soon be reorganised. The *Hantverksföreningar* would remain the focus of organised opinion among masters. From 1866 a tradition started of organising meetings of craftsmen on a national or Scandinavian level. The first Scandinavian meeting took place in 1866, the first Swedish one in 1870.[12] This first national meeting raised all the major demands for legal changes that the movement would seek:

1. Compulsory organisation. All independent craftsmen would have to be members of the local craft association.
2. Proven competence for masters. Anyone pursuing a trade independently would have to prove his or her competence. This competence could be proven in different ways, either through a proof of apprenticeship or through a special qualification for masters. The latter was the solution proposed by this first meeting.
3. Regulation of apprenticeship. The law of 1864 gave no special status to journeymen or apprentices, they were all referred to as 'workers'. The law assumed written contracts, but there was no sanction if none was signed. The maximum period a contract could be signed for was three years. The masters complained that this time was too short, and that apprentices frequently left their master to find better conditions with another.

This may be seen as the movement's maximum programme. There would be no return to the guilds, but the system envisaged would undoubtedly be very close to the law of 1846 which, once vehemently opposed by masters, was now sometimes held up as an ideal compared to the existing freedom.[13] This programme would, however, not usually be demanded in full. At different times different parts of it would be emphasised. And there was no unanimity about the demands. At the first meeting a few critical voices were heard, but their arguments were not based on explicitly liberal economic principles. They were more likely to stress that the masters ought not to go against 'the spirit of the time', or that regulations were useless. Possibly this is explained by a tactical need to push an argument that might be effective in a meeting dominated by 'restrictionists'.[14]

The petition proposed at this meeting would never be delivered and the next meetings would make less far-reaching demands for reform. The second meeting would be primarily concerned with attempts to spread voluntary craft associations, and no proposals for legal reform were made. Most speakers in the debate were critical of freedom of trade, but a fair number of representatives defended it, using such keywords as 'freedom' and 'equality'. The third meeting in 1874 would once more be clearly dominated by those critical of the new freedom, but no specific demands were made on the state.[15] The fourth meeting in 1876 would, however, be marked by a very different mood and appeals were once more made to the state for legal regulations. Two of the issues from the 'maximum programme' were put forward, compulsory organisation and apprenticeship regulation. Masters demanded compulsory contracts and a five-year maximum period. A clear majority of the participants supported restrictive proposals, and only about a quarter of the speakers in the debates could be considered opposed to legal regulation in principle.[16] The meeting resulted in a petition delivered the following year, demanding compulsory organisation and apprenticeship regulation. The petition was sent by state authorities to local authorities and craft associations around the country for comment, and we can thus get a glimpse of local support for the craft programme at the meetings. A clear majority of craftsmen and craft associations were in favour of the whole petition. In a few cases they would disagree on some point. Some were opposed to compulsory organisations, some to compulsory contracts. This might be explained by the fact that the proposed organisations were not given any specific tasks, and might easily appear superfluous if not associated with a wider system of regulations. Compulsory contracts would of course also constitute a limit to a master's opportunity to use young workers flexibly, and might thus be hard to accept. Rarely were craftsmen opposed to the whole programme and only one association was in principle opposed to any restrictions.[17]

The reaction of local authorities to this petition were relatively encouraging, a clear majority accepted some of the proposals. But the government was not willing to take action and only in 1890 was it officially considered and dismissed. Probably as a result of this major effort the national meetings now declined in importance, and between 1876 and 1892 only one meeting took place, in 1884. The lack of response to this relatively modest petition was certainly discouraging to those craftsmen seeking increased restrictions. At the meeting in 1884 the defenders of free trade were clearly stronger than at any previous meeting. A long debate took place over the effects of the law of 1864, but a proposed resolution, saying that nothing was to be gained from restrictions and a return to past conditions, failed to carry a majority. No other action was taken.[18]

From the records of the meetings a relatively clear picture emerges. 'Restrictionists' dominated during the whole period and defenders of 'freedom of trade' were always present. Sometimes there were only a few, at other times they were relatively influential, but they were never in a majority. Furthermore it appears there was a group that steered clear of all attempts to demand legal protection, knowing very well that this was quite futile. This attitude seems to have been strong in Stockholm, where in 1864 the *Hantverksförening*, as we have already seen, was not opposed to the new law. Criticised for not being active enough in pushing for reforms, the chairman defended the Stockholm association by referring to the futility of previous petitions and concluding by citing the proverb, 'What you cannot change, you have to suffer.'[19]

In 1874, the Stockholm association also arranged for an existing newspaper to become the official one of the Swedish craft associations. This was a somewhat surprising choice since the editors were clearly promoting liberal economic principles. After a few years the paper dropped the crest of the craft associations, complaining that the craftsmen had never shown any interest in it. It appears that the editors were also sometimes aware that they had little support for their liberal views among Swedish craftsmen.[20] That the Stockholm association was willing to promote a liberal paper as an organ of the masters' movement might also indicate that Stockholm craftsmen were more 'realistic' than many of their colleagues in smaller cities.

The 1890s would see a new mobilisation of the masters and in 1898 a permanent national organisation, *Sveriges Hantverks- och Industriorganisation* [Swedish Organisation of Crafts and Industry], was created. This re-mobilisation of the masters' movement began with a national meeting in 1891. The mood was now in favour of quite extensive restrictions, and demands went further than in the 1870s. Apprenticeship was once more an important issue. In the 1870s demands had been limited to an increase in the contract period, now a compulsory proof of workmanship in order to become a journeyman was proposed too. The meeting also advocated compulsory *Hantverksföreningar*, seen as essential to guarantee the control of apprentices' proofs of workmanship. These demands for control were followed up by the further one that only those who were apprenticed to a trade should be allowed to practise it independently with employed workers, or if not apprenticed, they would have to provide proof of sufficient skill. The voices heard arguing against these proposals were quite weak, and in part they argued that such demands would compromise the masters in the eyes of public opinion, making it more difficult to get support for more modest proposals for reform. What was proposed was now more or less a revival of the old law of 1846, and it was first time the 'maximum programme' had reappeared since 1870.[21]

At the next meeting in 1893, these proposals were developed by an elected committee into a proposal to change the law of 1864 so as to require skill in the trade to be proved by a new master, and a proposal for a new apprenticeship law. The idea of compulsory organisations had quietly been dropped, perhaps because they would in any event be necessary if the other proposals were accepted, and because there was no reason to bring this to the public's attention and so invite criticism for reviving 'the guild spirit'.[22]

The proposed new apprenticeship law would be a major theme in the later masters' movement, while restrictions on masters were not pushed for in the same way. The reasons were probably tactical; regulations of working conditions for young workers would certainly not appear quite as provocative as the other demands. The meetings however show that the wishes of masters went far further. The proposed apprenticeship law was introduced as a bill at the *Riksdag* in 1895, supported by an organised campaign of letters from craft associations to their local parliamentary representatives. It clearly had overwhelming support among craftsmen, but the *Riksdag* was only willing to propose voluntary proofs of workmanship for apprentices. The new organisation of 1898 would have the apprenticeship law as one of its main goals.[23]

Clearly neither Ericsson's nor Söderberg's conclusions can be accepted. There is considerably more continuity over the period than either of them admits. 'Restrictionist' tendencies were dominant during the whole period, and if anything more so during the 1890s. But scattered voices defending freedom of trade were heard throughout the whole period, perhaps being most vocal at the 1884 meeting. In that sense there might be some justification for Ericsson's suggested turn to the right around the turn of the century.

There is also considerable continuity in the arguments of the 'restrictionists', and they echo some of the themes from the movement in the period around 1850. Free competition is seen as a false ideal and economic principles are seen as closely linked to moral ones. Competition has to be regulated and supervised in order to be fair and equal. In particular it is seen as necessary to protect skill as an asset of the craftsmen. Free competition cannot guarantee the preservation of skills. The moral supervision of young workers remains an important issue. Authority has to be preserved. The attitude toward the state remains in principle quite positive.

The craftsmen were presumably forced to adopt the dominant language of 'freedom' as a positive value, but twisted it in accordance with their needs. Freedom without restrictions would lead to 'licentiousness' [*självsvåld*]. True freedom had to be ordered: as one craftsman put it, 'Ordered freedom is freedom, unordered freedom is no freedom.' This was perhaps not a very fortunate way of putting it, but it was quite typical of the 'restrictionist' way of arguing. In this way they could claim that they were the promoters of 'real' freedom of trade.[24]

Another important political debate in which the craftsmen called for restrictions was that of customs or free trade. The craftsmen appear as consistent protectionists in this area.[25] There is obviously a connection between the call for customs duties and for legal regulation of the crafts, but apparently there was far more unanimity about customs than there was about other regulations. At the meeting in 1884 there was much wider support for customs protection than for regulation of the crafts. A clear majority of the participants in the debate were protectionists, despite the fact that in every other way this was the least 'restrictionist' of all the meetings.[26]

The movement of the 1890s was certainly characterised by scepticism concerning the free market, coupled with a belief in the potential role of the state to create harmonious conditions. But to see the masters' movement exclusively in its relation to the state and politics would tend to conceal an extremely important aspect of it. It can be argued that almost all the issues brought up by this movement concerned relations between masters and workers (apprentices and journeymen). Already in the agitation following the law of 1846, the crucial issue was keeping journeymen from setting up shops of their own. The paramount position of the apprenticeship question also illustrates how important relations with workers were, and the perceived need to tie them closer to their masters. The proposal to regulate mastership was also argued along the line that freedom would lure young workers prematurely away from dependent work.

A standing criticism of the new freedom was that it had destroyed previous good relations between masters and workers. Already in 1874 one master complained that 'employers and workers now face each other as two enemy camps',[27] and a leading representative of the movement would claim in a speech of 1897 that, 'instead of being, as in the past, members of the same family, employers and workers now face each other as distrustful and not seldom bitter enemies.'[28]

The trade union movement of course exacerbated this feeling of animosity. It had its beginnings in the 1880s and the urban crafts were its most important source of strength. Masters were thus among the first employers to face a strongly organised, socialist workers' movement. Relations with the unions would perhaps be the major issue of the 1890s. The masters' attitude to unions was a rather mixed one. There are no signs of direct enmity towards workers' organisations as such so long as they were willing to accept the unity of interest between masters and workers. Their ability to organise was even held up as an example to masters.[29] This relatively friendly attitude is not difficult to understand. The masters' movement was itself hoping to organise production in the trades in accordance with their own approach to it, which they believed to be one that was suitable for all to follow. In these attempts journeymen organisations could be seen as allies.[30] But the actual practice of the unions was more problematic. Masters complained that unions were denying masters the right to hire and fire their own employees. In the paper of the movement, *Handtverks- och Industritidning*, complaints about 'trade union tyranny' were often heard.[31] The masters' movement wanted to re-establish relations with their workers through the mutual acceptance of organisations and the establishment of boards of mediation and arbitration within the trades. This demand was a major one of the organised movement, along with the establishment of an apprenticeship law.[32] The threat from the socialist unions made anti-socialism into an important aspect of the masters' ideology. This added a new dimension to the critique of liberalism. Through its insistence on liberty, and its emphasis on rights rather than obligations, it had fostered the new socialism; socialism was the natural child of liberalism.[33]

In research on the ideology of the petite bourgeoisie, a lot of interest has been focused on the ideology of the *Mittelstand*.[34] This implied a view of the petite bourgeoisie as a group in society mediating between the divisive forces of capital and labour and being the true source of stability in society. Ericsson has pointed out that this ideology also can be found in Sweden,[35] but it might be worth pointing out that references to such a view of society are very rare in the 1890s.[36] The arguments are seldom based on such an explicit conception of society. It is perhaps more surprising that this way of arguing appeared in the 1870s. However, the crafts were identified as the heart of the middle class, and there was no discussion of a unity of interest with small shopkeepers.[37]

From this brief history of the masters' movement we can clearly see that it was never characterised by an acceptance of liberal economic principles. Free competition in the market would destroy the crafts, and the state was called upon to intervene and regulate in the interests of the masters. Voices were sometimes heard advocating the advantages of an open market economy, but they were never in a majority. It is actually much more surprising to see the tenacity with which restrictive policies were advocated even if it must have been obvious that there was little chance of them being converted into practical policies. Even if the state showed no sympathy for their strivings, craftsmen held on to the view that the state could serve to protect the crafts against the threat of open competition in the market place.

It is thus difficult to accept Ericsson's view that masters turned away from economic liberalism towards the end of the century. But he is right to the extent that the masters' movement went further in its demands for restrictions than it had previously. The reason for this is probably not a change of heart among masters; it is more likely due to the fact that a changed general political climate would make the demands of masters more politically practical. The 1880s marked the decline of the political dominance of free trade in politics and the victory of protectionism. The Swedish historian Rolf Torstendahl has claimed that the 1890s mark the transition from the period of classic industrial capitalism to organised capitalism in Sweden. This implied new concepts of the role of the state and an increase in labour market organisations.[38] The revival and further development of the masters' movement around 1890 nicely fits this pattern.

III

Even if we find considerable continuities in the language used around 1850 and in the 1890s, there are also many changes. The movement cannot be reduced to activities directed towards the state. A number of practical issues of interest to masters, not requiring state intervention, were also discussed at their meetings. There are no attempts to restore the lost world of the guilds. The rich culture of the guilds was eroded long before 1846, and at that date they existed primarily to represent economic interests. The demands were in this sense also quite limited to an economic self-interest. The guilds were no living heritage; they belonged to a past that might be viewed in a sentimental light, but not as a thing to be restored. In almost every issue of *Handtverks- och Industri-Tidning* there were excerpts from old guild archives. These would serve to legitimise the role and importance of craftsmen, but would also serve as reminders of a past no longer valid. The heritage remained, but it had been transformed.[39] This can best be seen in the most important change in the movement towards the end of the century, namely the growing importance of relations with the workers. While relations with the state had been the dominant theme of the movement up to the 1880s, the new need to regulate relations with the craft unions now virtually overshadowed this problem.

Seen from the perspective of economic issues, the Swedish craftsmen might appear as a group dominated by conservative, almost reactionary people, with views so extreme that they could hardly find support anywhere outside their own group. Analysing the role of craftsmen in other contexts will, however, serve to considerably modify this picture, as Ericsson has perceptively pointed out.[40] In particular he points to their important role in a number of popular movements, such as dissenting churches and the abstinence movement. But no attempts have been made to study these relations closely. Any such attempt must involve a close study of one or more localities, as it will involve a close study of the relationships between different organisations, paying attention to the role of individuals within different organisations. This part of this essay will provide the outline of such a study for the city of Malmö, analyse masters' involvement in other organisations and political movements, and attempt to evaluate what this might reveal about their political attitudes.

Demand for the reform of the Swedish parliament was a major political issue in the mid-nineteenth century. The demand was to replace the corporate representation of Estates with a representation of individuals. Reformers did not envision universal suffrage; rather the franchise should be limited in accordance with wealth and income. The conflicting principles concerned different views of society. On the one hand were supporters of a view that society consisted of corporate bodies, on the other there was the view that society consisted of individuals.

From a purely theoretical view point the guilds belonged to the corporate conception of society. This did not prevent a large number of Malmö masters supporting parliamentary reform. In 1848 a nationwide petition registered support from 20 to 25 per cent of Malmö masters, among them their leading representatives in the city.[41] The *Malmö Hantverksförening* at this time supported attempts to reverse the reform of 1846. It thus appears that Malmö masters could very well at the same time support proposals commonly labelled both 'liberal' and 'conservative'. A new petition calling for parliamentary reform in the early 1860s once more mobilised relatively strong support among masters in Malmö, and this time roughly a third of them signed the petition.[42]

In 1848, leading masters also promoted the creation of an educational association, The Educational Circle [*Bildningscirkeln*], in Malmö. It was part of a widespread though short-lived movement in Swedish towns in the mid-century.[43] The purpose was to bring together people from different social classes and to bring education, both of mind and manners, to workers, particularly in the crafts. The Circles should promote understanding and harmony between classes. In the formation of the first Educational Circle in Stockholm in 1845, radical journeymen played an important role, but when the movement spread to other Swedish towns it was dominated by people from the middle class. Politics was usually kept out. In this sense non-political, the Circles were still built on a vision of a society of equal individuals, and in this sense they can be considered 'liberal'.[44]

This did not prevent leading masters in Malmö from playing an important role in the local Circle. Four masters were among the signatories of the appeal to form the association.[45] Since the Circle particularly wanted to attract craft workers (other workers appear not to have been welcome as members), their interest is quite understandable. To them this initiative was an attempt to reestablish relations with their workers in new circumstances.[46] They saw little if any conflict between this and their restrictive economic views.[47]

The Educational Circles were short lived and most did not survive for more than a few years. Some of their ideas would reappear in the *Arbetarföreningar* [Workers' Associations] that sprang up in Swedish cities, particularly in the 1860s. These also attempted to spread education and 'elevating' entertainment to workers. But they were also far more practical. Some of the propagandists were very much influenced by different co-operative efforts in England, France, and Germany. The greatest influences were Hermann Schulze-Delitzsch and the co-operative movement in Germany. This ideology stressed self-help while abstaining from all appeals to state support. It proposed a whole set of different co-operative efforts, such as sick and burial benefit societies, consumer co-operatives, people's banks [*Volksbank*], co-operative buying of raw materials, and as the crowning achievement, producer co-operatives to help workers become independent in a rapidly changing economy. This early labour movement is usually referred to as 'liberal' and given its focus on self-help and the denunciation of class conflict this seems to be justified.[48]

As well as in the Educational Circle, masters played an important role in the Malmö Workers' Association (MWA). This was founded in 1867, and even if the initiative came from workers, middle class people came to dominate the governing board.[49] An 1869 register of members allows us to analyse the social composition of the membership.[50] The crafts formed the most important source of recruitment for the MWA, accounting for 42 per cent of its membership. Some 9 per cent of the members were masters, journeymen being the dominant group from the crafts. Other workers made up 30 per cent of members, and the remainder mostly came from middle class groups. The MWA thus had deep roots in the working class, but with a very much wider recruitment.[51] While masters formed a relatively small group within the MWA, a considerable number of Malmö masters belonged to it, in fact just under half of them. The members were somewhat better off than the average master and several of the wealthiest craftsmen were members, showing that the attraction of the association was not limited to the less well-off strata of masters.[52] One way to further our understanding of craft masters' political attitudes is by looking at electoral campaigns in Malmö. After the parliamentary reform of 1865, elections to the second chamber of parliament were conducted every third year. In the first decades these were rather tame affairs, with no clear ideological dividing lines. Candidates would not publicly declare their political views. The franchise was also restricted and only men with a certain income or property above a certain value were given the vote. This initially excluded workers but many masters were voters right from the beginning. With increasing incomes more people acquired the right to vote over time. By 1880 two thirds of all craft masters in Malmö had an income sufficient to make them potential voters.[53]

Already in the first elections in Malmö there are signs of activity among craftsmen. Nomination meetings involving craftsmen would be convened, and other meetings would be called by the Workers' Association. It is apparent that craftsmen formed an 'opposition' group. They acted to promote the election of a craftsman to parliament, and claimed that public officials were not well suited to represent Malmö. However, the precise nature of this opposition was very vague, and it should be seen primarily as a social rather than a political kind of opposition. It was also not very effective, and Malmö elected merchants and public officials.[54]

In the 1880s it is easier to see the outlines of a political opposition centring on attempts to mobilise a popular constituency of craftsmen and workers. At electoral meetings in 1881 actual political questions are discussed and the candidates are asked about their opinions on political matters. A Reform Society is active in the local campaign. The most important issues concerned suffrage, where reformers wanted to widen the electorate, and defence issues, where reformers were opposed to compulsory military service.

In 1884 the Social Democrats, who were beginning their political activities in Malmö at this time, got involved in this popular opposition. We also find many master craftsmen active in this context. The official meeting of the master craftsmen did not support the opposition, but preferred the 'establishment list'.[55] These candidates would also ultimately be elected. The meeting of the Workers' Association also supported the establishment, which would cause accusations of 'conservatism' from reformers. The organisations of the masters and the Workers' Association were thus no longer the centre of opposition. But prominent master craftsmen would be important in this group.

While 'establishment' candidates had regularly been elected, they would be increasingly challenged by opposition candidates from 1887 onwards. From 1887, the Social Democrats actively promoted candidates. In the 1890s a liberal electoral committee [*Den frisinnade valmansföreningen*] is active. There are several attempts to unite the liberal and socialist left, but only in 1893 is this a success. The left advances a slate with three liberal candidates and one socialist one, and is met by an establishment list in the first clearly confrontational election in Malmö's history. But old habits die hard. In the last elections of the 1890s we still find the old pattern of trying to find consensual slates where different 'interests' are represented and where personal abilities are more important than political opinions. It is apparent that the 'establishment' attempted to include liberal candidates as well as more moderate ones on their lists in order to counter the socialist threat. In 1899 three slates are proposed to the voters, one of them by the socialists. Two names (both 'liberals') appear on all of them! The Social Democrats are trying to build on the popular constituency that already existed in Malmö, and attempting to build alliances with liberals.

In such a setting it is not easy to label the political opinions of candidates. From our perspective it is interesting to note that all master craftsmen who are politically active can be found within this popular left. They are active at the popular meetings together with Social Democrats, at the meetings at the Workers' Association, at the meetings of the Democratic Committee in 1893 and later on the Liberal electoral committee. This is true also of the printer C. A. Andersson, who was elected to parliament in a by-election in 1880, who usually appears on the 'establishment slate' but fails to get widespread support from the left. He has been labelled a 'moderate liberal'. This is also true of his successor as a craftsman representative, the painter A. Antonsson.[56] The tailors Agri and Bouvin appear to have been more radical, especially the latter who was on the liberal-socialist slate in 1893. Of course, this would not suggest that all politically interested craftsmen in Malmö were on the left. In the confrontational election of 1893, the *Hantverksförening* voted to support the establishment list.[57] Still, the politically active craftsmen were involved in the craftsmen's organisations, for example by serving on the board of the Craftsmen's Association, and represented Malmö craftsmen at the national and regional craft meetings. They were therefore well established among their colleagues.

That craftsmen often belonged on the political left is a conclusion supported if we look at the popular movements. Malmö, like the south of Sweden generally, had relatively weak dissenter and temperance movements. In Swedish research, these movements are often grouped together with the labour movement and referred to as *folkrörelser* [popular movements]. They represented a democratic organisation of society from below, and are often considered as politically liberal. At least they were in favour of widening the electorate in order to get support for their particular political demands. To some extent they were all movements of protest and reform.[58] We find these movements active in the popular left in Malmö too.

No studies have been made of the social composition of dissenting churches and the temperance movement in Malmö. Existing studies generally concern cities in central Sweden. Here craftsmen formed a very important group in both movements. In the late nineteenth century, independent craftsmen and workers actually dominated most of the urban associations studied, perhaps with independent masters playing a larger role in dissent than in the temperance movement.[59] There is no reason to believe that the pattern in Malmö was much different, and from the lists of members of the board of directors in directories, it appears that this generalisation also holds for Malmö.[60]

One striking fact about these different associations is the extent to which both masters and journeymen within the crafts participated in the same organisations. This suggests that they shared much the same social circumstances. The distance in living conditions between lesser masters and workers was probably very small, and they often lived in the same working class districts of the cities. No great dividing social lines existed.

Another form of association in which masters were active in the later decades of the century were in the associations of house owners [*fastighetsägarföreningar*]. These represented the interests of house owners in dealings with both local authorities and tenants. However, they also served as important organisations in parliamentary electoral campaigns, often being considered liberal. As house owners, craft masters formed an important group in these associations. Toward the end of the century the associations turned more conservative, primarily as a reaction against advancing social democracy, which was seen as a threat to private property.[61]

What do we make of this conflicting evidence? Were masters 'conservative' and 'liberal' at the same time without realising the contradiction, or were they split between groups with different political leanings? In German research a similar problem has been interpreted in two different ways. Friedrich Lenger has suggested that German masters in the revolution of 1848/49 were economically 'conservative' but politically 'liberal'. He finds no necessary contradiction between enmity to freedom of trade and radical politics.[62] Another position is to claim that the contradictory evidence suggests that different groups within the crafts held different views. This solution is suggested by Jürgen Bergmann in a polemic with Lenger where he holds that economically conservative craftsmen would normally hold conservative political and social views. In the revolution, the crafts were divided between different political attitudes.[63]

The evidence in this article certainly suggest that masters in Sweden did not see any difficulty in holding economically 'conservative' views and participating in 'liberal' organisations. Those craftsmen who took the initiative to form the Educational Circle in 1848 all served on the first board of directors of the *Hantverksförening* in 1847, one as chairman. Of the 28 masters on the same board, 11 signed the reform petition of 1848, among them not only the chairman but also the vice-chairman.[64]

Neither was it a problem to participate in the masters' movement and in the MWA at the same time. Of the eight masters who participated at the first four national meetings of the masters' movement, six had been members of this association. At one time two of them were actually chairman and vice-chairman. Whether all were 'restrictionists' is not clear, but the representative in 1870, who had been vice-chairman of the MWA earlier in the year, supported the 'maximum programme'. All those who served on the board of directors of the *Hantverksförening* in the 1880s had been members of the MWA in 1869.[65]

It is however necessary to stress that these organisations were not overtly political ones. They attempted to keep out of politics, and their emphasis on education and self-help could well be acceptable to groups promoting different political causes. Neither is it necessarily the case that masters who signed petitions for parliamentary reform would have perceived this as incompatible with holding economically restrictive views.[66] In none of these cases did the 'liberalism' of the movements imply a radicalism that might have been irreconcilable with the 'conservative' views advanced by masters when arguing for restrictions in economics. There was, however, clearly a tension. The liberal press would denounce the meeting of the craftsmen in 1870 and compare it unfavourably with the meeting of the Workers' Associations that same summer. At the latter no demands for state intervention were made; they wanted to rely on self-help. But the rhetoric of 'ordered' and 'true' freedom might perhaps bridge this apparent gap.[67]

Also in the 1880s and 1890s, many of those craftsmen I have identified as 'liberal' actively participated in the masters' movement, playing leading roles in their organisations. Two of the most active, the painters Antonsson and Agri, were on the board of the *Hantverksförening* in 1890, Agri as vice-chairman.[68] There is evidence that two more of the twelve members had at least occasionally been active on the left.[69] We also find them as Malmö representatives in the national and regional meetings of the masters' movement.[70] The printer C. A. Andersson, as previously noted labelled by an historian as a 'moderate liberal,' introduced the bill containing the apprenticeship law proposal from the masters' movement in the *Riksdag* in 1895.

Still, politics in this period tended to become more 'modern' with clearer political oppositions. This must have tended to link positions on different political problems together into more coherent general political attitudes. One would therefore expect it to become more difficult to combine 'liberal' politics with 'restrictionist' economic ideas.

There are also clear indications that the politically active Malmö craftsmen, along with the Malmö Association as a whole, belonged to the least 'restrictionist' wing of the masters' movement. Andersson clearly stated in the *Riksdag* debate on the apprenticeship law that he was opposed to any restrictions on the right to establish an independent business, and Bouvin was one of the few critical voices at the 'restrictionist' meetings in 1891 and 1893. The Malmö Association in 1893 was as a whole opposed to proposals for qualifications for masters, while it supported the apprenticeship bill and compulsory organisation.[71] But even if many of these Malmö masters were among the least 'restrictionist' at many of these meetings, they would support some of the causes of the masters' movement

One should also be wary of being too concerned with simple dichotomies between 'liberal' and 'conservative' and 'traditional' and 'modern'. Artisans are often seen as backward looking people maintaining tradition in opposition to modernity, and conservatism against liberalism and socialism. One might easily forget that many of the restrictions proposed by Swedish masters at the end of the last century are actually in force in Germany today. They are apparently quite compatible with a smoothly functioning capitalist economy. Why should Swedish masters necessarily have seen such restrictions as incompatible with a market economy? As Adelheid von Saldern has pointed out, the German masters' movement cannot automatically be seen as an economically anti-modernist movement.[72]

In the Swedish case this can be illustrated if we look at one organisation formed primarily by master craftsmen. This is *Malmö industriförening* [Malmö Association of Industry]. It was founded in 1855 by craftsmen, teachers, intellectuals, merchants and industrialists. While open to everyone, it was clearly dominated by craftsmen and small industrialists.[73] It would co-operate with *Malmö hantverksförening* and rent rooms in a house owned by Malmö craftsmen, *Hantverkssocietetens hus*. We find many of the same individuals active in both the *Industriförening* and the *Hantverksförening*. The *Industriförening* was clearly not a backward looking organisation. Its purpose was to promote industry by helping to develop skills. It organised industrial exhibitions, primarily for craftsmen. It held a lottery, where craft products were prizes. It awarded prizes to apprentices who had shown skill when producing their voluntary journeymen pieces.[74] It donated money to finance visits abroad for artisans to study new techniques. It started a library, which in its early years concentrated on scientific and technological works, and organised lectures on the same subjects. The purpose was to link the crafts to the scientific advances of the period. It is certainly a programme that demonstrates a concern among Malmö craftsmen to be competitive in a market economy, linking them to economic progress. The 'restrictionist' attitudes they held were in no way seen as incompatible with this 'progressive' activity.[75] The incoherence of such activities and the 'restrictionist' programme is very much a construction of later historians who wish to create tidy categories.

It is also obvious that the masters' movement was not ideologically homogeneous. It was not a political movement as such, and would probably attempt to unite people with different views. Of course there was also room for internal conflicts within the movement. This also holds true for the associations of property owners, the temperance movement, and the dissenting churches. Even if it is correct to label them as 'liberal' in some sense, they could probably encompass members of different political persuasion. When politically active, members of the same organisation could promote different causes. In Gävle, the craftsmen who were members of a dissenting church, *Missionsföreningen*, were politically active in promoting the protectionist cause, while others were free traders.[76]

In the German context David Blackbourn has warned against identifying the attitude of the *Mittelstandbewegung* [middle class movement] with that of the petite bourgeoisie. The movement represented those who were better off, and many masters without employees and small shopkeepers would tend to have more radical politics.[77] Even though we have little evidence for Sweden, this seems quite likely. The gap between self-employed craftsmen with no employees and journeymen barely existed. Many workers would probably work for themselves if they could not find employment. The organised masters' movement was also relatively weak in the 1880s, and only revived in the early 1890s.[78] As I have argued above, it was clearly a movement representing employers, and relations with workers seem to have been an absolutely crucial aspect of its programme. To many small craftsmen this might have made it an irrelevance.

Some evidence from Malmö might hint at such differences in recruitment. The *Hantverksförening* only organised a minority of masters. In 1890 it was less than a third of them. At least the board of directors consisted of masters with large workshops and high incomes; on average they paid 47.7 crowns in income tax and employed ten workers. This contrasts very markedly with the masters who were prominent in the temperance and dissenter movement. Twelve identified leaders paid an average income tax 14.0 crowns and only employed 2.4 workers.[79] This would clearly suggest that recruitment to the masters' movement was very different from recruitment to the popular movements. In these it was much more likely to find masters who were less well-off, and who shared many of the living conditions of the workers who formed the majority of members. In the city of Nyköping this also appears to have been the case.[80]

Even if this is so, it might have little to do with differences of political opinion. While the masters' movement might well have been of more interest to more substantial masters, its 'restrictionism' does not equate to a general 'conservatism'. Generally for the whole period, there are plenty of indications that Malmö craftsmen can be found on the town's political left. They formed part of a popular environment, where it was natural to seek alliances with workers. These attempts did not cease even when socialism became a major political force from the 1880s onwards. This would however create tensions between masters and workers. However, this political attitude did not prevent Malmö masters from participating in the increasingly conservative national movement.

It should of course be pointed out that developments in Malmö might not be typical. There are indications that Malmö masters were less 'restrictionist' than many other masters. More work is clearly needed, particularly at the local level where it is possible to trace the activities of individuals in order to trace interconnections between different organisations.

IV

This final section will attempt to place Swedish developments in a comparative context. The general picture of the political alignments of the petite bourgeoisie suggests that these differed substantially between countries. In England the petite bourgeoisie played a prominent role in the radicalism of the early nineteenth century and was still important in Chartism. Based on an ideal of small-scale production, these radicals promoted a democratic society, opposed to all kinds of privilege and monopoly. After the middle of the century their presence was less visible, politically they probably supported the Liberals, and only at the beginning of the twentieth century was there a turn to the Conservatives. At no time did they give up their commitment to the economic principles of freedom of trade.[81] In France the situation in the early part of the century is rather similar. Many petit bourgeois were supporters of the radical republican tradition. Only toward the end of the century did they move toward the right and started demanding state intervention in order to protect small producers and shopkeepers.[82]

The pattern in Germany is quite different. The organised movement of craftsmen was quite conservative, calling for state intervention to protect the trades. Already prominent in the revolution of 1848/49, this movement would gain momentum towards the end of the century, and also achieve some important legal support. Scholars warn against a too facile identification of all petit bourgeois with the organised movement. In the revolution the craft movement was clearly conservative, but masters were also active on the revolutionary left.[83] Haupt and Lenger even suggest that we might talk of a 'liberal' phase in the German craft movement between 1850 and 1870.[84] Blackbourn and Lenger also point out that even toward the end of the century not all craftsmen would follow the organised opinion.[85] These reservations are certainly important but still cannot erase the marked differences between Germany on the one hand and England and France on the other.[86]

If we look at the organised movement of craft masters it is clear that there are great similarities between Sweden and Germany. In economic matters the organised opinion of Swedish masters was clearly in favour of legal restrictions, and appeals were made to the state to ensure the survival of the craftsmen. The demands made were also strikingly similar. The German movement asked for compulsory organisation [*Zwangsinnungen*], qualifications for mastership, and apprenticeship laws.[87] As we have seen, these demands were also made in the Swedish movement.

In discussing the reasons for different national patterns it has been common to refer to corporate traditions, in particular the guilds, and their quite diverse histories. The early erosion of the guilds in England, their abolition in France during the Revolution, and their late survival in large parts of Germany seems a likely explanation of both the survival of corporate traditions among German craftsmen, and the strength of their organisations.[88] The case of Sweden would certainly help support such an interpretation. The Swedish guilds survived almost up to the middle of the century, and the trades remained substantially regulated up to 1864. This is the time when freedom of trade was finally introduced in several German states.[89]

It is very likely that these corporate experiences would help shape the consciousness of Swedish craftsmen, in particular concerning the state. While craftsmen had often been critical of the actual practices of the state in regulating the crafts (the Guild Law of 1720 was not universally approved), it is quite clear that their demand for stricter regulations on setting up businesses would necessitate state actions. No other authority existed to guarantee such controls. Therefore we can identify a very common phenomenon when we discuss the attitude to the state of craftsmen, that they were on the one hand critical of the state as it was, on the other hand very positive to its activities in principle.[90]

As burghers, the masters were also given a role in local government, and participated in the election of the Burghers' Estate in parliament. In Stockholm there were even seats reserved for craftsmen.[91] This Estate would prove the craftsmen's best ally in the defence of guild legislation. The preservation of at least some aspects of corporate regulations would thus seem to have been necessary to the craftsmen.

As I have argued above, much of the cultural heritage of the guild period was eroded by the early nineteenth century. As organisations defending the economic interests of the crafts they did however survive, and this aspect of the corporate heritage was certainly still alive up to the end of the guild era. It is also clear that the survival of the guilds and their replacement with compulsory *Hantverksföreningar* helped masters maintain a solid organisational basis for protest. Many of these associations would survive as voluntary organisations, and through national meetings would secure the artisans a place in the national political forum even before they had a national organisation.

These traditions also served to maintain a craft identification among masters. In local urban politics in the corporate era they had maintained cohesion as *craftsmen*, an organised interest with specific rights, but economically, socially and politically inferior to the merchants and public officials who formed dominant groups in Swedish towns. This identity would probably be more important to most masters than their identity as members of individual trades or guilds.[92] Based on this identification a number of institutions were established in a town like Malmö. In the 1870s Malmö craft masters had a voluntary trade association [*Hantverksföreningen*], they owned a large property, they had a society for old age pensions, they had a reading society [*Hantverkarnas läse- och klubbsällskap*], and many participated in another trade organisation [*Industriföreningen*].[93] Some of these institutions were directly inherited from the corporate period, others were newly created. This strong identity as artisans perhaps helps explain why there are no indications that small shop-keepers were seen as a group with a close affinity to craftsmen. In other words, Swedish craft masters did not see themselves as forming a part of a petite bourgeoisie. Small shopkeepers, on the other hand, did not have a corporate tradition of their own to fall back on. The burghers of Swedish towns had been divided into merchants and craftsmen [*handlande och hantverkare*], and small shop-keepers would be a subordinate part of the former group.

It is my contention that this late corporate presence would have definite effects on shaping the political consciousness of master craftsmen. In the same way as in Germany it would help maintain some sort of consciousness of a corporate presence and of the crafts as a particular group in need of protection. The similarities to Germany are hardly surprising. Ever since the Middle Ages the Swedish crafts had been heavily influenced by Germany. The guilds carried on German traditions and Swedish journeymen frequently travelled through Germany or the wide area of Central and Northern Europe where German guild traditions dominated. The masters' movement was also influenced by the German movement, references to Germany were common, and most likely the Swedish movement was encouraged by developments in craft legislation in Germany toward the end of the century.[94] Their demands would now appear as less outdated and unrealistic.

In emphasising the guild tradition, I think it is necessary to add that this cannot be reduced to the actual legislation, but also has much to do with economic developments within the corporate structure. As Heinz-Gerhard Haupt has pointed out, in both England in France guilds had developed into extremely oligarchic organisations, as compared to Germany and Sweden where a greater cohesion was apparent in many trades. In England and France the workers rather than the masters would be the upholders of corporate restrictions in the trades.[95] While the crafts in Sweden did not correspond to any idealised picture of relative equality between masters, economic developments had not led to an internal split; the guilds still encompassed and represented all masters independent of their scale of operation. This is also important in understanding the apparent homogeneity of masters' attitudes.

If similarities between Germany and Sweden are quite striking there are also striking differences. One is the almost complete lack of success of the Swedish movement. While the legislative protection of the German crafts must not be exaggerated, the German movement scored notable successes. Several parties courted the *Mittelstand* and developed programmes for their protection. Nothing similar happened in Sweden. Haupt suggests that the German successes had a lot to do with the organisational strength of the craftsmen given by the recent corporate past.[96] The Swedish case suggests that this is hardly a sufficient explanation, and that the general context of petit bourgeois political activities is far more important. While this is too large a theme to develop here, it is quite clear that the failure of the Swedish movement had to do with its inability to form political alliances, or to make it interesting to any political group to court their support.[97] This in turn probably had to do with some characteristics of Swedish politics. Representatives of the farmers dominated the Swedish parliament and many of the big political questions of the period reflected their concerns, like protectionism, property taxation, and military reform. Urban interests were often represented by liberals, often with roots in the popular movements, and they did little to protect petit bourgeois interests. Comparison along these lines would probably prove fruitful.[98]

Another important difference compared to Germany is that if we take a broader view of the Swedish craftsmen, it is not as apparent that they should be placed on the political 'right'. The craft movements were very similar in their demands, and the Swedish movement also shows a marked turn to the 'right' at the end of the century. But this 'turn to the right' is not at all as clear if we look at other organised activities of Swedish craftsmen. The involvement of many craftsmen in the popular movements suggest that many should rather be placed on the 'left'. In Malmö it is clear that many craftsmen were active in a popular liberal context.

However, it is necessary to be cautious in generalising this pattern. Nevertheless, it would hardly be an alliance that would facilitate support for the economic programme of masters and this might, if not peculiar to Malmö, help explain their lack of success.

As a final reflection I would like to reiterate that we should not focus too exclusively on relations between masters and the state. As this essay has suggested, relations with workers were a dominant theme in the different activities of masters. The tension between the movement as a general interest organisation and/or as an employers' organisation would be crucial in the early national organisation around the turn of the century.[99] The rise of socialism as the dominant ideology of the workers would also affect craft masters. Attempts to form a broad popular alliance would be made more difficult. Their identity as employers of workers would be more important. This could also help explain why the movement was not equally appealing to all masters, and it is likely that it primarily represented masters with larger numbers of employees.

Notes

[1] This prevalent view is reflected in general histories of the nineteenth century, e.g. in Eric Hobsbawm's eminent trilogy: *The age of revolution 1789-1848*, 1962, ch. 6, s. IV; *The age of empire 1875-1914*, 1987, ch. 4 s. I and ch. 7 s. II; a Scandinavian example, Lars-Arne Norborg, *Det starka Europa* (*Bra Böckers världshistoria*, vol. 11), Höganäs 1986, pp. 149-50.

[2] The obvious points of reference are Geoffrey Crossick and Heinz-Gerhard Haupt, *The Petite Bourgeoisie in Europe 1780-1914*, London 1995; and *Shopkeepers and Master Artisans in Nineteenth Century Europe*, Geoffrey Crossick and Heinz-Gerhard Haupt (eds), London 1984.

[3] This point has been made by Heinz-Gerhard Haupt, 'Gesellschaftliche Bedeutung des Kleinbürgertums in westeuropäischen Gesellschaften des 19. Jahrhunderts', *Geschichte und Gesellschaft* 16 (1990), p. 310.

[4] For the crafts in Malmö in the late guild period, see Lars Edgren, 'Crafts in transformation? Masters, journeymen, and apprentices in a Swedish town, 1800-1850', *Continuity and Change* 1 (1986), pp. 363-383.

[5] In principle crafts should be confined to the towns, but the countryside in practice had a lively craft production, both through home industry and more professional craftsmen. Carl-Johan Gadd, *Självhushåll eller arbetsdelning?* [Self-sufficiency or division of labour?], Göteborg 1991; Maths Isacson & Lars Magnusson, *Proto-Industrialisation in Scandinavia*, Leamington Spa, 1987.

[6] Henry Lindström, *Näringsfrihetsfrågan i Sverige 1837-1864* [Freedom of Trade as a Political Problem in Sweden 1837-1864], Göteborg 1929; Tom Söderberg, *Hantverkarna i genombrottsskedet 1870-1920* [Craftsmen in the Period of Industrial Breakthrough 1870-1920], Stockholm 1965.

[7] Lindström, *Näringsfrihetsfrågan*; Söderberg, *Hantverkarna*.

[8] The petitions can be found in *Konseljakter* 18 January and 22 March 1850, 7 February 1852, 9 April 1856. Civildepartementet. (Riksarkivet). The national petitions were printed, *Petition angående vissa förändringar i Kongl. Maj:ts nåd. handtverksordning...*, Västerås 1850; *Underdånig petition angående ändringar i näringsförfattningarne...*, Stockholm 1853. I have discussed the campaign against the Law of 1846 in an unpublished paper, 'Hantverkarna och näringsfriheten 1847-1853' [Craftsmen and Freedom of Trade, 1847-1853], Dept. of History, University of Lund, 1979. See also Lindström, *Näringsfrihetsfrågan*; Söderberg, *Hantverkarna*.

[9] Arne Munthe, *Hundra år i hantverkets tjänst. Stockholms stads hantverksförenings historia* [One Hundred Years in the Service of the Crafts. The history of the Stockholm Crafts Association], Stockholm 1947, pp. 149-59.

[10] Tom Ericsson, *Mellan kapital och arbete. Småborgerligheten i Sverige 1850-1914* [Between capital and labour. The petite bourgeoisie in Sweden, 1850-1914], Umeå 1988, pp. 105, 147. Ericsson is however not quite consistent. He also claims that a more conservative outlook became more visible after 1864 (pp. 115-16) and that the petite bourgeoisie as a whole were illiberal in the second half of the nineteenth century (p. 170).

[11] Söderberg, *Hantverkarna*, pp. 124, 172.

[12] Söderberg, *Hantverkarna*, pp. 124-55.

[13] *Nerikes Allehanda* 27 July 1870 (Sefbom); *Förhandlingar vid tredje allmänna industri-idkaremötet i Göteborg den 17, 18 och 19 Augusti 1874*, Göteborg 1874, 8 (Hägg), 31 (Håkansson); *Förhandlingar vid femte allmänna industri-idkaremötet i Stockholm den 28, 29 och 30 augusti 1884*, Stockholm 1884, 21-22 (Friberg), 24 (Molin). See also note 18.

[14] For the proceedings of this first meeting we have to rely on reports in newspapers; *Nerikes Allehanda* 27 July 1870; *Nya Dagligt Allehanda* 28-30 July 1870.

[15] *Förhandlingar vid andra allmänna industri-idkaremötet i Stockholm den 25, 26 och 27 Augusti 1873*, Stockholm 1873; *...tredje...industri-idkaremötet 1874.*

[16] *Förhandlingar vid fjärde allmänna industri-idkaremötet i Stockholm den 24, 25 och 26 augusti 1876*, Stockholm 1876.

[17] *Konseljakter*, 29 September 1890, Civildepartementet (Riksarkivet). The association in Karlskrona accepted only some very minor proposals of the petition. The reaction from a number of craftsmen in Landskrona suggests the difficulty in interpreting opposition to the petition. They were not willing to accept either compulsory contracts or organisations, but ended with expressing their regret that the law of 1846 had been abolished!

[18] *...femte...industri-idkaremötet...1884.*

[19] *Norden* 24 December 1874. At the meeting in 1876 the speakers from Stockholm were evenly divided between 'restrictionists' and those opposed to appeals to the law; *...fjärde...industri-idkaremötet...1876.*

[20] *Norden* 12 October 1877, 3 May 1878, 4 April 1879.

[21] *Förhandlingar vid sjette allmänna industriidkaremötet i Göteborg 1891*, Göteborg, 1892. Söderberg offers a quite different interpretation of this meeting, he claims that the conservative spirit of the 1870s was foreign to it, and that demands were more practical; Söderberg, *Hantverkarna*, 172. My conclusion is almost the opposite.

[22] *Förhandlingarna vid sjunde allmänna industriidkaremötet i Norrköping 1893*, Norrköping 1893.

[23] *Bihang till riksdagens protokoll 1895* 8:2:2 no 15; *Andra kammarens protokoll 1895*, 3:26, 40-56, 3:27, 1-35; the statutes of the new organisation were printed in *Handtverks- och industritidning* 1898, pp. 4-5.

[24] A few examples spread over time: *Nya Dagligt Allehanda* 28 July 1870 (Widman); *Nerikes Allehanda* 27 July 1870 (Blomstrand); *...andra...industri-idkaremötet 1873*, 16-21 (Lindberg); *...tredje...industri-idkaremötet 1874*, 8 (Hägg); *...fjärde...industri-idkaremötet...1876*, 19-20 (the chairman), 27 (Granberg); *...femte...industri-idkaremötet...1884*, 23 (C Johnsson); *...sjette...industri-idkaremötet...1891*, 29 (Rubensson); *Förhandlingar vid åttonde skånska handtverksmästaremötet i Helsingborg den 20 juli 1892*, Helsingborg, 1892, 16 (O Jönsson, quoted in text); *Handtverks- och industritidning* 1898, 117; 1899, 177.

[25] Protectionist proposals were made at the first (1870) and fifth (1884) meetings. For craftsmen's attitudes to customs, see also the archives of the state committee set up in 1876 to investigate Swedish customs duties, 1876 års tullkommittés arkiv (ÄK 791), (Riksarkivet).

[26] *...femte...industri-idkaremötet...1884*. This protectionism would not necessarily extend itself to corn. The re-introduction of customs duties on corn was a major political question in Sweden in the 1880s.

[27] *...tredje...industriidkaremötet...1874*, pp. 16-17.

[28] *Allmänna skandinaviska handtverks- och konstindustriidkaremötet i Stockholm 1897*, Stockholm, 1897, pp. 23-24.

[29] *Handtverks- och Industritidning* 1898, 87, 109; *Allmänna Skandinaviska Handtverks- och Konst-industriidkaremötet i Stockholm den 5, 6, 7 och 8 juli 1897*, Stockholm 1897, 24.

[30] The early craft unions often had the explicit intention of organising production in a mutually satisfying way, and the interest of the trade remained important. Unions in the 1880s might even demand that masters organise. See e.g. the Shoemakers' Trade Union in Malmö, February 21 1888, *Malmö skomakarfackförbunds protokoll*, (Arbetarrörelsens arkiv i Malmö). At the third provincial meeting of Scanian craftsmen, representatives of local trade unions were invited in order to express their views, *Förhandlingar vid tredje skånska handtverksmästaremötet i Lund den 11 augusti 1887*, Lund 1887, 4.

[31] *Handtverks- och Industritidning* 1898, 53-54, 79, 186; 1899, 159, 372, 379, and 29 December. See also *...sjette...industri-idkaremötet...1891*, pp. 15-16.

[32] The statutes in *Handtverks- och industritidning* 1898, pp. 4-5. This policy was adopted already at the sixth meeting, *...sjette...industri-idkaremötet...1891*, pp. 19-20.

[33] *Handtverks- och Industritidning* 1898, p. 77.

[34] Geoffrey Crossick and Heinz-Gerhard Haupt, 'Shopkeepers, master artisans and the historian: the petite bourgeoisie in comparative focus', pp. 5-6; David Blackburn, 'Between resignation and volatility: the German petite bourgeoisie in the nineteenth century', pp. 35ff; both essays in *Shopkeepers and Master Artisans*, Geoffrey Crossick and Heinz-Gerhard Haupt (eds).

[35] Ericsson, *Mellan kapital och arbete*, pp. 138ff.

[36] An interesting exception is *Förhandlingarna vid åttonde allmänna svenska industriidkaremötet i Visby 1896*, Stockholm 1896, p. 35. The same spokesman advances the interesting idea that craft workers ought to identify with their masters and distinguish themselves from industrial workers in the same way as masters distinguished themselves from the great industrialists, *Handtverks- och industritidning* 1899, p. 42.

[37] *Norden* 11 and 25 July 1874.
[38] Rolf Torstendahl, 'Technology in the development of society 1850-1980', *History and Technology*, I, 1984; Rolf Torstendahl, 'Das Konzept der Organisierter Kapitalismus und seine Anwendung auf Schweden', *Geschicte und Gesellschaft*, 11, 1985.
[39] For the uses of history, see Tom Ericsson, 'Cults, myths and the Swedish petite bourgeoisie, 1870-1914', *European History Quarterly*, 23, 1993, pp. 233-51.
[40] Ericsson, *Mellan kapital och arbete*, pp. 147-48.
[41] The petitioners from Malmö are listed in *Malmö Allehanda* 13 and 17 May 1848.
[42] Listings in *Konseljakter*, 1 January 1863, Justitiedepartementets arkiv (Riksarkivet).
[43] Carl Landelius, *1840-1850-talets bildningscirklar och arbetarföreningar i Sverige* [Educational Associations and Workers' Associations in Sweden in the 1840s and 1850s], Stockholm 1936; Torkel Jansson, *Adertonhundratalets associationer* [Nineteenth-century associations], Uppsala 1985, pp. 186ff.
[44] The 'Circles' could be seen as potentially dangerous bodies, as one of the founders of the Malmö Circle testifies; Ludvig B. Falkman, *Minnen från Malmö under första hälften af innevarande århundrade* [Memoirs of Malmö in the first half of the present century], Malmö 1986, p. 193.
[45] *Malmö Allehanda* 2 February 1848.
[46] Lars Edgren, 'Hantverkarna och arbetarkulturen. En aspekt av klassformering' [Craftsmen and working class culture. An aspect of class formation], *Scandia*, 56, 1990, pp. 239-46.
[47] However, it would have been quite interesting to know what the masters felt when a debate on freedom of trade took place in the 'Circle' in 1849. The speaker introducing the subject promoted unlimited freedom of trade. The arguments of the debate are not reported, but the resolution is clearly a compromise; freedom of trade is good but regulations are needed to achieve 'good order', a formula quite often used by masters pressing for restrictions. Edgren, 'Hantverkarna och arbetarkulturen', p. 242.
[48] Axel Påhlman & Walter Sjölin, *Arbetarföreningarna i Sverige 1850-1900*, [Workers' Associations in Sweden 1850-1900], Stockholm 1944; Jansson, *Adertonhundratalets associationer*, pp. 196-203.
[49] In 1868, half the board consisted of middle class people, one quarter of workers, and one quarter of craft masters, *Malmö adresskalender 1868*, p. 68.
[50] *Medlemsmatrikel* 1869, Malmö arbetarförenings arkiv (Arbetarrörelsens arkiv i Malmö).
[51] A difficulty in the analysis is distinguishing masters from journeymen when only trades were used in titles. Of the 42 per cent of craftsmen, only one third reported their standing in the trade. The yearly statistical reports from the city magistrate on the local crafts has been used to determine who were masters. (Kommerskollegii arkiv. Kammarkontoret. Årsberättelser, handlande och hantverkare (Riksarkivet)). It has been assumed here that those craftsmen who are not listed here were workers. This seems to be realistic, however it is possible that some of them carried on their trade independently on a small scale, with no or very few employees.
[52] The membership lists have been compared with the yearly statistical report on the Malmö crafts in 1870 (cf. previous note).

[53] In this case I have used a database of craftsmen in Malmö in 1880, constructed from church and taxation records.
[54] The following discussion of Malmö elections is based on a study of local papers. I have used *Snällposten* for 1866 and 1869, *Sydsvenska Dagbladet* for all remaining years, and *Malmö Nya Allehanda* between 1866 and 1887. Elections took place in August 1866, August 1869, and in September 1872, 1875 1878, 1881, 1884, April 1887, September 1890, 1893, 1896, 1899. While it would have been desirable to study more papers, I have found that one paper is usually sufficient for the information I have been seeking.
[55] I have preferred to talk about the 'established' list or the 'establishment' list rather than to try to give it a political label (conservative). What I refer to is the list supported by the dominant groups in local government, that is merchants, big industrialists, and public officials. This list was usually voted for at an electoral meeting called by the *stadsfullmäktige* (the locally elected city council).
[56] Sten Carlssson, *Lantmannapolitiken och industrialismen. Partigruppering och opinionsförskjutningar i svensk politik 1890-1912* (Farmers' Politics and Industrialization in Sweden 1890-1902), Stockholm 1953, p. 432
[57] *Sydsvenska Dagbladet Snällposten* 23 September 1893.
[58] Sven Lundkvist, *Folkrörelserna i det svenska samhället, 1850-1920* [Popular Movements in Swedish Society, 1850-1920], Stockholm 1977, summarises the extensive research of the 1960s and 1970s. For regional distribution, see pp. 66-75.
[59] Lundkvist, *Folkrörelserna*, pp. 104-22.
[60] In three temperance organisations and three dissenting churches in 1890, 44 individuals are listed with titles in the address calendar of that year. Of these 12 were masters and 9 more were craftsmen. *Malmö stads adresskalender för 1890*, 69-70, 89-91; Statistical reports on the crafts in Malmö 1890 (cf. note 52).
[61] Ericsson, *Mellan kapital och arbete*, 135-38; Pär-Erik Back, *Sammanslutningarnas roll i politiken 1870-1910* [The Political Role of Organisations 1870-1910], Skellefteå 1967; Hans Wallengren, 'En kamporganisation i vardande. De organiserade fastighetsägarna i Malmö 1882-1914', [An interest organisation in the making. The organised property owners in Malmö 1882-1914], *Elbogen*, 19, 1989.
[62] Friedrich Lenger, *Sozialgeschichte der deutschen Handwerker seit 1800*, Frankfurt/M 1988, 86-7; see also David Blackburn, 'Economic crisis and the petite bourgeoisie in Europe during the nineteenth and twentieth centuries', *Social History*, 10, 1985, pp. 96-7.
[63] Bergmann, *Wirtschaftskrise und Revolution. Handwerker und Arbeiter 1848/1849*, Stuttgart 1986, pp. 233-50.
[64] The board of directors of the Hantverksförening: Hans Falck and Ernst Fischer, *Malmö Hantverksförening 1826-1926*, Malmö 1926, p. 61.
[65] Directors according to *Malmö stads adresskalender* 1883 and 1886. For the Board of Directors of the *MWA*, Protokoll, Malmö Arbetarförenings arkiv (Malmö stadsarkiv).
[66] It is another matter that 'objectively' the masters would be losers from such reforms. In the Burghers' Estate craftsmen would be assured of some representation which they would not have in the new two chamber parliament from 1866. Also in local politics the change from a corporate representation of burghers to the representation of individuals would result in a loss of influence for masters, Ericsson, *Mellan kapital och arbete*, pp. 133-34.
[67] *Nerikes Allehanda* 3 August 1870.

[68] *Malmö stads adresskalender för 1890*
[69] The cooper S. Andersson was proposed as a candidate for parliament at a popular meeting in 1884 (*Sydsvenska Dagbladet Snällposten* 9 September 1884) and in 1887 he proposed Agri as candidate (*Sydsvenska Dagbladet Snällposten* 22 September 1887); in 1890 the painter Borgström proposed the radical clergyman Meijer as a candidate (*Sydsvenska Dagbladet Snällposten* 9 September 1890).
[70] Agri and Bouvin were present at the national meeting in 1891 (*Förhandlingar vid sjette allmänna industriidkaremötet i Göteborg 1891*, Göteborg 1892), pp 88-91. Agri, Bouvin, S. Andersson and Antonsson would all be present at the regional meetings.
[71] Andersson: *Andra kammarens protokoll 1895*, 3:26, pp. 42-43; Bouvin: *...sjette...industri-idkaremötet ...1891*, p. 38; *...sjunde...industri-idkaremötet...1893*, pp. 18-21; Agri opposed legal regulations on masters in 1893, *...sjunde...industri-idkaremötet...1893*, p. 26; Antonsson spoke against restrictions at provincial craft meetings; *Förhandlingar vid andra skånska handtverksmästaremötet i Malmö den 31 maj 1886*, Malmö, 1886, p. 7; protocol of the Malmö Craft Association, 4 May 1892 and 6 March 1893, Malmö stads hantverksförenings arkiv, protokoll 1888-1895 (Malmö stadsarkiv).
[72] Adelheid von Saldern, 'The old *Mittelstand* 1890-1939: How 'backward' were the artisans?', *Central European History*, 25, 1992, pp. 27-51.
[73] *Malmö Industriförening* published yearly reports on their activities, containing excerpts from their protocols. These can be found at the University Library in Lund in a special section (they are not found in the ordinary catalogue). LUB Småtrycket (Teknol., Sällsk. [Malmö Industriförening]). No membership lists exist. Of 54 members of the board before 1900, 23 were master craftsmen; *Malmö Industriförning 1855-1955*, Malmö 1955.
[74] Even after 1864 the local craft associations awarded journeymen certificates, even if this was purely voluntary.
[75] The description of this association is based on the yearly reports mentioned in note 74.
[76] Ingrid Åberg, *Förening och politik. Folkrörelsernas politiska aktivitet i Gävle under 1880-talet* [Association and Politics. The political activity of the popular movements in Gävle in the 1880s], Uppsala 1975, p. 57.
[77] David Blackburn, 'La petite bourgeoisie et l'Etat dans l'Allemagne impériale, 1871-1914', *Le Mouvement Social* no. 127, 1984.
[78] *Handtverks- och industritidning* 1899, 2, complained that only about 10 per cent of all masters were members of the national organisation.
[79] This is based on listings of the leadership in different organisations *in Malmö stads adresskalender för 1890*. These are then identified in the yearly statistical reports on the crafts (see note 52). The average income tax of all masters was 17.6 *kronor*, and the average number of workers 3.4. The statistics under-report workers.
[80] Sven Hedenskog, *Folkrörelserna i Nyköping 1880-1915* [Popular Movements in Nyköping 1880-1915], Uppsala 1973, p. 94.
[81] Geoffrey Crossick, 'The petite bourgeoisie in nineteenth-century Britain: the urban and liberal case', in *Shopkeepers and Master Artisans*, Geoffrey Crossick and Heinz-Gerhard Haupt (eds), London 1984, pp. 71-81. Crossick and Haupt, *The Petite Bourgeoisie in Europe*, pp. 149, 153-5, and 162-3.
[82] Heinz-Gerhard Haupt, 'The petite bourgeoisie in France, 1850-1914: in search of the juste milieu?', in *Shopkeepers and Master Artisans*, Crossick and Haupt

(eds), pp. 108-13; Crossick and Haupt, *The Petite Bourgeoisie in Europe*, pp. 146, 149-151, and 160-161.

[83] For conflicting interpretations of this, see Lenger, *Sozialgeschichte der deutschen Handwerker* and Bergmann, *Wirtschaftskrise und Revolution*.

[84] Heinz-Gerhard Haupt and Friedrich Lenger, 'Liberalismus und Handwerk in Frankreich und Deutschland um die Mitte des 19. Jahrhunderts', *in Liberalismus im 19. Jahrhundert. Deutschland im europäischen Vergleich*, Dieter Langewiesche (ed.), Göttingen 1988, p. 317.

[85] Blackburn, 'La petite bourgeoisie et l'Etat..''; Lenger, pp. 158-59.

[86] This contrast is important in Crossick and Haupt, *The Petite Bourgeosie*.

[87] Blackburn, 'La petite bourgeoisie et l'Etat...', p. 17; Lenger, *Sozialgeschichte der deutschen Handwerker*, p. 155.

[88] Crossick and Haupt, 'Shopkeepers and master artisans', p. 24; Haupt, 'Bedeutung des Kleinbürgertums', pp. 298-305.

[89] Lenger, *Sozialgeschichte der deutschen Handwerker*, p. 89; Heinz-Gerhard Haupt, 'La survivance des corporations au XIXe siècle: une esquisse comparative', *Revue du nord* LXXVI (1994).

[90] Blackburn has reflected on this apparent inconsistency in petit bourgeois attitudes in Germany, 'La petite bourgeoisie et l'Etat'. For Swedish artisans in the late guild period, Ernst Söderlund, *Hantverkarna*, 2 [Craftsmen], Stockholm 1949; Lars Edgren, *Lärling - gesäll - mästare* [Apprentice, Journeyman, Master], Lund 1987.

[91] In France craftsmen were usually excluded from electoral rights during the July monarchy which might have helped to promote radicalism, Haupt and Lenger, 'Liberalismus und Handwerk', p. 321. In England parliamentary reform would also mobilise craftsmen for radicalism. The Swedish situation with corporate representation would probably make masters less disaffected with political conditions.

[92] Lars Edgren, 'Craftsmen in the political and symbolic order : the case of eighteenth-century Malmö', in *The Artisan and the European Town, 1500-1900*, Geoffrey Crossick (ed.), Aldershot, 1997, pp. 131-150

[93] Falck & Fischer, *Malmö hantverksförening*.

[94] The leading proponent of restrictions in the 1870s, the master shoemaker S. A. Hägg, closely followed developments in Germany; *Norden* February 16 and March 23 1877; S A Hägg, *Några tankar om handtverkeriernas i Sverige ställning...* [Reflections on the Situation of the Crafts in Sweden], Uppsala 1874, pp. 18-22. Influences from Denmark and Norway were also important as witnessed by Scandinavian meetings in 1866 and 1897 in Stockholm.

[95] Haupt, 'La survivance des corporations', p. 805; Crossick and Haupt, 'Shopkeepers and master artisans...', p. 24; Haupt and Lenger, 'Liberalismus und Handwerk...', p. 319.

[96] Haupt, 'Bedeutung des Kleinbürgertums', pp. 302-03.

[97] Ericsson, *Mellan kapital och arbete*, p. 145. This contrasts not only with Germany, but also with France, Haupt, 'Bedeutung des Kleinbürgertums', p. 315.

[98] Haupt, 'Bedeutung des Kleinbürgertums', provides an interesting example of such a comparison between Belgium and France in order to understand the failure of the Belgian *Mittelstandbewegung*.

[99] Söderberg, *Hantverkarna*, pp. 193-225.

JØRGEN FINK

In Defence of the Middle Class. But who and how?

In 1915 universal suffrage was at last introduced in Denmark.[1] The old privileges of the wealthiest part of the electorate were now abolished and voting was no longer an exclusively male privilege. Henceforth all adults, male and female, rich and poor were accepted as voters with equal rights without any discrimination. Fifty years of struggle over democratic rights thus came to an end.

Only one of the four political parties, *Højre* [The Right], opposed universal suffrage, but even this party voted for it. This was part of a deal that introduced proportional representation. To attain this, the party had to support universal suffrage, although it continued to oppose it in its political programme. This was somewhat awkward as the principle had now not only been adopted, but had been adopted with the help of the votes of The Right.

In this situation one of the party's young journalists, Asger Karstensen, took the initiative to reconstruct the party. The party would have to accept universal suffrage and establish itself as a democratic party of the middle class. This was his demand, and he managed to convince the not very active leadership of the party that this was necessary. Thus *Højre* was transformed into *Det konservative Folkeparti* [The Conservative Democratic (literally people's) Party], and between 1915 and 1920 Karstensen tried hard to make the new party into a real party of the middle class.

Initially he had some success. This could be seen in the political programme of the new party. The programme itself was very short containing only twelve points, but the political statement that accompanied and explained the programme was outspoken and stated clearly that the new party was a party of the middle class:

'All political parties now [as universal suffrage and the new constitution have changed the political conditions of the nation] have to base their work on the principle of universal suffrage, but

185

the expanded electorate may become a danger to the individual search for an independent living, free enterprise and personal responsibility by opening the door to the ruthless intrusion of the social-democratic [labour] and social-liberal parties. Consequently all sound conservatives in our society have to join in the defence and support of the middle class in the towns and in the countryside as modern Denmark first and foremost has been built upon the social and cultural achievement of this class.'[2]

The programme thus left no doubt that this was a party of the middle class. The problem was that no one really cared about the programme. This became clear when the name of the new party had to be decided. The Democratic Party [*Folkepartiet*] was Karstensen's suggestion. The Conservative Party was the other. In the end they had to compromise and The Conservative Democratic Party became the solution. So the party programme was no guarantee that the party would stick to its middle-class position, and it demanded hard work if this was to be accomplished. This then was Karstensen's task for the next five years.

His opponents were members of the old party who had drifted into the new without enthusiasm. They would have preferred to have gone on as before and pursued an ordinary reactionary policy, that is a good old-fashioned one. They had no clear policy but were generally *against*. They had no leader, but when the ideological struggle in the party became more intense they backed Alexander Foss in his fight against Karstensen and the new middle-class line. Foss was a great Danish industrialist, chairman of the Danish Federation of Industrialists and an impressive figure in public life. His political line was free enterprise without conditions, and as Karstensen's middle-class policy was an obstacle to that, Foss started to fight against Karstensen's influence in the party and in the press.

Asger Karstensen was not a member of parliament when the transformation of the party took place. He was elected to the steering committee of the new party, and that became the main platform for his influence. He made this influence felt, and after a while conservative MPs dared not act in important political matters without consulting the steering committee. This became untenable. If Karstensen was to wield power over conservative MPs, he had to become a member of the group. So in 1918 he was elected a member of the lower chamber of the Danish parliament.

Alexander Foss had been elected to the lower chamber in 1915 but was far too busy to attend. In 1918 he switched to the upper chamber which was less time-consuming. The conservative members of parliament from both chambers normally held sessions in common and these sessions became one of the battlefields for the ideological struggle in the party. The other battlefield was the press. The struggle was an ideological struggle between a democratic middle-class line and an undemocratic upper-class line, but it was not acted out as such. The ideological question was never discussed. The battle was waged around the political questions of the day and the focus of the battle became a proposed trust Act, or rather antitrust Act.

Trust acts belonged to the spirit of the time. Big business had come of age and had created new realities that demanded political and legal regulation. The USA was the pioneer both in the growth of big business and in the attempts to regulate it. This proved difficult. Acts against trusts and monopolies could aim either at protecting consumers against exploitation or protecting small producers against ruinous competition. The American Sherman Antitrust Act from 1890 was at first difficult to interpret, but after 1897/8 it was interpreted by the Supreme Court as an instrument for the protection of consumers. This had two consequences. The Act was used against small business forbidding price agreements and retail price fixing of every kind, but big business found new ways of evading it through mergers and holding companies. The result was the great merger movement at the turn of the century. It was thus seen that antitrust legislation was not necessarily helpful to small business. In 1911 the Supreme Court tried to interpret the Act as also protecting small business. The Standard Oil Trust was declared illegal and had to be dissolved because it was in unreasonable restraint of trade. The point here, however, was not the outcome (that a big trust had to be dissolved) but the premisses of the verdict, introducing the rule of reason. This did not prevent the creation of trusts, on the contrary, they were legalised in so far as they were not unreasonable. So this did not prove helpful to small business either.

These experiences from abroad should have been a warning, but they were not. In Denmark as in other European countries antitrust regulation emanated from the wartime economy of the First World War. The war had made public regulation of the economy necessary in all countries, but except among revolutionary movements there was general agreement that after the war it was 'back to normalcy'. Normalcy was understood as markets of free competition. But where monopolies had taken the place of the free market, there was no normalcy to go back to, and in those cases public regulation would have to continue in the shape of antitrust Acts. This was the common wisdom of the time. All the four political parties of Denmark demanded antitrust regulation in their programmes.

In 1919 an antitrust Act was presented to the Danish parliament. It was read in the lower chamber and finally adopted by it in the spring of 1920. From there it passed to the upper chamber, where it never had a final reading. So in the end nothing came of the efforts. This was due in the first place to the determined resistance of the Danish industrialists. The antitrust legislation caused a bitter clash in The Conservative Democratic Party and triggered the ideological struggle between the middle-class and the upper-class wings of the party.

This battle the middle-class wing lost. For it the course of events was a total disaster. There were several reasons for this. One was that the antitrust regulation was mixed up with the national question of reunion with parts of the Duchy of Slesvig. There was absolutely no intrinsic connection between those two questions, just a temporal coincidence. But that was enough. The national question caused a split in the middle-class wing and isolated its leading members in the party. Another reason was, as already mentioned, that the antitrust legislation was met with very determined resistance from the industrialists who were able to mobilise almost all elements of the Danish business community against it. The master artisans and shopkeepers sided with industry on this question.

But a third reason was that the middle-class wing, or rather the leading politicians of the middle-class wing, disagreed about fundamental questions such as: (1) who belonged to the middle class; (2) how they could be protected; and (3) whether they needed protection at all. This of course weakened their position and made them easy targets.

The ideologies of the middle class wing

The leader of the middle-class wing of the party was Asger Karstensen. His name has been mentioned already. He was a political agitator and strategist, energetic and bold but without any knowledge of or interest in the more detailed and cumbersome political issues. In particular he lacked a knowledge of economics. In economic matters he relied on the help of others. When writing the programme of the new party in 1915 his greatest help in this respect had been the economist Dr Arnold Fraenkel. Later, in the antitrust campaigns of 1918-20 he was totally dependent on L.V. Birck, who was professor of economics at the University of Copenhagen. Unfortunately those two economists hated each other or rather Fraenkel hated Birck and Birck despised Fraenkel. This too weakened the position of the middle-class wing.

To Karstensen the importance of antitrust legislation was self-evident. It was part of his political credo which was simple and straightforward. Capital would, if left unrestrained, continue its concentration and thereby ruin many independent artisans and shopkeepers. In social terms this meant that the number of workers would swell, the number of masters and owners would shrink and in a society of universal suffrage the political consequence would be that some day society would wake up to a socialist majority. Consequently it was a political necessity to protect the middle class (the old middle class of shopkeepers and artisans) against the overwhelming competition of big business, and this was to be done by antitrust legislation.

Karstensen was not the only one to entertain this conviction. It was a common point of view among people concerned about the fate of the old middle class. The idea had been launched by Karl Marx in the *Communist Manifesto* as a prediction of the inevitability of socialism. Karstensen, like so many others, accepted this analysis but tried to find political ways of avoiding the unavoidable. It was a simplistic view that paid little respect to the changes in the character of the market economy that had developed since the day of the *Communist Manifesto*. In particular, Karstensen showed no awareness of price agreements or retail price fixing and other 'soft' conspiracies in restraint of trade that were so crucial to the existence of small business. Karstensen had no acquaintance with the many trade associations of master artisans and shopkeepers who were the *loci* of these price agreements. After his defeat in the struggle in The Conservative Democratic Party he approached these groups but was repelled by their narrow and petty political horizon. They on their side distrusted him and were tired of benevolent and condescending outsiders who acted as self-proclaimed spokesmen of the middle class. Consequently they had tried to establish a political party of their own and succeeded in creating the Business Party [*Erhvervspartiet*] that won one seat in the general election of 1918 and three or four seats in the three general elections of 1920.

To Karstensen then, to sum up, the middle class was the old middle class, and it was much in need of protection, and this protection should be an antitrust act (whether the middle class itself wanted it or not).

Arnold Fraenkel was a different kind of person from Karstensen. He had a thorough and philosophical nature, held a doctorate from the University of Leipzig and was an erudite man. He wanted to take the foundations of his ideological point of view as far back in history as possible grudgingly coming to a halt when he reached the Creation. He wrote three books about the middle class and the trust question, and his point of view was highly original. To him the problems of the trust were neither what they did to the small producers nor what they did to consumers. The last point admittedly might be a problem but not a big one then. No, the real problem was that the trusts, monopolies and great companies were a menace to the character of their employees. Here was the real danger. The trust constituted a threat to the individual social ambition of employees. Individual social ambition was Fraenkel's key concept. To him this was what constituted the middle class. It was the class of people driven by individual social ambition. This was a political and not a sociological definition of the middle class. It was open to all people who acknowledged this individual ambition, whether they were master artisans, employees, white- or blue-collar workers.

Master artisans and shopkeepers did not rank highly in the ideology of Fraenkel. They were doomed. He understood the concentration of capital as literally a biological process that it would be foolish to try to stop. He shared Karstensen's fear that universal suffrage paved the way to socialism and he too saw the middle class as the only bulwark against the rising tide of socialist workers. But in his eyes the middle class was not the old middle class of independent businessmen. Independence could not in the long run be the foundation of a middle-class life. The political task then was to find material rewards other than independence on which a middle-class existence and identity could be constructed. This was the problem, and it was a problem easier to state than solve. Fraenkel himself was hesitant in answering this question. Later, in 1928, he suggested monthly instead of weekly salaries, but probably knew that this was a rather dull answer to a question starting with the fundamental characteristics of human nature and Genesis itself. But his way of stating the problem was politically relevant, and the employee problem became in a sense the most burning political question of the inter-war years. It was a fight for the soul of employees that became the decisive political battlefield between left and right in Danish politics in the 1920s and 1930s.

To Fraenkel, then, the middle class was not the old middle class of independent small businessmen, but the new middle class of employees. They were much in need of protection, but this protection could not be furnished by an Act of parliament, and certainly not by an antitrust Act. What was needed was responsibility from the employers' side towards their employees and this could not be achieved by legislation but only, if at all, by persuasion and enlightenment.

L.V. Birck was the third of the leading politicians of the middle-class wing of The Conservative Democratic Party, but in a sense he did not belong to this wing or to any other wing for that matter. For better or worse he went his own way in politics as in other fields of life. He was definitely against Karstensen's somewhat narrow policy and his endeavour to protect the old middle class. 'A policy that only is a policy of the middle class in distress is equally absurd and will meet the same opposition from me as a policy that will be the policy of great industry or tariff protection.

All policy must be a policy of state encompassing the whole of society.'³

His points of view were far closer to Fraenkel's, but, as already mentioned, their mutual relations were bad. This might have been so in any case, but anti-semitic expressions from Birck definitely made the relationship more strained. Fraenkel was of Jewish origin and although Birck apologised and denied being anti-semitic he had spoken out in a way that could not be understood in any other way. His words were not directed at Fraenkel but were said in a rather sensational incident in August 1918 that took place in a public commission in charge of wartime economic regulation. Birck was a member of this commission and before him was Max Ballin, a wealthy industrialist from a Jewish family and owner of a large shoe factory. Arguments between them became more and more heated. When Ballin called Birck a liar Birck totally lost his temper. He would have attacked Ballin physically by throwing a chair at him if other participants in the meeting had not stopped him. He shouted: 'I am a white man and you are a Jew, and a professor at the University of Copenhagen cannot tolerate accusations of that kind from you.'

The shortcomings of Birck were thus evident; his strength was his moral courage. He exposed doubtful economic activities and was unafraid and incorruptible. In 1908 he had deposed the Minister of Justice who shortly afterwards confessed to being a simple impostor, and Birck never attacked without reason. His criticisms of Ballin's economic arrangements were not without foundation either.

Since August 1914 Birck had been a member of the public commission in charge of wartime economic regulation, and he wanted to continue this work by establishing an antitrust committee after the war. This was the main purpose of the antitrust Act that Birck drafted and that was presented to parliament in August 1919. Fraenkel turned against this proposal whereas Karstensen gave it his full support.

As mentioned above, Birck's ideas about antitrust legislation were quite different from Karstensen's. Karstensen wanted to protect small businessmen against the big ones, but this was not what Birck wanted. Like Fraenkel, Birck was not against trusts as such: 'I am not an opponent of trusts, on the contrary; I understand that they are able to organise production. I admire their practice of joint purchasing and their advanced methods. But I know that a considerable part of their income stems not from these matters but from their economic power and the abuse of it towards competitors and customers'.[4]

He had no intention of protecting small business. His aim was to protect customers from exploitation by the trusts, and he wanted the trusts to charge fair prices. In the war years he had seen many attempts made by businessmen to evade economic regulations, and consequently he took great care when drafting the Act to make sure that evasion was impossible. This however meant that the price agreements of small businessmen were also covered by the Act. Birck tried to convince the spokesmen for the artisans and shopkeepers that this was not the intention, and that the Act only aimed at big business, but as the Act was actually drafted it potentially hit small business hard, and the representatives of small business became bitter opponents of it. This probably did not mean much to Birck who actually disliked the old middle class, but it greatly weakened the position of the middle-class wing.

To Birck the middle class was not in danger. His expectation was that the numbers of the middle class would increase, in particular the petit bourgeois part of it, whereas the numbers of the working class would diminish. So he did not accept the notion that big business was the limbo of socialism, as Karstensen put it. As early as 1906 Birck had said that proportional representation would be an effective obstacle to a socialist take over by ballot, and the introduction in 1915 of universal suffrage, accompanied by the introduction of proportional representation, caused him no political alarm.

Birck despised the old middle class, admired the technical middle class of engineers, foremen and others, and said that as long as this class was loyal to the upper class, society was not in danger. This technical middle class was not in his opinion in need of protection, and he was in general against any policy that would cater for the interests of a single class. A policy should be a policy for the whole of society. His advocacy of an antitrust Act was not for the benefit of the middle class but was directed against the moneyed upper class whose greed he found excessive and who in his opinion had forgotten the spirit of service that it owed to the state and society to which it belonged.

The antitrust Act and the decline and fall of the middle-class wing

In less than a month the middle-class wing of The Conservative Democratic Party totally lost its position. The beginning of the end came in the last days of February 1920 at the final readings of the Antitrust Act in the lower chamber of the Danish parliament. The majority of the conservative MPs turned against the Act even though antitrust legislation was part of the party's programme. This was the outcome of the bitter struggle between the middle-class wing and the big-business wing led by Alexander Foss. This in itself was not fatal to the middle-class wing whose general position was weakened but not beyond repair. It still had opportunities within the party. What started its downfall were the speeches of its three leading politicians in the debate in parliament. Fraenkel and Birck started to quarrel. For once Birck was not the aggressive one. Fraenkel explained that he for one was not against antitrust legislation, but that he could not support this draft because it was rather unclear. Everyone knew that Birck was the author of the draft, and he gave an ironic response to Fraenkel's attack but was in no way rude or impolite. Fraenkel however used the response as a pretext for a personal attack on Birck.

'The honourable member [Birck], who is a professor at the university, has only recently, particularly since some clashes in the commission for the regulation of wartime economy [the Ballin incident], found out that there are such things in the world as trusts. Not that he is in any way shy concerning the issues he takes up (they range from the philosophy of religion to economic and political matters), but he seems until very recently to have been unaware that there are things like trusts and great enterprises.'[15]

Birck made no reply. The outcome of this quarrel was that Birck was expelled from the party. This was strange seen in the light of the debate, because it was Fraenkel and not Birck who was the aggressive one, but the debate was simply the last straw. What really cost Birck his position in The Conservative Democratic Party was his stance on the national question concerning the duchy of Slesvig. A referendum was held in the northern part of Slesvig in February and March 1920, and Birck was the only conservative MP who demanded that the referendum should be respected both where it favoured Denmark and where it favoured Germany.

His expulsion from the party of course weakened the middle-class wing, but it was further weakened by Karstensen's speech in the antitrust debate. He used the opportunity to gloat over his chief antagonist in the party, Foss, saying that the acceptance of the antitrust Act by the lower chamber was a painful defeat for the big-business wing of the party and that this wing, in his opinion, was really in for it. However, at the time of the debate in parliament Foss had been struck down by apoplexy and was seriously ill. Consequently he had no opportunity to defend himself against Karstensen's attack. Gloating has never been good manners in Danish public debate and gloating over a sick man of course even less so. There is little doubt that Karstensen made the mistake of his life on this occasion. In any case he made himself a target for vehement attacks. Amongst other things an old customs affair was dug up. In itself it was really a trifle. In 1917, when an editor, Karstensen had tried to interpret customs regulations relating to newsprint to his own advantage. He had asked the Customs Department whether his interpretation was acceptable and been told that it was. However, other editors found the interpretation too clever and became angry with him, as a result of which he then gave up the practice he had adopted. It later turned out that he had saved approximately the equivalent of eight pounds, so it was really nothing, but the incident was used as a pretext for vehement attacks on his moral standards. This totally undermined his position in the party, and he was on the verge of expulsion like Birck. He lingered on in the party until July 1920 and then left it voluntarily.

In no time the middle-class wing had collapsed. As indicated above, there were several reasons for this. Inner disagreements between leading politicians of the wing was one of the important ones, the other was the total lack of a social or political foundation. The middle-class wing tried to speak for the middle class, but it had no authority to do so. This became painfully clear when the antitrust Act had been adopted by the lower chamber of the Danish parliament and passed on to the upper chamber at the beginning of March 1920. Three parties had carried the Act through the lower chamber, and these three parties together had a majority in the upper chamber too, so the final endorsement was soon to be expected (although it actually never came). In this situation, Danish industrialists launched a barrage against the Act. They mobilised the press and the other sectors of business. A committee was set up on March 5th with representatives from organisations of the smaller shops, the bigger shops, hotel owners and master artisans from the capital. Industry and wholesale were in charge of the committee, and although the shopkeepers modified the stance of the committee towards the antitrust Act, they eventually joined in a deputation of the committee to the upper chamber of the Danish parliament, where they expressed great concern about the proposed Act. The master artisans of the capital even sent a letter of their own stating that they could not accept that their price agreements would be covered by the antitrust Act. The representatives mentioned could not speak for the entire old middle class, but they represented the most important portion of the middle class and they all turned against the Act. Not a single middle-class association raised its voice in favour of it.

So there was Asger Karstensen marching into battle to defend and support the middle class (and so following the party programme) and in the middle of the battle he found himself all alone, abandoned by everyone. He would come to the rescue of the middle class, but no middle class came to rescue him. They were either watching silently or howling at him in unison with his foes. He spoke for them, but he was not their spokesman. The middle class Karstensen knew and liked was the blacksmith of the village of his childhood. He was not in touch with the urban middle class, and when after his defeat he tried to be, he found to his dismay that he did not like them. His love of the middle class was an abstract love and a love that was not reciprocated. More than ever the old middle class gathered around its own political party, the Business Party, which attained its best result ever at the general election of April 1920. So Karstensen ended up representing no one and his political influence vanished.

Only Fraenkel stayed on in the party and his line won in the long run. In the inter-war years The Conservative Democratic

Party developed into a middle-class party not in a narrow sociological sense but in a broader political one. It became a party of middle-class values and middle-class orientation open to all who shared those values.

Notes

[1] This essay is based on Jørgen Fink, *Storindustri eller Middelstand? Det ideologiske opgør i Det konservative Folkeparti 1918-1920* [Big Industry or Middle Class? The ideological clash in The Conservative Democratic Party 1918-1920], Århus 2000.

[2] Jørgen Hatting, *Fra Piper til Christmas Møller. Det konservative Folkepartis historie i et halvt århundrede* [From Piper to Christmas Møller. The story of The Conservative Democratic Party in half a century], vols 1-4, Copenhagen 1966, vol. 1, pp. 32 ff.

[3] L.V. Birck, *På fredens tærskel. En finanstale* [At the Threshold of Peace. A budget speech], Copenhagen 1918, p. 24.

[4] L.V. Birck, *På fredens tærskel*, p. 17.

[5] *Rigsdagstidende 1919-20. Folketingets forhandlinger* (The Danish Hansard), pp. 3965 ff.

CHRISTINA FLORIN

Multiple Identities. Female Professional Strategies in an Historical Perspective

Introduction

The occupational groups of professions dominated by women that came into existence with the foundation of modern industrial society in Sweden in the late nineteenth century found it more difficult to secure official status than their male counterparts did, even if the women concerned were recruited from the middle classes and sometimes even belonged to a higher stratum of the bourgeoisie. How can this be explained? Why were male professions more successful?

We may look upon professionalisation and gender in various theoretical ways.[1] We can either assume a discursive perspective and emphasise the hidden but significant symbolic gender structures that may be found in the traditions, language and cultural patterns of professions. Or else we can analyse the process historically/sociologically and study how women and men have actually behaved, when they have striven to mobilise collectively in order to obtain professional recognition. In the first approach, the aim is to get to the bottom of the gender encoding of the professional culture. Are, for example, the successful professions, through their long historical traditions, so identified with the male gender that a process of professionalisation is the same as a masculinisation? Are men's attempts at excluding women a result of a discursive struggle for power where what is perceived as feminine is rejected, because it does not fit into the male-defined order of power within the discourse in which the struggle for positions takes place?

Or must we pose the questions in a different way as is done in the other approach? Its point of departure is that professionalisation is a strategy based on gender-neutral premisses. A profession is an occupational group that wants to protect a certain knowledge base and tries to exclude those who lack the right qualifications or sufficient theoretical knowledge to be let in. It is a matter of appropriating new prestigious assignments within the profession or excluding the groups seeking to come in but lacking the right qualifications. When men try to exclude women by saying that women are not suited to this, that or the other profession, they no longer stick to the professional rules of the game, with education and qualifications as the guiding principles, but choose alternative strategies, for example gender strategies. They claim that, because of their strength, their health, their specific male essence or similar properties, men must reserve certain occupations for themselves, and forget that women have the same knowledge base and the same education as their colleagues.

It is a well-known from earlier research that in the industrialised countries at the turn of the century the male professions in various ways tried to keep women out, and, if they were let in, they were kept at a lower level.[2] The collective historical answer to this process was that women created their own profession-like organisations. There arose an historically new situation, namely a *gender-based splinter organisation* in many occupations.[3] The occupational groups that I deal with in this essay are those female occupations where the members joined interest organisations to improve their positions. Sometimes they competed with men, sometimes not. Certain occupations were from the beginning too closely identified with the female gender for men to even to wish to compete for them. What did women do then to try to become professional? Were they able to stick to the strict rules for how a profession should behave? Could they base their efforts solely on education and qualifications as weapons?

Our theoretical tools for analysing the historical organisation of different professional groups become more difficult to handle when women are included. Some female groups adopted male strategies as norms, while others did not. It is also important to distinguish between *being* a profession and *acting* professionally. Certain occupations, which do not possess the necessary qualifications for becoming proper professions, may still act in accordance with the rules of professionalisation, even if they do not succeed, or only achieve a partial success. In women's attempts at professionalisation, we must therefore look for patterns other than those encountered when dealing with the male professions. On the basis of various examples of the professional strategies of female civil servants, teachers, nurses, midwifes and so on, I will primarily let the sociological perspective govern my approach, even though the discursive interpretation will also be touched upon. I will thus concentrate on what strategies the women used.

Naturally the professionalisation projects must also be analysed in terms of the historical situation in which they came about. The gender order that was dominant when the first female professional projects began cannot be neglected. Women started from an historical level that was structurally entirely different from men's. They had no control of the public sphere they were to enter as the men had got there first. This fact sets its mark on the women's way of organising themselves and the strategies they chose. They had to organise themselves by means of several different types of mobilisation and their relation to the state was different from men's.

The role of the state in professionalisation projects is always important, since the state becomes a mediating institution able to decide whether the professions enjoy a monopoly or not in their occupational market.[4] At the turn of the century the state played the role of 'gender actor', regulating relations between the genders as well as determining the exclusiveness of professions by deciding what kind of education and training was required for one occupation or another. And the state was not a gender-neutral institution, especially not at the turn of the century when women had no access to political power.

The gender-structure imbalance

A picture from the offices of the central authorities may illustrate the gender imbalance between men and women in Sweden at the turn of the century. The male state bureaucrat in the picture instructs the female typist how to put the ribbon into the typewriter. It is he who represents the abstract and theoretical knowledge and she the practical. There is a certain patriarchal atmosphere in the picture and the male civil servant leans in a somewhat protective manner over his typist. Both were strongly bound by gender-cultural ideas about what was masculine and what was feminine, and the leading role of superior was part of the natural order of things in the male culture. Just as at home, the woman was supposed to prepare and arrange the information before it was served to the man. Both performed a kind of gender choreography with fixed gestures before each other, where he showed his masculinity and she her femininity in different ways and where sexual undertones were often present even in an impersonal governing system such as the state bureaucracy. His prescribed masculinity consisted of having responsibility and representing the state in all its complexity, while her femininity was expressed in her inferior position and routine tasks. Between the bureaucrat and his secretary there was a kind of mutual dependence.

Source: *Från svenska statsförvaltningen* 1913

In terms of class, the differences between the two in the picture do not seem to be very great. Just like the men the state typists came from bourgeois families, but the men still had a long lead over them.[5] The educational system favoured men (women were not admitted to secondary grammar schools[6]), the state service structure favoured men (women were not qualified to become higher civil servants[7]), the political system favoured men (women did not have the right to vote), according to civil law married women were subordinate to their husbands, and so on. All the work in the office was organised in terms of the concept of two different sexes: different salary scales, social benefits, career ladders, working hours and work places. These inequalities were not linked to ideas of the different physical strength of the sexes; there was no biological rationality behind the management. The office work did not become physically heavier as it became more complicated, rather the reverse.[8] The imbalance was structurally and ideologically conditioned and built into the male authority, power conditions in the state, in professional organisations and in institutions. The imbalance was present also in the different conceptions of the sexes of themselves and of each other, in their subjective identities.

It is this kind of gender-structural point of departure we must have when we wish to understand women's strategies designed to improve their situation. When women were choosing a way of advancing their cause, they first had to relate to male structures and male colleagues and show consideration for them in a way that men did not have to do with respect to women. They had an extra dimension to consider and this influenced their choices. There was a split in women's gender identities. On the one hand they were included in the abstract concept of 'human being', which was connected to the central tenet of the Enlightenment (although its origins were earlier) that people were essentially equal, so that there was a potential similarity between men and women. On the other hand, their specific culture carried within it conceptions of the sexes being both essentially different and placed in a hierarchical order. Historically the experiences of a woman were as both a human being and 'the other', that is, 'not-man'.[9] Such subjective experiences of reality resulted in women having both to cross the borders of men's domains and at the same time defend their own.

Gender relations were also complicated by sexuality and love between men and women in their private lives. In a way they were therefore bound structurally to each other as sexual beings[10], and therefore women's societal subordination was not always a shared basis for their struggle. Power relations between the sexes could become invisible. Mutual understanding and conflict with regard to the other sex were thus characteristic of female strategies.[11] In addition women (and men) also bore several identities, deriving from class, nationality, generation, religion, and so on, and this could also form the basis of organisation in an occupational group. Taken together all this can make the concrete actions of female civil servants sometimes appear ambiguous and irrational when examined from the point of view of theories based on the perspectives of male actors.

I will now consider some female groups of professionals and describe their strategies during the first phase at the beginning of the twentieth century and reveal the complexity and ambiguities of their actions. But first, a few words about why certain civil servant professions became feminised at all.

The most obvious change in the pattern of recruitment to the lower professions at the turn of the century was the increasing proportion of women.[12] There were many reasons for the lower civil service echelon becoming feminised. Economic factors were important. Women were considered to be able to sell their labour for less because they were regarded as a different kind of workforce, defined on the basis of their family affiliation and not as primary providers. Another reason was the demographic change that Sweden had undergone which resulted in different marriage patterns. This created a new type of workforce: the unmarried middle-class woman. Bureaucratic changes in the state and in industry brought with them new routine tasks which women were thought to be able to manage just as well as men.

Gender-ideological reasons were also tied up in all this. Many employers thought that the virtues ascribed to women, such as conscientiousness and patience, were valuable assets in civil service and professional work. This type of work also suited the women themselves, since the working conditions generally corresponded to female cultural notions of what was masculine and feminine.

Professionalisation patterns of some different female professions

The first to organise themselves were the midwives.[13] Lisa Öberg, who has studied the professionalisation of midwives in a Swedish context, shows that they employed several strategies, namely professional, trade union and social class ones.

Great structural changes took place in obstetrics at the end of the nineteenth century and the midwives themselves were very active in advocating hospital instead of home deliveries. But women faced competition from another professionally advancing group, physicians. In this particular area of medicine, Swedish midwives and physicians had earlier enjoyed a relatively equal status. Both used obstetric instruments, and both received similar training in delivery in the middle of the nineteenth century. But towards the end of the century there emerged a competition for this know-how. With the aid of science and bureaucracy, the physicians 'colonised' the midwives' old area of expertise, namely delivery, and made it into a scientifically specialised discipline within medicine: obstetrics. Midwives were no longer allowed to handle complicated deliveries and the period of training for doctors was extended and made more theoretical. The time they had to spend gaining practical experience was also lengthened. The former freedom of midwives became constrained within the institutional framework of a new kind of hospital bureaucracy, while the power of physicians over subordinate occupational groups such as nurses, midwives and nursing assistants increased.

The fate of the midwives was inevitable. Men could use these new power bases for their own professionalisation. The educational system, the Board of Health and Welfare, the Swedish parliament, and the medical associations were all institutions from which women were excluded. But the midwives themselves also benefited from this development, even though they ended up in a position subordinate to that of the physicians. The position of the midwives was automatically improved as a result of the professionalisation of the physicians. They also received longer training and a higher status. The number of births attended by untrained staff steadily decreased. The midwives gained a degree of influence over their own professional culture at the level where they were placed and they themselves contributed from below by creating their own code of ethics, establishing themselves as a professional group of irreproachable, sober and moral people. Midwives who misbehaved lost their professional licences and those without proper training were banned from the organisation of midwives. The profession now attracted more middle class girls and the ideology of the vocation further raised the status of the profession. On the other hand, the midwives were not very successful in their union demands. Their salaries remained low, while physicians could make demands for increasingly high ones.

Let us turn to another group of female professionals. The growth of elementary schools in Sweden during the latter half of the nineteenth century led to a growing number of teachers. Schoolmistresses in Elementary Schools is an interesting occupational group to study, because they entered a male domain at a stage when this occupation had not yet assumed a definite shape.[14] As a female group, female elementary school teachers were in a unique historical situation, as from the very beginning they enjoyed a relatively equal position relative to their male colleagues. They had the same education, the same state salaries, the same official duties and the same retirement age. Many of them came from urban families of civil servants, although many farmers' daughters made a career in this profession. Men were often recruited from the agrarian class in the rural parts of Sweden, which meant that the women as a group brought a different cultural capital to their profession. For this reason the feminisation of the profession was not felt to be a disadvantage.

What strategies did the female schoolteachers initially opt for? Well, they went to the Swedish Comprehensive Union of Elementary Schoolteachers, a mixed-gender teacher organisation (founded in 1880). There they worked side by side with men as colleagues. It is true that the issues they brought up, such as social issues and charity, were close to the female culture, but they also became involved in other issues such as professional ethics, cultural issues and educational matters. The professional view that it was knowledge and educational competence that mattered served to guide the organisation during its first 25 years. Men and women co-operated in a project about 'primary school'[15] and in attempts to raise elementary schools to the level of a cultural institution. It was possible to advance both professional issues and feminisation at the same time. At least to begin with.

At the turn of the century conditions began to change, however. With the aid of the state, male elementary schoolteachers managed to raise their status above women's. A gender strategy began to manifest itself within male ranks. The national principle of equal pay was abandoned. In order to prevent poor local authorities from employing a woman rather than a man for financial reasons, they were given an extra government grant to cover the difference in salary. The women were given fewer seats on the board of the national organisation, which made it harder for them to voice their opinions. A kind of early quota system was introduced at the teacher training colleges in order to retain men within the profession.

How did the women then respond to this masculinisation of the profession? There was a shift from gender co-operation to gender conflict. Many female schoolteachers took matters into their own hands and formed an organisation of their own, the Swedish Union of Female Elementary Schoolteachers. Trade-union, professional and gender strategies went hand in hand in the new organisation. Female schoolteachers demanded an immediate return to the principle of equal pay while at the same time claiming that women were different and hence better suited to the teaching profession than men. They propagated the cause of feminising the curriculum while at the same time demanding that female teachers be given career opportunities in order to become head teachers and inspectors.

They also dissociated themselves from female infant school teachers (who were considerably less qualified), thereby bringing about a kind of professional exclusion downwards. Female infant school teachers were not recruited to the new national organisation, although they were members of the larger comprehensive one. Female infant school teachers eventually formed a union of their own and there was a complete split within teacher groups due to the gender-based separation of organisations. There were also other dividing lines between teachers which made it difficult to form a unified basis for common mobilisation, such as class distinctions, conflicts between urban and rural areas, vocational teachers against class teachers, and so on.

A group that did *not* have to compete with men on equal conditions were the nurses. Instead they challenged other female groups within the same sector. They make up an enigmatic occupational group when their strategies are analysed. As Agneta Emanuelsson describes in her thesis, they built up hierarchies and fenced themselves off from other women in nursing, namely nursing assistants and assistant nurses.[16] They used a clear professional strategy, a class strategy, a religious strategy and a gender-cultural strategy. They adopted male professionalisation as a pattern when organising themselves and they advocated a formal theoretical education that would raise their status.

The nurses formed an exclusive organisation, the Swedish Association of Nurses, which only admitted those with a higher theoretical education. They commanded respect among people in general by emphasising their female culture and their caring and motherly abilities as valuable qualities in the hospital environment.[17] They developed almost feudal characteristics in their occupational culture, for example the strongly symbolic nun-like uniform, the strict ethics of the religious calling, the celibacy, the military hierarchical order and hygienics. In this way they mystified their knowledge base and established a professional distance between themselves and others.[18] They also exercised a significant degree of control over their professional skills through participation in the planning of the curricula of the private training institutions.

But the model of organisation in this profession may also be analysed in terms of class conflict. It was noble and upper-class women who took command of the organisation and formulated the discourse in the educational system that was built up in the private sector. By creating the image of a pious and moral professional woman who brought the ideology of home and nursing to a social institution, the profession was attractive to the daughters of the middle classes. For this reason they kept up a strict strategy of exclusion against other female groups in nursing. By their self-sacrificing ethic the nurses were able to approach the area of male medical science without having to redefine the bourgeois feminine ideal. They were consciously professional according to a male norm, but through their motherly and Christian image they still represented the feminine. They thus created a class barrier between themselves and nursing assistants, who instead organised themselves together with men into the large Swedish Trade Union Confederation. The nurses thus chose strategies based on their gender position and created their own niche vis-à-vis the men, the physicians, but also on the basis of their class position in relation to the nursing assistants.

A forgotten female group in the history of civil servants are dairy managers. Thanks to Lena Sommestad's thesis we now have detailed knowledge of the way in which these female overseers disappeared from history in the 1930s.[19] From having been a female occupation at the turn of the century (women have always worked with milk and milk products), the officials in the industrial milk trade became a male professional body during the interwar period. Female dairy managers at the turn of the century were unusual in that they did work that was considered typically male; they were at once managers, overseers and machine operators, and the Swedish dairy industry was built up by a female work force that had been trained at special dairy schools.

During the 1930s the dairy trade was no longer in harmony with the female ideal of the time. The urban and middle-class image of the 'feminine' had a stronger impact and the full-time wife, mother and housewife became normative. Occupations where activities were closer to the female culture, such as those involving children, nursing and service, became favourite occupations for girls who wanted an education. The dairy manager, who represented the agrarian farmer's wifely ideal, became old-fashioned. The substantial structural changes that took place in the dairy industry must also be taken into account. Large-scale production and rationalisations changed the organisation of the dairies, and the small dairies, where the women had worked, disappeared. The men's takeover was facilitated by the fact that the state dairy institutes, which they attended, had become more theoretically oriented, and this contributed both to the men's professionalisation and to the masculinisation of the profession.

A bit caustically one might say that female dairy managers chose no strategy at all. It is true that there were women who joined the professional organisation, the General Swedish Union of Dairy Managers (13 per cent in 1921), but they reached no advanced positions. The women's more craftsmanlike skills became outdated when the dairy industry was rationalised, and no strong protests against the masculinisation of the dairy industry were heard from female quarters.

So far I have dealt with female occupations that may be said to constitute an expansion of the female cultural sphere of caring. But other areas were also opened up to female labour where the arrival of women was actually a bit unexpected, such as the state bureaucracy! Modern bureaucracy, as it developed towards the end of the nineteenth century, was a meeting place for men: a male power system that was supposed to render the administration of state and industry more effective. When women entered civil service departments and ministries, the gender differences were always evaluated to women's disadvantage and they were given the lowest positions in the hierarchy. The state's 'masculinity' was, however, complicated. It contributed to women having a subordinate position, but it could also function as a tool for change.

As early as the 1880s individual women had become employed as *clerks* in government administration, but the big wave of employment came at the turn of the century. A government system with extended duties became overburdened with work that the permanent bureaucrats could no longer manage, and the positions were filled from below with well-educated female workers who had to handle routine tasks. The number of clerks with a permanent position in the government administration was slightly more than 300 at the turn of the century. If all part-time employees are included, the number was probably more than 500.

The women employed in public service organised themselves in a very active union called Women in Government Service.[20] They mixed both professional and trade-union strategies, as Bengt Nilsson has shown in his thesis on the Swedish typists or clerks. They thought in terms of gender equality relative to the men and demanded a professional promotional system with permanent posts and an established status in accordance with the same hierarchical principles as men had. But they also worked a great deal on trade-union monetary issues in order to obtain social rights, regulated working hours, holidays and pensions.[21] The issues of status and protection of the knowledge base were not as prominent for the clerks employed in public service, since they had to tussle with a great number of men with similar problems in the service structure. There were thus also men at lower levels in the state administration who had both professional and trade-union conflicts with bureaucrats with a higher education.

The members of Women in Government Service possessed an expert knowledge, which they had acquired in everyday practice. They had a complete mastery of the complicated officialese and an insider knowledge of how things were done and of the bureaucratic culture which they could utilise. They were not unsympathetic towards ability grouping but advocated different service classes based on fixed qualifying conditions and free competition between the sexes. The women employed in public service also had their social rights regulated, even if it was not until fairly recently that they arrived at the same level as men.

Female clerks in private employment had a much more difficult situation. They were even more dependent on their male superiors, since their work was subject to short-term profit interests and their opportunities of working for political changes were more restricted. The clerks organised themselves at first together with the shop assistants into the National Swedish Union of Clerical Employees, which eventually came to be only for clerks. The strategies of the Union of Clerical Employees were primarily concerned with women's political issues and the union carried on a number of activities that were not primarily connected with their working lives but with their social life.[22] The union arranged courses, musical evenings, club activities, meals, a debating society for training people in socially advantageous civic knowledge, and so on. The union functioned both as an extended family and a home while at the same time being a trade union. It was the clerks' route to political change.

The last group I will analyse does not constitute a unified occupational body but a group of women who were all connected by the fact that they had an academic degree. In their respective professions they should thus have had the same professional opportunities as male academics, if the latter had stuck to the rules established by the bourgeois meritocratic society, namely to each according to his/her ability. It was knowledge and education that should be decisive, not hereditary or other principles. What, then, was the situation of academic women in Sweden?

Women who had taken a higher academic degree organised themselves into an association called the Swedish Association of Female University Graduates.[23] They pursued a purely professional policy for the ideals they advocated in matters concerning posts and qualifications. They claimed that female university graduates had the same qualifications as male academics and that qualifications should therefore be decisive when appointments were made, not gender. Academic women demanded a constitutional amendment in order to gain access to higher government posts that were reserved for Swedish men. After many years of political struggle, which at times became rather heated, their demands were finally met and the Qualifications Act came into force.[24]

These women used all the rules of professionalisation. They formed an interest organisation and united across educational and occupational borders. In these particular matters they were equality feminists, that is, they did not claim that women's special characteristics were given by nature but emphasised instead the similarities between men and women. By using their knowledge and qualifications as weapons they were eventually able to undermine the male power monopoly of higher government posts. The development in society at large of meritocratic ideas that qualifications and skills should have priority over ancestry and family ties helped them along in their political struggle.

The female academics allied themselves with men who were sympathetic to women's emancipation and in this way they were able to obtain some degree of influence over the Swedish establishment, although they had no formal political rights. They could respond to men's scientific studies, which claimed that women were weaker and not suited to certain responsible positions, by carrying out studies of their own that proved the contrary. They showed that existing definitions of what was masculine and feminine were not eternal truths but historically and socially determined. With humour and satire as their weapons the academic women also poured some ridicule on their male opponents. With their professional qualifications they demanded a position in the institutions of power, but it was not until the 1940s that female academics were given a visible share of the higher posts in the academic world.

Multiple identities

Can we finally see any common patterns in the organisation of female professionals at the turn of the previous century? They all did different things. Some female groups based their strategy primarily on qualifications and knowledge, that is, they assumed a purely professional policy, some strove to impart a solid middle-class character to their profession, some took their stand on the religious calling or mystifications of women's culture. They often mixed professional strategies with trade-union issues such as salaries, pensions and working conditions. A group such as the dairy managers simply gave up and let the men take over. Some emphasised the similarity of the genders, while others called attention to the differences and claimed that certain essential female characteristics made them more suitable for this or that occupation. Some wanted to make the home a model for the inner life of the organisation, while others concentrated on women's political work by joining their unions to larger political organisations and networks.[25] What the women had in common was that they mixed strategies and used different identities as bases, class, culture, gender, professionalism, religion, women's policies, and so on, sometimes in agreement with the men, sometimes in conflict with them.

What was, however, a common point of departure for all female occupations was that they all had to operate within structures that were built up according to norms that had been formulated in institutions where middle-class men had been influential for generations. The women who came into public life at this time struggling to obtain professional recognition were far behind the men when it came to gaining control of the public sphere. The women thus started on a different historical level just as women who wanted to enter areas where men already had a structural lead did. Their choices were marked by their lack of influence on certain arenas such as government policies, the market, theoretical education, the higher professions and other male power bases. They were both like and unlike men and thereby they had to serve several 'masters', the state and the market as well as men. Women had to bear multiple gender identities. That is the reason why they behaved differently, as I interpret it.

When they entered the male institutions they wanted to preserve something of their feminine identity. They created environments around themselves that were to remind them of the female culture they had left. The nurses wanted to make the hospitals home-like institutions, the clerks formed a union that was to be a second home for unmarried women and assist them from the cradle to the grave, the schoolmistresses decorated their classrooms with plants and flowers. My comparison of the strategies of different groups of female civil servants indicates that professionalisation and gender may be seen both as a concrete historical project between real men and women (or between women and women, or between men and men) contending for material resources, but also as a discursive struggle about who should interpret and give a meaning to the gender constructions.[26]

Notes

[1] For a more detailed description of these theoretical points of departure, see Christina Florin, 'Kön och professionalisering. Två teoretiska angreppssätt' in Pirjo Markkola et al. (eds), *Från sexualitet till världshistoria. Rapport från det 4:e nordiska kvinnohistorikermötet i Tammerfors*, 1995, pp. 275-281.
[2] Cf.Anne Witz, *Professions and Patriarchy*, London 1992.
[3] Christina Florin, 'Kvinnliga tjänstemän i manliga institutioner,' in *Kvinnohistoria. Om kvinnors villkor från antiken till våra dagar*. Stockholm 1993, pp. 136-152; Ylva Waldemarson, 'Kön, klass och statens finanser – en historia om statligt arbetsgivarskap och statsanställda kvinnor 1870-1925,' in Kvarnström, Lars, Ylva Waldemarson & Klas Åmark (eds), *I statens tjänst. Statlig arbetsgivarpolitik och fackliga strategier*, Lund 1996.
[4] On the role of the state in the professionalisation, see among others Michael Burrage & Rolf Torstendahl (eds), *Professions in Theory and History. Rethinking the Study of the Professions*, London 1990; Rolf Torstendahl & Michael Burrage (eds), *The Formation of Professions. Knowledge, State and Strategy*, London 1990.
[5] Bengt Nilsson, *Kvinnor i statens tjänst – från biträden till tjänstemän*, (Acta Universitatis Upsaliensis 179), Uppsala 1996, pp. 41-45, 77-81.
[6] Christina Florin & Ulla Johansson, *Där de härliga lagrarna gro. Kultur, klass och kön i det svenska läroverket 1849-1914*, Stockholm 1993.
[7] Greta Wieselgren, *Den höga tröskeln. Kampen för kvinnans rätt till arbete*. Lund 1969.
[8] Kirsten Geertsen, 'Kvinnor på kontor. Könsarbetsdelning på de offentliga kontoren 1900-1940', *Arbetarhistoria*, no. 3, 1989.
[9] Gro Hagemann, 'Om utfordre fornuften – kvinneforskningen som kritisk motoffentlighet,' in *Festskrift til Ottar Dahl*, p. 110. Oslo 1994.
[10] Anna Jónasdottir, 'Gemensamt och specifikt i kvinnoförtrycket', *Häften för kritiska studier*, no. 2, 1988, pp. 35-45.
[11] Cf. Monica Edgren, *Tradition och förändring. Könsrelationer, omsorgsarbete och försörjning inom Nörrköpings underklass under 1800-talet*, Lund 1994, pp. 42ff.

214

[12] Tom Ericsson, *Den andra fackföreningsrörelsen. Tjänstemän och tjänstemannaorganisationer i Sverige före det första världskriget*, Umeå 1983, pp. 24-29.
[13] Lisa Öberg, *Barnmorskan och läkaren. Kompetens och konflikt i svensk förlossningsvård 1870-1920*, Stockholm 1996.
[14] Christina Florin, *Kampen om katedern. Femininiserings- och professionaliseringsprocessen inom den svenska folkskolans lärarkår 1860-1906*, Stockholm 1987.
[15] At the turn of the century 'primary school' was the name of the form of education that the elementary school teachers wanted to introduce, a primary school common to the children of all social classes.
[16] Agneta Emanuelsson, *Pionjärer i vitt. Professionella och fackliga strategier bland svenska sjuksköterskor och sjukvårdsbiträden 1851-1939*, Stockholm 1990.
[17] Kari Melby, 'Women's work, equal and different. Female teachers and nurses in Norway 1912-1940,' in *International Congress of Historical Sciences. Chronological Section II*, conference report, Madrid 1992, pp. 333-343.
[18] Christina Florin, 'De gåtfulla sjuksköterskorna,' *Historisk tidskrift*, 1991, p. 4.
[19] LenaSommestad, *Från mejerska till mejerist. En studie av mejeriyrkets naskuliniseringsprocess*, Lund 1992.
[20] Cf. Nilsson, Bengt *Kvinnor i statens tjänst – från biträde till tjänsteman*, Uppsala 1996. See also Christina Florin, 'Statsbyråkratins erogena zoner. Staten som testplats för manligt och kvinnligt,' in Broberg, Gunnar, Ulla Wikander & Klas Åmark (eds), *Bryta, bygga, bo. Svensk historia underifrån*; Stockholm 1994; Kvarnström, Lars, *Män i staten. Stationskarlar och brevbärare i statens tjänst 1897-1937*, Stockholm 1998; Waldemarson 1996.
[21] Besides Bengt Nilsson, see also Tom Ericsson, 'Kvinnor i facklig kamp. En studie av föreningen Kvinnor i statens tjänst,' *Scandia*, no. 1, 1981.
[22] Ingela Nilsson, 'Svenska kontoristföreningen,' unpublished undergraduate paper, Department of History, Umeå University 1993. Annika Rodhe, 'Svenska kontoristföreningen. Fackföreningen från vaggan till graven,' unpublished undergraduate paper, Department of History, University of Stockholm 1997.
[23] Christina Florin & Ulla Johansson, 'Kunskap och kompetens som vapen,' *Häften för kritiska studier*, nr 3, 1990.
[24] Greta Wieselgren, *Den höga tröskeln. Kampen för kvinnors rätt till arbete*, Lund 1969; Tord Rönnholm, *Kunskapens kvinnor. Sekelskiftets studentskor i mötet med den manliga universitetsvärlden*, Umeå 1999.
[25] Cf. the strategies of Norwegian schoolmistresses and housewives. See Kari Melby, *Kvinnelighetens strategier. Norges husmorsforbund 1915-1940 og Norges Laerarinneforbund 1912-1940*, Trondheim 1995.
[26] Cf. a previous article on this. See Christina Florin, 'Mångdubbla identiteter. Kvinnliga tjänstemän och deras strategier i ett historiskt perspektiv,' in Johansson, Anders (ed.), *Fackliga organisationsstrategier*, Stockholm 1997.

JAN EIVIND MYHRE

Middle Classes and Suburban Lives: Norway 1840-1940 in a Comparative Perspective

Introduction

Two major societal processes, one topographical and one social, were simultaneously at work in shaping Norwegian society from the middle of the nineteenth century to the middle of the twentieth. The processes of middle-class formation and suburban growth are often regarded as twin processes in the sense that suburbia was largely a middle-class phenomenon and that the rise of the middle classes to a considerable degree took place in the suburbs. This view has become almost a cliché.

The interdependence of the two processes is mirrored in geographical and sociological theory. Geographers have produced a number of urban land-use models where social residential segregation plays an important part; the concentric zone scheme, the sector scheme and the multiple nuclei scheme are among the best known. They have also developed a number of theories to explain the character of social areas.[1] Sociologists, on the other hand, have studied the social characteristics of the middle class, its way of life, its relation to other classes and its perception of itself.[2] In all three aspects, the suburban dimension seems to loom large.

How general is the supposed tie between the suburbs and the middle classes? There is every reason to believe it is restricted to certain parts of the Western world (North America, Australia and New Zealand, some parts of Europe) and to certain decades in the nineteenth and twentieth centuries. But even within these boundaries the connection needs to be questioned and explored, for even a cursory knowledge of Norwegian urban development reveals that the middle classes were not the only people in the suburbs.[3] This is the task at hand.

217

The present investigation will concern itself mainly with the Norwegian experience, albeit from an international perspective. Most of the information is taken from Christiania (or Kristiania, from 1925 named Oslo). The chronological scope is from around 1840 to 1940, encompassing the three generations who witnessed the rise of the Norwegian capital from a town of 38,000 to a city of 450,000 (including suburbs). The period is distinguished from that of the pre-industrial (mainly poor) suburbs that preceded it and that of the satellite towns and almost limitless urban sprawl that followed the Second World War. My concern is *suburbia*, not *exurbia*. This period may be called the classic suburban epoch. The Swedish and Danish suburban experience coincides chronologically with the Norwegian one, while the English and North American 'classic' suburbanisation began a few decades earlier.[4] 'Suburbia', F.M.L. Thompson writes, 'rose between 1815 and 1939, an unlovely, sprawling artefact of which few are particularly fond.'[5] Applied to Norway, however, this statement is not very appropriate.

The concept of the *suburb* is touched upon above and will be further delineated below. Is it possible to say something short and satisfactory about the middle classes? At this stage I believe it suffices to say that the people of the middle classes are tied together by a common animosity towards the workers and by values and ways of life which may be called bourgeois or simply middle-class.[6] Our problem will not be significantly altered by the various answers to the question of whether there was a Norwegian upper class or not. Norway had no aristocracy, but it would indeed make sense to identify a distinct Norwegian social elite consisting of an educated upper crust of senior civil servants (particularly in the nineteenth century), the upper echelons of the money-based bourgeoisie and some private professionals (especially in the twentieth century). Such a class, however, would not in any event constitute a bulky element within the Norwegian social geography.

Pre-modern suburbs

In order to offer a contrast to this classic suburban epoch, I will give a short sketch of the pre-modern suburb. In the pre-modern towns and cities of Europe the middle class, or rather, the *burghers* and the civil servants, generally lived in or near the urban centres, close to their businesses in the harbour, the market place, the major streets or the public institutions. In Christiania and other towns in Norway, quite a few burghers had farm-like summer residences on the rural outskirts of the town, called *løkker* [enclosed areas] in the Norwegian capital. The true suburbs were mainly the realm of the lower classes.[7] Working-class suburbs of this kind had existed since the middle ages and were built on the outskirts of Christiania until the 1870s.

The suburbs of the Norwegian capital in the first half of the nineteenth century neatly illustrate Braudel's sweeping statement: 'Just as a strong tree is never without shoots at its foot, so towns are never without suburbs. They are the manifestations of its strength, even if they are wretched fringes, shantytowns. Shoddy suburbs are better than none at all ... To reach the suburbs was always to take a step downwards, in Bremen, London and elsewhere.[8]

The suppressive character of the relationship between town and suburbs is well expressed by the Norwegian poet Henrik Wergeland in his poem 'The Suburbs lamenting Christiania'. It was partly political and partly economic: 'The thought of building your supremacy on yoke, your power on coercion, did not stem from a brain, but from the belly of a merchant.' It was, however, also a question of social status. Wergeland addressed the town: 'Why adorn your crown with the weeping of poverty?'[9]

Not all suburbs were completely slum-like; some were *faubourgs* including thriving artisans and shopkeepers. Nevertheless, suburbs meant marginality in practically all the senses of the word.[10] They were physically marginal, situated on the edge of the urban settlement. They were in some cases even a temporary settlement. The houses as well as the people signalled economic marginality. This social and cultural marginality is illustrated by a statement made in 1841 by the municipal council of Aker, Christiania's rural neighbour, which played host to the suburbs. It read: 'The suburbs are an abandoned wreck, which all authorities push aside, a cesspool without cobblestones, without lighting and without enlightenment ... the nest of immorality, depravity and corruption.'[11] They were wretched and disorderly.

The suburbs were poor, despised and unwanted, in many ways the opposite of what suburbs were going to signify only a few decades later.

The modern suburb

From around 1840 a new type of settlement emerged on the western outskirts of Christiania, slowly at first, then with increased speed from about 1860. The new houses could not be identified as second-rank settlements, neither a *faubourg* of petty shopkeepers and artisans nor a pure slum of the kind described above, as they were fairly large villas. The buildings were not a direct continuation of the existing town either, and finally, the new settlement was not to be confused with the older summer residences, although they might look like them. When H.C. Petersen, the Attorney General, in 1832, decided to reside all year in his summer mansion outside the town, he started a trend. But most of the new suburban villas in the first generation were built as parts of larger schemes. People at the time considered this phenomenon a new type of suburb which housed, to begin with, the upper middle class and the social elite.

What then, were the defining characteristics of this new kind of suburb, destined to prevail in large parts of Christiania's vicinity for the next century? I will point to two topographical traits. First, a suburb was a settlement *outside* the city, while at the same time belonging to it through sharing the same labour market and being a part of the same urban social structure. 'Outside' usually means outside the limits of the city. This entails that suburbanites have different legal rights from city-dwellers, although not necessarily fewer rights. (City limits, by the way, is not an unambiguous term, as the legal confusion concerning Christiania's borders prior to 1859 illustrates, when the political, commercial, ecclesiastical, criminal and building districts were distinct entities.) But what about *former* suburbs, the ones that became incorporated through the extension of the city limits, a commonplace phenomenon in Norway in the nineteenth and twentieth centuries?[12] There are good reasons to continue to regard them as suburbs, which brings us to the next point.

The classic suburb differs from the typical larger Norwegian nineteenth or early twentieth-century town or city in its type of settlement. Whereas the latter consisted of dense, contiguous built-up areas of brick tenement buildings or smaller wooden houses facing the streets, the former was made up of villas or other small homes for one or a few families, often situated on spacious plots, giving the area a semi-rural look. The houses were not particularly oriented towards the street or road. We also have to distinguish between 'inner' and 'outer' suburbs. Inner suburbs were built adjacent to or in-between existing urban environments, that is, they were geographically a part of the nineteenth-century city.[13] This normally meant that the place of work, as well as the city centre, was within walking distance. Outer suburbs were settlements in need of transportation to reach work and the city centre. The classic suburb, in the sense of the word used here, was an outer suburb. The suburbs of the late nineteenth and early twentieth centuries, in other words, represent a very different way of building and planning an urban environment, a quite different urban concept from the one characterising the older central city. The classic suburbs were spacious, green, secluded and private.

The rise of suburbia – a middle-class phenomenon?

Was the classic suburb a middle-class phenomenon? At the outset I would like to make two preliminary observations. In the first place, there is lots of evidence to the fact that groups outside (and below) the middle class inhabited many of the newly-created suburbs in the century between 1840 and 1940. Some of these suburbs were even dominated by working-class families, in a more or less organised fashion. There existed workers' organisations for the purpose of enabling labourers to get their own homes [*egnehjemsbevegelsen*]. Examples were the printers' village at Nadderud in Bærum and Holtet haveby [garden village] at Ekeberg. Philanthropic undertakings aimed to house workers in pleasant surroundings (Ullevål hageby, Arctanderbyen at Ekeberg). Large companies would sometimes build houses for their employees, workers or functionaries, especially at the edge of smaller factory towns (in Christiania, Haslebyen built by the Freia company). Speculative enterprises involved the selling of cheap and small plots to workers who built their own homes, often from beginnings in the shape of shacks or cabins (Risløkka, Haslum, Solemskogen).

The second point concerns the question of the *embourgeoisement* of the workers. Were the presence of *egnehjem* [owner-occupier houses] and other kinds of workers' suburbs a result of the spread of middle-class values through society? Some workers' settlements dreamt of creating a 'socialist republic', but were not very different from other suburbs. Others did not manage to sell enough plots to fellow trade unionists, and offered them on the open market. The philanthropic and municipal efforts to build suburban homes for workers certainly emanated from middle-class values.

Representatives of the middle class certainly imagined that the suburbanisation of workers would have the effect of making workers complacent and adherent to middle-class values. August Nielsen, the municipal leader of housing development in Aker, commented in 1928 upon a proposal to build 'skyscrapers' [*skyskrapere*] in the urban periphery. Nielsen found the proposal economically interesting, well-planned from a sanitary perspective, and promising as regards the efficient use of land. From a social point of view, however, he considered it hopeless. Our suburbs of the future must still be owner-occupier houses [*egnehjem*] with gardens, he stated. 'The *egnehjem* is, and will remain in the future, the best and cheapest medicine against both tuberculosis and bolshevism, and in keeping with the best in our national character.'[14] The idea that the *egnehjem* development, with ordinary people owning their own houses in suburban surroundings, was essentially a preventive measure against socialism, has been quite common, but has proved untenable.[15]

In which areas then, economic, social, cultural, or political, should we look for ties between suburbs and the middle classes? I will look at four major areas, each containing both topographical and social factors. The first concerns the role of the natural (rural) environment. The second deals with urban planning and urban structure. It will include the question of organised development, the relation of home to workplace (the role of commuting) and the legal side of separating city and country. Area three considers the relationship between geographical and social distance and the lifestyles and consumption patterns among suburbanite types. Finally, the question of the mentalities and ideologies of the suburban dwellers will be looked at, including such issues as the alleged individuality and family orientation among the middle classes.

Suburbs as nature

Suburbanism, according to quite a few observers, is a way of life that worships rural, natural surroundings; trees, grass, flowers, clean air, silence, at the expense of brick, concrete, asphalt, cobblestones, dirty air and noise. The names of suburban homes built on Christiania's periphery in the decades around the turn of the century give a clue: *Skogsbo* [forest home], *Furulund* [pine grove], *Solheim* [sunny home], and *Fagerås* [beautiful hill]. Other names include *Pax, Fredenshavn* [peaceful haven], *Helsebot* [cure], and *Granly* [fur tree shelter]. In other words, the suburbs were places with a taste of the forest, bringing peace and good health, a place to which to retire after a day's work [*Retiro*].

What is the background to this worship of nature in an urban context? It might be an offshoot of the enthusiasm for nature of the romantic era. In Christiania many a summer residence in the western outskirts (the *løkker*) became year-round homes during the nineteenth century. The so-called national romanticism of the mid-nineteenth century and the nationalist 'counter-cultural' (counter to the urban bourgeois European culture that produced romanticism) nationalist movements from the late nineteenth century shared an idolisation of the Norwegian countryside. So, there was obviously an element of *pull* in the rise of suburbia; semi-rural life was ideologically attractive.

On the other hand, there was certainly a *push* element as well. In the second half of the century, downtown dwellings became increasingly unattractive as manufacturing, wholesaling and retailing activities pushed inhabitants outwards, and as noise (horse drawn carriages on cobblestones), smell and dirt (from factories) and rising crime-rates made inner cities less inhabitable. Although many people had no choice but to stay, suburban life was becoming a dream for many, and a possibility for quite a few.

In Norwegian society, a distinct anti-urbanism surfaced during the last decades of the nineteenth century. It was based partly on a critique of the social conditions of the larger cities, partly on an identification of the urban with what was not considered Norwegian, an aspect of the political and cultural struggle around national questions. Is it possible to connect anti-urbanism with the movement towards the suburbs?

They may be a connection, but if there is, it is not very strong. To the extent that the nationalist so-called countercultures were anti-urban, they did not embrace the suburbs as an alternative. Suburbs were urban, too. Counter-cultural organisations, like many other types of organisations, created building associations that contributed to suburban development.[16] Several members of the literary intelligentsia were definitely anti-urban, but certainly did not worship suburbia. No poets have lauded Grefsen or Hasle or Jar, Christiania/Oslo suburbs considered nice but boring. From Olaf Bull to Rudolf Nilsen or Sigurd Hoel, poets and authors praise the inner city (when they don't condemn it), Karl Johans gate (the main street), St. Hanshaugen (a central park) or Vika (working-class, rowdy), to name a few Oslo localities. Even the rural poet Einar Skjæraasen wrote: 'Was not the city marvellously pretty, fantastically new...quivering with Olaf Bull...'[17]

There are exceptions, but we may probably discern an element of irony in these words of the originally middle-class communist Jon Michelet: 'Once you have taken a breath from the clear air of the West End, felt its safe afternoon light and tasted its abundant puddings, you will always have an aching longing to go back.'[18] Poets often go to extremes, of course, but one might ask whether the attraction of pine trees, raspberry bushes and green lawns is a petit bourgeois passion, far removed from the world of literary people. The latter would probably consider suburbia a way of fulfilling the rural dream in a banal way.

A man born in 1908 said about his childhood at Røa, a distant western suburb of Oslo: 'In the old days, Røa was way out in the countryside. But even though we didn't go to town very often, it was easy to get there [by tram]. Around Røa you could find excellent places for picking wild berries, going fishing and skiing. It's easy to understand why Røa became an attractive place to live.'[19] Having both city and wilderness close at hand seemed to be the ultimate attraction. The attraction remained even though hygienic and other facilities remained at a low standard for some time. One contemporary observer explained this by pointing to the fact that many suburban dwellers had a rural background.[20]

Nature worship was quite prevalent among the middle classes as well as the elite in Norwegian society from the second half of the nineteenth century on, a fact very much tied to the phenomenon of national identity, which was, even more than in other countries, connected with nature. Unlike its social superiors, working-class culture, including the labour movement, took an ambiguous attitude towards the worship of nature, including the one represented by suburbanism. The inner city was sometimes praised as the true home of the (industrial) working class, because of its man-made environment and collective way of life. At the same time, workers longed to get away from small and dirty dwellings. Anton Tschudi, the well-known speculator, advertised in the labour newspaper *Socialdemokraten* in 1912, trying to sell cheap plots at Haslum in Bærum: The area offered 'the best gardener's soil [*gartnerjord*] near Kristiania ... the most beautiful forested areas with sheltered valleys and hills with wide views to the Kristiania fjord'.[21] Quite a few workers heeded the call, although all they could afford was to live in shacks, at least for the time being.

Planning and commuting

To what extent was the classic suburban development in the century preceding 1940 a *planned* process? Were middle-class settlements more planned than working-class suburbs or mixed suburbs? A point of departure for discussing this is the 1928 map (reproduced below) belonging to August Nielsen's abovementioned article. The map has two interesting features. First, it expresses the idea of *zoning*, the separation of various land-use functions. Residential, industrial, and commercial areas ought to be geographically separated. Second, the suburban areas were of two kinds. Vertically hatched areas were named 'garden towns' [*havebyer*], probably denoting organised or synchronised development (planned in a certain sense). The white areas symbolised rural settlement *or* villas, more casual suburban settlement (unplanned). Areas vertically dotted are industrial areas, three in all along the railway lines to the west, north and north-east.

Byproblemer Akersdalen — Oslo.

Plan av Oslo og Aker hvor boligbydannelser er angitt.

Instead of building inside the city limits (the cross-hatched area) or at the edge of the town, where there was in fact ample space, urban development took place in the outer environs of Christiania/Oslo, mainly as organised suburban settlements. There were four main types of such organised development, three of them usually taking the form of stock companies.

First, there were projects combining housing and transport, as mentioned above, which invariably favoured middle-class customers, in some cases even higher middle-class.[22] Second, there were private building societies normally based on middle-class professions (such as high school teachers) or functionaries working for a particular company. However, some of these were working class based, usually on trade unions, like the well-to-do printers. Third, philanthropic or municipal suburban housing projects aimed at educating as well as housing the working class, but in many cases ending up with middle-class customers because of high prices. Finally, there was the private parcelling out of small plots to families with modest means, mainly working-class. This activity was mainly speculative, but with certain social considerations, as in the case of Anton Tschudi, a major buyer and seller of land in the decades before the First World War. When the plots were cheap, it normally meant they were far removed from town.

To sum up: the organised suburban development had a majority of middle-class participants, but this aspect of suburbanisation still cannot in any way be labelled a one-sided middle-class phenomenon. It was still less a collective middle-class venture, although some limited ventures were initiated by, and reserved for, middle-class occupations, and some others tried to keep workers out (see below).

The building of suburbs entailed the separation of home and workplace, thus creating a demand for transport. In some cases, the means of transport were there beforehand, therefore making possible the development of suburbs. This was the case with the railway lines connecting Christiania with other cities and counties. A north-eastern line was opened in 1854, a western one in 1872, a southern one in 1879 and a northern one in 1900. All of them created suburbs, but had to await the 1880s and 1890s for the suburban urge to appear. The formation of a group of commuters does not in itself have a class dimension, but distance and means of transportation do. Transportation costs increase with travel distance, while land prices decrease. The expenses involved in buying land or commuting to town may be too high for low-income groups.

A different class perspective on commuting is represented by railway timetables. Around the turn of the century, the earliest trains from the west arrived in the capital shortly before 9 am, in keeping with the needs of office-workers and businessmen. The printers, however, had to be at their workshops by 7. For two years they fought a battle with the railway company before achieving their goal: an early morning train. In 1902 the first train left Stabekk station at 6 am, arriving in the city at 6.45.[23] Working hours for sections of the middle classes also fitted in well with travelling home for lunch. In around 1900, the commuting fathers and husbands of Ljan had time off between 2 and 4 in the afternoon.[24]

In some instances, suburbs did not further transportation or vice versa. Suburban development and the building of tramways were simply parts of the same organisational effort, as the cases of Holmenkollbanen in the 1890s and Akersbanene in the 1920s (both north of the capital) show. All such combined projects aimed at satisfying the needs of the middle class, as can be seen from the ambitions of the developers as well as from the tram timetables.

Commuting normally meant travelling from one municipality [*kommune*] to another. The commuters soon developed urban expectations of their host *kommune*. The suburban, rural, municipality, however, was neither equipped nor willing, particularly in the early stages of suburbanisation, to provide urban services to the new settlements. Such services were necessarily more expensive per capita than services in more densely inhabited urban areas. In any case, the municipalities surrounding Christiania/Oslo preferred wealthy suburbanites to poor ones. This could be achieved by a combination of two measures: tempting people with low taxes, and discouraging workers from settling by creating red tape or not giving public guarantees for loans from the state-owned bank (*Arbeiderbruk- og boligbanken*, founded in 1903) to prospective house-owners of modest means. By the late nineteenth century, rural municipalities no longer offered fewer legal rights than urban ones did.

Social and geographical distances

How much does class show on the outside? Was life in suburbia better suited to emphasise class differences? One might argue that spacious plots and individual homes gave their inhabitants an opportunity to display their wealth or taste. The appearance of a home was more important in the suburbs than in the inner city. Once again, the names of the suburban houses give an indication of this attitude: *Fjellborgen, Digreborg, Baldersborg*. '*Diger*' means 'big', '*fjell*' means 'mountain', '*borg*' means 'castle'. Their homes were their castles. Exclusiveness might also be achieved by using foreign names, such as *Bellevue*. Class could be demonstrated through the size of the house, its architecture, its location, the garden, and so on. This is perhaps true also with the lower middle classes, even though they often earned no more than better-off workers did. However, middle-class people tended to spend relatively more of their income on housing than working-class people did.

The aesthetic quality of the suburbs was a subject of ridicule in early twentieth-century England. 'Contemporary social and architectural critics', F.M.L. Thompson writes, 'were fascinated and appalled by the mindless, creeping nature of the sprawl with its apparently insatiable capacity for devouring land, destroying the countryside, and obliterating scenery for the supposed purpose of enabling more people to live in quasi-rural surroundings.'[25] John Betjeman's words from 1937 on one of the suburbs are well known:

> Come, friendly bombs, and fall on Slough
> It isn't fit for humans now,
> There isn't grass to graze a cow
> Swarm over, Death![26]

Although some of the Norwegian suburban settlements (working-class cabins and the like) were regarded with contempt, the general impression is that of satisfaction, even admiration. One reason may be that the unevenness of the landscape hid much from view. And as an exception to the good will enjoyed by the suburbs, there was criticism of the unplanned appearance of some of them. The architecture in much of Bærum, a municipality to the west of Oslo, seemed vulgar with the houses put up at random and poorly adjusted to the landscape, complained an Oslo architect in 1929.[27]

As a matter of fact, most suburban settlements were not allowed to be randomly placed in the area surrounding Oslo. Already from 1869 *bygningskommuner* [building municipalities] could be set up in rural areas to impose building regulations designed to prevent chaos with regards to communications, aesthetics, and the risk of fires. This happened at a number of places in Aker.[28]

Although some sections of the middle class were affluent enough to spend considerable amounts on conspicuous homes, most functionaries and small businessmen had only modest incomes. More important than owning impressive homes, perhaps, was maintaining a geographical distance from the working class. This is our next point.

It is sometimes said that in a society where distinctions between social classes (estates, strata) tend to become blurred, there arises a need to make geographical distance mirror social differences. In pre-modern societies people knew their rank and place in society, the theory goes, and so there was less need for geographical segregation. The burghers of pre-industrial towns, more than their predecessors, needed more workers close at hand, servants and helpers of all kinds. In modernising Norway, particularly after the turn of the century, a need for keeping workers at a distance may have been urgently felt. When the Oslo city authorities wanted to buy a villa in the southern suburb of Ljan, the local inhabitants protested vehemently, fearing that the municipality might use it for social welfare purposes. They pointed to the restrictive covenants attached to the property.[29]

Such restrictive covenants were indeed a major means by which socially unwanted elements could be kept at bay. The 1923 sales contracts between the *Akersbanene* developer (a municipal company) and the estate buyers at Sogn, north of Oslo, included the following. Only villas were allowed to be erected, only one house on each plot. Attics and basements were not to be made habitable, thereby preventing people from letting rooms to workers, or perhaps preventing low-income groups from affording villas by taking lodgers. No activities were allowed that might disturb neighbours by such things as smoke, smell, and noise. No entertainment, manufacturing or other commercial activities were permitted. Any division of plots required permission from the seller. The contract also contained clauses on matters of aesthetics.[30] However, we do not know to exactly what degree such restrictions were actually enforced. There are reasons to believe that developers anxious to sell plots could ignore some of them and get away with it. Status uniformity was not easy to either obtain or maintain.

Status uniformity, in the strict sense that workers were unwanted in projects that were mainly middle-class, was probably not the issue. The point was tidiness, cleanliness, quiet: some working-class suburbs also imposed restrictions similar to those mentioned above on their inhabitants. Class differences could be emphasised in an number of ways, and by both sides. The inhabitants of the garden village of Holtet (named 'the red village' because of its trade union origin) were not always on good terms with their neighbours in the middle-class area of Bekkelaget. For example, they refused to allow their children to join the scout movement, which they considered bourgeois.[31]

More commonly, of course, it was the middle class that frowned upon working-class neighbours. In 1901, the *velforening* [local welfare or residents' organisation] at Vestre Stabekk complained to the police the day after the printers at Nadderud had had a celebration: 'There was much drinking, fighting and uproar. The roads and ditches were scattered with empty bottles. Likewise, individuals of both sexes seemed to have settled down for the night in various outdoor places.' The party did not repeat itself, and subsequent relations between the two neighbouring groups of suburbanites turned out to be friendly and co-operative.[32]

This was the rule between the various settlements, because almost all suburbanites, and particularly those living in organised settlements, seemed to have one trait *in common*. Their values and lifestyles may be characterised as decent, respectable, tidy, orderly. This was also true of workers, notwithstanding their wrongheaded opinions, in the eyes of the middle class. Holtet hosted several communists (some of whom were definitely middle-class). There the medicine against bolshevism did not seem to be effective, at least not in the short run.

Families, individualism and ownership

The middle classes and suburban life were united in the cultivation of the private and the individual, or so the stereotype has it. The individualistic orientation of the middle classes is set against the collective attitude of members of the working class. Suburban housing conditions, with relatively ample space both outdoors and indoors, were well suited to a private lifestyle, although they did not necessarily promote it.

The Norwegian suburbanite was usually a house-owner, although quite a few, on closer inspection, rented their homes.[33] In theory, the status of owner made him economically less dependent on others, a positive quality in all quarters. On the negative side, contemporary critics, like the radical architect Erik Rolfsen, called attention to 'a certain emptiness and isolation' which they associated with suburban living.[34] Another architect spoke about 'the lonely villa child', as part of an argument in favour of building parks in suburban areas where people could meet.[35]

What do we actually know about the various suburban communities? I have an answer: they were *communities*, and not just a heap of houses where the attention of the inhabitants was directed towards the family *or* the central city. To be sure, only 'the red village' and similar settlements celebrated the First of May, but in nearly all kinds of suburban colonies there was a felt need to undertake collective projects of one kind or another. Sometimes, for example with the provision of street lighting, this constituted the beginning of a community feeling in previously unorganised settlements.[36]

Local welfare or residents' organisations [*velforeninger*] had many tasks on their agendas: water supply, the problem of sewage, waste disposal, road maintenance, road lighting, snow clearance, collective transport, a local school; normally public tasks that proved too heavy a burden on the formerly rural municipalities surrounding Oslo. The organisations acted as pressure groups for lobbying the municipal council, which usually gave them financial support, before gradually providing normal urban services to the suburbs. This process was barely finished by 1940. Areas with unorganised suburban settlements soon created their own organisations or were admitted to neighbouring *velforeninger*.

There were social arrangements too, for adults as well as children. Sports clubs, choirs, housewives' associations, boy scouts and girl guides soon appeared. Participation in some of the activities must have felt obligatory. Free riders, even in these middle-class communities, were frowned upon. Before the advent of the age of private cars, railway stations or tram and bus stops were social gathering points. The great daily event in Ljan at the turn of the century was the coming of the evening train at 7.20, bringing husbands and fathers back from work in the city. Almost everyone was there.[37] If families and homes were important to the people of the suburbs, there was certainly a public sphere, too. This was partly social, as shown above, partly topographical, with open plots left available for the purpose of socialising (some even built meeting rooms).

English descriptions of suburban life are gloomy accounts of family- or city-centred lives, with little neighbourly love. Thompson again: 'The suburbs appeared monotonous, featureless, without character, indistinguishable from one another, infinitely boring to behold, wastelands of housing as settings for dreary, petty, lives without social, cultural or intellectual interests, settings which fostered a pretentious preoccupation with outward appearances.'[38] Perhaps combined efforts were not necessary in England, taken care of by the developer or local authorities. At any rate, the Norwegian suburbia seemed slightly different. Suburbanites seem to have had a particularly strong organisational bent, preventing, among other things, housewives from dying of boredom. Suburbia, rather than being a social disaster, might in some respects have been a social inventor. Clearly, the nature and strength of city orientation among Norwegian suburban dwellers needs to be investigated. Certainly, people needed to go into the town for specialised shopping or amusement. How pretentiously occupied they were with outward appearances, we do not exactly know.

The attitude of the labour movement to suburban life was ambiguous. Socialist architects, among others, feared that owning their own homes made workers bourgeois in outlook and were in fact relieved when the municipal garden suburb project at Ullevål hageby turned out to be too expensive for most workers. On the other hand, several suburban projects, like Holtet haveby, were initiated by radical forces within the labour movement, hoping to create small socialist republics. Outside the larger cities, in small towns and especially company towns, there was no ambiguity involved. Home-ownership was the only alternative to renting a basement or living in company-owned houses.

The rise of the classic suburb coincides with the emergence of the housewife-family as a dominant family type. The suburbs were made not only for one-income families, which were fairly common even before the suburbs evolved, but also for families where the wife did not participate in her husband's work in any way. Working-class households needing a second income could hardly find anyone to look after the children. It is telling that working-class suburbanites frequently counted printers, iron-workers and others with a solid income amongst their numbers. The relatively few middle-class wives with a job could normally afford a maid.

Normally, in the meaning of both being a norm *and* the most usual thing, during the day the suburbs were the women's and the children's world. Many suburban houses had female names, perhaps as a token of this: *Sirilund, Kristinedal, Dukkehjem* [doll's house]. This world, however, was a male creation, a place where husbands could rest after a hard day's work. Despite occasional accusations of loneliness, suburban environments were considered rather ideal for children. Unattended play in rural surroundings became a model childhood in the second half of the nineteenth century. For children to have their own bedrooms was in keeping with the new psychological views on children's needs advanced in the inter-war years. For the lower middle class, in particular, this could more easily be realised in the suburbs.

Conclusion

Was the rise of suburbia in the short century between 1840 and 1940 a middle-class phenomenon in Norway? Quantitatively speaking, before the turn of the century the classic suburb was almost uniquely middle-class. After 1900 the pattern is more mixed, but there was probably a middle-class majority. Statistically, we may therefore say that suburban growth tended towards being a middle-class phenomenon.

This is unsatisfactory. Was 'suburban reality ... a social patchwork' while the 'suburban dream was a middle-class dream'?[39] Did workers end up there by accident or by *embourgeoisement*? We must discuss the various aspects of suburban life and the values and attitudes attached to it. Whether we speak of worshipping nature, self-ownership, or communal attitudes, we end up with an ambiguous picture.

Although life in suburbia from one side looks like a return to nature, we may also look at it from a modernising or a civilising perspective. Suburban living may be described in terms such as tidy, proper, decent, hygienic, clean, solid, respectable. The civilising aspect of the *egnehjem* movement was not a uniquely bourgeois programme, but something that the labour movement struggled to achieve.

In his classic text on urbanisation from 1899, Adna Ferrin Weber described the suburban development as a classless ideology. Even though the middle classes were there first, suburbia was a place for workers, too.[40] Still, suburbanisation is often understood as a middle-class project. Was it the prospect of social segregation from the lower orders that united the middle classes in their suburban dream?

Notes

[1] Excellent introductions to this field are offered by Harold Carter, in his *The Study of Urban Geography*, London 1975 (1972), chapters 9 and 11; and in *An Introduction to Urban Historical Geography*, London 1983, part IV.
[2] David Lockwood, *The Blackcoated Worker. A study in class consciousness*, Oxford 1989 (1958); C. Wright Mills, *White Collar. The American Middle Classes*, New York 1951. Norwegian sociologists are, or have been, interested in class, but not particularly the middle class. See Tom Colbjørnsen et al, *Klassesamfunnet på hell* [The Waning of Class Society], Oslo 1987. Concerning the historians' interest, see Myhre's article earlier in this volume.
[3] Knut Helle, Finn-Einar Eliassen, Jan Eivind Myhre and Ola Svein Stugu, *Norsk byhistorie 700-2000*, Oslo 2004.
[4] Paul M. Hohenberg and Lynn Hollen Lees, *The Making of Urban Europe 1000-1950*, London 1994; Lars Nilsson, *Den urbana transitionen. Tätorterna i svensk samhällsomvandling 1800-1980*, Stockholm 1989 (Sweden); Per Boje and Ole Hyldtoft, 'Økonomiske, geografiske og demografiske aspekter. Danmark', in Grethe Authén Blom (ed.), *Urbaniseringsprosessen i Norden, bd. 3*, Oslo 1977, pp. 178-244 (Denmark).
[5] Kenneth T. Jackson, *Crabgrass Frontier. The Suburbanization of the United States*, N.Y. 1985; Robert L. Fishman, 'American Suburbs/English Suburbs: a transatlantic comparison', *Journal of Urban History*, vol. 13/3, May 1987, pp. 237-251; F.M.L. Thompson, 'Introduction: The rise of suburbia', F.M.L. Thompson (ed.), *The rise of suburbia*, Leicester 1982, p. 2.
[6] See the introductory articles, but also Jan Eivind Myhre, 'Finding the Middle Class. Norway in a comparative perspective, c. 1870-1940', *Scandinavian Journal of History*, 3/1994, vol. 19, pp. 237-249.
[7] On the Christianian pre-modern suburbs, see Jan Eivind Myhre, 'Wanted and Unwanted Suburbs: Annexations and Urban Identity. The case of Christiania (Oslo) in the 19th century', *Scandinavian Economic History Review* 2/1996, pp. 124-139; in French as 'La banlieue souhaité et non-souhaitée. Annexion et Identité Urbaine. L'example de Christiania (Oslo) au XIXe siècle', *Histoire - économie et Société*, 15/3, Juillet-septembre 1996, pp. 417-435.
[8] Fernand Braudel, *The Structures of Everyday Life, Vol. I of Civilization and Capitalism 15th - 18th Century*, London 1985, p. 503.
[9] Henrik Wergeland, Forstædernes Klagesang over Kristiania, *Samlede Skrifter*, Første Bind, Christiania 1852, pp. 341-343. Author's translation.
[10] See e.g. John L. Merriman, *The Margins of City Life. Explorations on the French Urban Frontier, 1815-1851*, New York 1991.
[11] According to Jan Eivind Myhre, *Hovedstaden Christiania. Oslo bys historie bind 3, 1814-1990*, Oslo 1990, p. 197.
[12] Christiania/Oslo had major extensions to its city limits in 1859, 1878 and 1948.
[13] Christianian examples include the upper middle class suburb of Fagerborg and the working-class suburb of Balkeby (of philanthropic origin). Liv Hilde Boe, Fagerborg, *St. Hallvard* 3/1979; Tom Bryn, Balkeby, *St. Hallvard* 1/1989.

[14] August Nielsen, Byproblemer Akersdalen-Oslo, *St. Hallvard* 1928, p. 55.
[15] Øystein Bergkvam, *Egne hjem-bevegelsen i Norge 1900-1920. Tradisjon eller nye strømninger?* Main thesis [*hovedoppgave*] in history, University of Oslo 1999.
[16] The counter-cultures embraced Norwegian dialects (against the urban Danish-like language), temperance, low church movements and other cultural expressions considered rural and therefore Norwegian.
[17] 'Var ikke byen eventyrlig pen, fantastisk ny...dirrende av Olaf Bull', from *Kvit natt* (White night, 1941), Bernhard Hagtvedt (ed.), *Møte med tigerstaden. Oslo i innflytternes øyne*, Stavanger 1950, pp. 49-50.
[18] 'Har du først pustet inn Vestkantens klare luft, kjent dens trygge ettermiddagslys og smakt dens rikelige puddinger - da vil du alltid bære på en sår lengsel etter å komme tilbake', quoted from Fredrik Wandrup, *Oslo sett fra luften*, Oslo 1986, p. 52. Michelet is writing about the far, suburban, West End.
[19] Eivind Heide, *Bydel 36 gjennom tidene. Røa, Voksen, Huseby, Hovseter, Holmen*, Oslo 1980, p. 97.
[20] Emil Smith, *Disse fjerne år*, Oslo 1936, pp. 230-231. Smith wrote about the generation prior to 1914.
[21] Harald og Kristin Røgeberg Winge, *Haslum gjennom 60 år*, 1973, p. 24.
[22] Kari Amundsen, Berit Anderson, Ingeborg Hvidsten og Alf Stefferud, *Complet færdige Huse. Strømmen trævarefabrik – ferdighusproduksjon 1884-1929*, Oslo 2002, pp. 112-125.
[23] Jan Eivind Myhre, *Bærum 1840-1980*, Oslo 1982, p. 196.
[24] Finn Erhard Johannesen et al, *Fint folk i bratte bakker. Ljans historie*, Oslo 1990, p. 92.
[25] Thompson 1982, p. 3.
[26] Quoted from Peter Hall, *Cities of Tomorrow. An Intellectual History of Urban Planning and Design in the Twentieth Century*, Oxford 1988.
[27] Arno Berg, according to Myhre 1982, p. 191.
[28] Elin Børrud, Hagebyen som forsvant i funkisen. Historien om Sogn Haveby, *Byminner* 4/1996; *Aker 1837-1937. Kommunens styre og forvaltning gjennom hundre år*, vol. I, Aker 1940.
[29] Johannesen et al 1990, p. 160.
[30] Johan L. Stang, *Sogn - en del av Oslo*, Oslo 1980, pp. 117-119.
[31] Michael Hopstock, *Holtet haveby. Den røde by*, main thesis in history [*hovedoppgave*] at the University of Oslo, 1994.
[32] Michael Sars og Reidar Nordheim, *Stabekk. En historikk*, 1974, p. 69.
[33] Johannesen 1990; *Utsikt over Nordstrands historie*, Oslo 2000.
[34] Knut Kjeldstadli, *Den delte byen. Oslo bys historie, vol 4, 1900-1948*, Oslo 1990, p. 409.
[35] Jan Eivind Myhre, *Barndom i storbyen. Oppvekst i Oslo i velferdsstatens epoke*, Oslo 1994, p. 66.
[36] *Selskabet for Sandvikens Vel 1896-1946*, Sandvika 1946.
[37] Johannesen et al 1990, pp. 93, 95.
[38] E.g. Alan Jackson, *The Middle Classes 1900-1950*, 1991, p. 318; and Thompson, 'Introduction' in Thompson 1982.
[39] Thompson 1982, p. 20.
[40] Adna Ferrin Weber, *The Growth of Cities in the Nineteenth Century*, N.Y. 1899, pp. 473-475.

JAN EIVIND MYHRE

Uncertain Status: Norwegian Teachers between Professions and Middle Classes

Two perspectives

'Teaching ... is a middle class occupation,' proclaimed an article in a Bergen paper in 1973, albeit referring to statistics from as early as 1950. Then 39 per cent of (elementary) school teachers[1] were sons and daughters of farmers and 20 per cent had teacher parents. Some 12 per cent of teachers were the children of workers, 9 per cent of businessmen, 5 per cent of clerks (functionaries) and 3 per cent of academics. The author continues: 'More than half of Norwegian teachers live and work in the countryside. The strong ties to the countryside and the middle class, the political leanings of teachers, their personalities and moral and religious convictions, must influence their teaching by way of affecting the choice and treatment of educational material.'[2]

Here the teacher is at once situated in both the countryside and the middle class. This is of course no impossible juxtaposition, but still a problematic and unlikely grouping in Norwegian history. We normally associate the middle class with towns and cities, their social structure and the urban way of life. The farmers of Norway, for long rightly named peasants, are not usually labelled middle class, at least not until well into the twentieth century. Norwegian teachers, on the other hand, have long had an ambiguous social position. On the one hand, it is difficult to place teachers (socially speaking) anywhere other than in the diffuse (lower) middle class, at least from the time of the important school Acts of the mid-nineteenth century, which elevated the social status of elementary school teachers.[3] On the other hand, for a long time teachers were quite oriented towards the rural districts in their general outlooks. Not only did most of them work and live there, they had been born there and were culturally and politi-

237

cally attached to the countryside. At least until the middle of the twentieth century, they were seen as 'the intelligentsia of the farmers' movement',[4] the political vanguards of nationalism and democracy in late twentieth-century Norway.

One of the more peculiar traits of teachers as a middle class, therefore, is their rural anchoring. However, during the last 150 years an increasing proportion of teachers have worked in the towns and cities, and ever fewer have retained a sense of identification (in terms of descent, gender or culture) with their colleagues in the countryside. In a sense, then, the stage was set for splits within the occupation. This is exactly what happened, and this split was expressed in organisational terms. I will return to this fact later, and here be content with stating that this split is pivotal in assessing the teaching occupation as a middle class one.

The two main categories among teachers (we may preliminarily and approximately call them city and country teachers) represented two different ways of looking at the occupation, and also two ways of trying to assert its status and standard of living. Both categories naturally wished to improve the occupation's social standing. To achieve this, for more than a century teachers have employed two strategies, separately or combined. The first I will call a trade union strategy, tied to the teachers' struggle for a solid middle class standard of living. The second strategy consisted in searching for the status of a profession. A profession, preliminarily, is an expert occupation, and is characterised by managing to convince its clients (customers) or its employer that the service it renders is indispensable to them and society at large. Normally, admission to a profession is well guarded, and only (higher) education gives the right of entry. Finally, and no less important, the profession enjoys a (near) monopoly on its services.[5]

The two major perspectives on the teachers as middle-class actors on the societal stage are these. One is the traditional rise-of-the-middle-class perspective, where one part of the middle class is made up of small business people (often self-employed), and another comprises a new group of wage earners, public or private clerks doing non-manual work. Their most important common characteristic was an emphasis on their social distance from the working class. Economically speaking, many lower-middle class people were on a par with workers. The petty artisan or shopkeeper could easily succumb; poorly paid functionaries tried their best to hide how badly off they were. Distance from the workers was established by creating a separate culture of their own, often a pale copy of that of the bourgeoisie. The status of the functionaries as middle class, however, also had more tangible aspects. They normally enjoyed being paid every month, as different from the weekly or daily payment of workers.[6] English speakers sometimes use the term '*salariat*', from salary, to distinguish them from wage earners.

Norwegian farmers are, of course, a group of preponderantly small independent businessmen. Taking this last term as their point of departure, Danish historians unhesitatingly locate their farmers in the middle class, at least since the time of the breakthrough of capitalist farming in the middle of the nineteenth century. In Norway, however, the greater difference between town and country, economically, socially and culturally, makes such a location unreasonable, at least until the mid-twentieth century. Not that Norwegian peasants/farmers have not had to buy and sell to survive for centuries. But family farming meant subsistence farming in Chayanov's sense. The survival of the farm meant everything, and the cost of manpower in a family farm (almost all Norwegian farms were family farms) was not a fixed item in the budget. This was different from doing business in a town.[7] The social and cultural divisions between town and country in Norway hardly need further elaboration here; Norway had 'two cultures' until the second half of the twentieth century. In certain respects they are still with us in the twenty-first. Rural society in Norway from the middle of the nineteenth century onwards did not resemble a capitalist class society.

It was especially the middle that was missing. On the south coast (Sørlandet, or Agder) there were sea captains and their wives (called '*madam*', as against '*frue*' for the upper classes and '*kone*' for the lower classes). Elsewhere in the countryside the middle layers were thin indeed, consisting of a few functionaries, like clerks and teachers.[8] Despite their middling status, however, rural teachers were not cultural aliens to the countryside, and did not identify much with the urban middle classes, their urban teacher colleagues being ambiguous exceptions.

Delimiting the middle classes upwards is a difficult pursuit when it comes to nineteenth and twentieth-century Norwegian history. In the twentieth century we might identify an economic upper class consisting of rich businessmen, owners of factories, ships and banks. In the nineteenth century, however, Norway was characterised by the absence of a sizeable land-owning class (nobility had been formally abolished in 1821), and for a long time also by the absence of a strong capitalist upper class. In their place, the senior civil servants [*embetsmenn*] operated as an *Ersatz Aristokratie*, the leading political and social class in the country. These senior civil servants were in many respects the forerunners of the modern professions, lawyers and ministers being their foremost representatives. Their assets were themselves, their expertise and their education; we are talking about an educational bourgeoisie (the German *Bildungsbürgertum*) rather than a business bourgeoisie (*Wirtschaftsbürgertum*).[9] They enjoyed a monopoly in their educations and professional lives, and managed to convince most others that they were indispensable, elevated above private interests and always working in the best interests of their parishioners, the electorate, society at large, and the state.

One might thus call the *embetsmenn* the fathers of the professions and semi-professions of our days, not excepting the teachers. The similarities between a senior civil servant in the 1860s and a teacher from the 1910s are many, even though the dissimilarities are easy to find as well. The senior civil servants in the countryside (at least half of them lived there in the mid-nineteenth century) were not part of the rural way of life, and looked to their peers in town when it came to culture. And urban teachers, like other professions and similar occupations, were obviously not upper-class in the second half of the twentieth century.

In making the teachers a profession or a *semi-profession*[10], which is my second major perspective, I have two aims. The first is to place teachers in the middle class from this direction too. Professions are middle-class occupations, even though professionalisation as a process concerns society as a whole and is not confined to the middle class. The other aim is to underline the fact that the perspective of the professions points beyond the class society, towards the professional society [*profesjonssamfunnet*]. This society is characterised by human capital in the shape of the education and expertise possessed by the professions, which has perhaps become the most important form of capital. The social structure in professional society takes the form of a number of parallel hierarchies, professions, competing for a place in the sun.[11] The professionals may be publicly or privately employed.

The social formations of professional society, as the English historian Harold Perkin portrays them, do in fact resemble Norwegian pre-industrial estate society, as presented by Jens Arup Seip and Sivert Langholm, for example. The senior civil servants, businessmen and artisans each made up a vertical hierarchy, the civil servants' column reaching highest and the artisans' lowest. The 'estate' of the civil servants [*embetsstanden*], as it was normally called, could be subdivided into smaller hierarchies, according to profession or occupation.[12]

My main point is this: teachers' roles in society, their self-appraisal and their strategies to improve their social standing and standards of living, were shaped by both their position as a middle-class occupation in town and country and their status as an aspiring profession. The two are not always easy to separate. Both concern social elevation and achieving economic or cultural benefits. It is not enough to say that the strategies belong to the class society and the professional society respectively. Although class society precedes professional society in time, the two coexist through the whole of the twentieth century. There are other dimensions applicable to teachers that may blur our dichotomous perspective, while still others serve to enhance it. I am referring to the geographical distinction (or rather opposition) between Western Norway (*Vestlandet*) and Eastern Norway (*Østlandet*, also representing the rest of the country), the sex or gender dimension , and the dimension that runs from the academic/elitist to the popular. This last is an opposition that has plagued teachers' organisations through all of their history. An example would be the mention of the prominent educator Torstein Høverstad (1880-1959) in Gro Hagemann's book on the history of teachers. In her discussion, Hagemann emphasises Høverstad's position as a spokesman for the plain and anti-academic strain in the teachers' organisations. In a biographical sketch below his portrait in the book, however, Svein Sæter lays a one-sided emphasis on the educator's strong formal academic standing.[13]

At a later stage, perhaps surprisingly, I will launch the popular, plain or common [*folkeligheten*] as an important part of the teachers' identities as professionals. First, however, we need to look more closely at the historical experiences of teachers, and what the middle-class perspective and the professional perspective really entailed.

The teachers and the middle class

When I locate the teachers in the middle class, and when teachers themselves and their contemporaries did so too, I mean to place teachers in a vertical social structure between an upper class (in Norway this means an elite of higher civil servants and/or a capitalist haute bourgeoisie) and an underclass, called working people or working class [*arbeidsfolk* or *arbeiderklasse*]. In the nineteenth century one would speak of commoners or common people [*allmuen*], a category that would also contain people above the ranks of workers.

In the first half of the nineteenth century, teachers did not stand out from other common people. More often than not, the local priest would recruit as teachers young men who were no good at other things. Until schools for teachers [*seminarier*] were established in all dioceses from the 1830s, and in many cases for a generation longer, teachers belonged to the rural underclass, and were recruited from there. As late as 1879, Torkel Halvorsen Aschehoug stated in parliament [*Stortinget*] that teachers principally 'emanated from the working class', shared its views and therefore naturally acted as its spokesmen. For Aschehoug, this was a reason for giving the vote to the teachers, but not to workers.[14] For a number of other parliamentary representatives who discussed electoral reforms in the two decades following the 1860s, the important attribute of teachers was their belonging to the 'middle ranks' [*middelstanden*]. As one MP said in 1873, they 'stood at a level of education [*Dannelsestrinn*] higher than the other classes being discussed, and therefore deserved the right to vote.'[15] There was one problem, however. Teachers were poorly paid and earned less than many workers. A major consideration among the legislators was that only people who could sustain a living without support were eligible to vote. This explains why the parliament introduced a census system in 1884, requiring a minimum taxable income for potential voters.[16]

This means that the material standard of living among teachers in late nineteenth-century Norway did not match their social or cultural status. Teachers were increasingly viewed as educated, enlightened and entrusted with the important task of teaching children. The social standing of children was definitely on the rise in the second half of the century.[17] Schooling was given high priority in Norwegian society from the mid-nineteenth century. The School Act of 1860 required all children to be taught to write (most of them could already read). As a consequence of new and ambitious legislation in 1889, within a few years almost all Norwegian children went to the same, public, elementary schools, now called *folkeskolen*.[18] The monumental school buildings erected in Norwegian towns from the late nineteenth century on bears witness to the importance attached to education in Norwegian society.

For a long time, however, teachers' salaries were modest, although in real terms their wages rose faster than those of most other occupations. In the late 1870s they surpassed able seamen, and in the course of the 1880s their salaries caught up with those of telegraphers.[19] In the first decade of the twentieth century they could no longer be considered poor, at least as far as the men were concerned.[20] Teachers still felt undervalued. Urban teachers, in particular, would compare themselves with other educated (and less educated) groups with higher incomes. For all teachers, whether rural or urban, the question of payment was always at the forefront of their minds. The activities of The Norwegian Teachers' Association testify to this. Teachers and their organisation were rarely satisfied. However, a modest salary could be compensated for by a steady livelihood. As public employees, this is exactly what most teachers had. Female teachers during the inter-war years were an exception to the rule, because employers gave priority to breadwinners, and most female teachers were unmarried, thus being at risk of losing their jobs. In times when there was a surplus of teachers, as in the 1920s and 1930s, newly educated teachers faced difficulties in finding work. The question of pensions was a major issue for the organisations from day one, and an area where the teachers' efforts proved gainful.

The security of the teachers' position was symbolised by the fact that they were paid monthly, unlike the workers who were paid by the week, day or hour. Receiving a salary was of course a well-known mark of the middle class. In 1890, the country's first general organisation for functionaries, *Kristiania Bestillingsmannsforening*, decided that being paid by the month or year was a criterion for membership. Teaching was one of its 52 approved and named occupations, and teachers were represented in its first management.[21]

Norwegian political history from the 1870s on, and especially after 1884, is full of sturdy teachers, the heirs of Ole Gabriel Ueland and Søren Jaabæk, prominent parliamentarians and teachers and farmers. Already around 1880 there were about 13 teachers in the *Storting*, elected on the basis that they were farmers as well.[22] Between 1907 and 1940, 10 out of 17 ministers for church and educational affairs had been educated as primary school teachers.[23] Literature, mainly fiction, depicting the important position of teachers as local intellectuals, the spiritual leaders of rural communities, became a part of the Norwegian cultural heritage.

However, this heritage may have led us to overestimate the standing and status of teachers in Norwegian society around the turn of the century. As one of the teachers said at the formation of the Norwegian teachers' association in Trondheim in 1892: 'Certain other classes in society look down on a teacher.' He expressed the hope that the new organisation would put an end to this. The teacher in question, Qvam, did not specify which class he had in mind, and his statement may be a testimony to high social ambitions.[24] But if we accept that teachers in general did not enjoy the social status posterity has attributed to them (not even in rural areas, nor even in their heydays up to the 1920s), and in any event occupied a lower position than Qvam and his colleagues wished to have, how are we to explain this? What prevented Norwegian teachers in the late nineteenth and early twentieth centuries from having a higher social status?

To begin by focusing on the modest salaries may seem like putting the cart before the horse, meaning that low status is followed by meagre pay. The relationship is, of course, more complicated. Social status and income may influence each other. And sometimes their relationship may even be weak. *Pauvres honteux* are still *honteux*. But in that case, the exclusiveness is usually old, while our teaching profession was relatively new. For the teachers, their modest pay to a degree indicated a modest social status. Again, why was their salary so meagre?

Three explanatory factors lie close at hand; gender, descent and education. In addition, all three worked to divide the teachers, a fate not very conducive to material success. Already from the late 1870s female teachers were in a majority in the towns. Women had far lower wages than men; in fact their low salaries were used as an argument to hire women instead of men. Female salaries also served to raise or sustain the salary levels for male teachers. This was explicitly stated by their employers, that is the urban municipalities. That is why the men felt threatened when the women fought for equal pay within their common organisation in the 1890s.

Female teachers possessed two characteristics that their male counterparts lacked. First, they were mainly townspeople, based in towns and recruited from towns. Secondly, they emerged from the higher echelons of society. Quite a few must be characterised as daughters of upper class families, their fathers being senior civil servants or rich businessmen. With their social and cultural capital, these women succeeded strikingly early in achieving equal wages with men in the towns. And the men were probably right to believe that equality was achieved literally at their expense. Teachers' salaries came from what was usually perceived as slender public purses. Urban purses, by the way, were the least slender ones, especially in the larger cities, which meant better wages for city teachers. Many teachers saw this as unfair, and a majority of teachers worked in rural districts until after the Second World War. It therefore became a priority for the organisation to see that teachers were placed on a uniform state wage scale. They finally achieved this in the wake of a governmental wage committee recommendation in 1948. They also wished, in vain, to become government employees instead of municipal ones.

On both issues teachers were divided along gender lines and along the urban-rural split. The two coincided well. Male town teachers were not that afraid of equality between the sexes because they believed that the towns could afford it. All urban teachers were opposed to geographical equality because they feared wage reductions and because the costs of living were much higher in urban areas than in rural ones. These rivalries led to three break-ups in the history of the teachers' organisation. The first took place in 1912, when female teachers formed their own association. The second happened in 1954 when both male and female teachers of Oslo broke away, and the third occurred a year later when a small group in North Norway (in *Nordland*) opposed what they saw as a too centralised organisation.

The lines of conflict erected on the dimensions of man/woman, town/country and centre/periphery were followed by yet another, the question of teachers' education, both its duration and, in particular, its content. The length of their education was increased at almost regular intervals, demanded by an almost unanimous occupation. The 1930s and the 1960s were particularly important periods in this respect. Disagreements arose when there were attempts at making the education, and thereby the teaching occupation, more academic. The urban teachers, nearly all female teachers, and the teachers of Eastern Norway wanted a longer education, an education approaching academic levels, and consequently higher entrance requirements for teachers' schools. They wanted a larger share of students with *examen artium*, the graduation exam for the *gymnasium*.

This must be regarded more as a strategy for increasing wages than as a strategy for developing the schools (see below). I will therefore call it a trade union strategy. The urban teachers and their fellow partisans wished to turn the national teachers' organisation into a pure trade union. But although their organisational pattern was borrowed from the labour movement (as for example in 1911), the teachers did not usually see themselves as trade unionists.[25] And they did not lose their non-proletarian virtue until they went on strike for the first time in 1954.[26] Some of the teachers wished to raise their academic status, and thereby their salary, it was thought, by letting their education approach that of the *gymnasium* teachers [*lektorer*]. They would make cultivating their distinctiveness as primary school teachers a priority. That would be to choose quite another strategy.

That the social standing of teachers should be raised was a commonly held opinion within the occupation during the interwar years. A representative from the town of Fredrikstad wrote in

1927 that the teacher was no longer the obvious leader in the rural districts, neither culturally nor politically. He 'no longer stands out among the others, he disappears in the crowd.' The reason for this, he held, was that the education was second-rate. It was too short and fell short of professional standards.[27] The remedy, this teacher said, was to make the education and the occupation more academic. This would raise teachers up to the protected middle class, in terms both of income and social status. The background for the anxieties of this teacher was a general societal development characterised by urbanisation and a higher level of education. The rural municipalities experienced this too; the teachers there no longer worked almost exclusively among farmers and fishermen. Teachers were so to speak caught up in society and no longer stood out as the local educated elite.

What does it mean to say that teachers, through their associations, pursued middle-class status? Academic kudos has been mentioned; long pay periods and well-ordered pensions also tasted of the middle class. However, fighting for higher wages and struggling for shorter hours (or *leseplikt*, the number of weekly classes) savoured just as much of the working class, of course. For teachers, like many others, the salary was a means to create a style of life we may call middle-class, consciously different from that of the working class. Teachers did not do manual work and they possessed book learning. Otherwise we know surprisingly little about the teachers' lifestyles and values beyond the ones attached to their work. These values speak for themselves; the teachers preached industry, moderation, cleanliness and godliness, for long periods also democracy, nationalism and the values of the Norwegian so-called counter-cultures, like temperance and a national language [*målsak*]. As late as 1950, more than half of all teachers voted for *Venstre* [liberals] or *Kristelig folkepart* [Christian People's Party] as against only one fifth of the total electorate.[28]

In many ways the trade union route to a middle-class position has become dominant among teachers. A relatively long basic education (two years at teachers' college, three years from 1973 and four years from around 1990) and frequent additional courses and the *gymnasium* or equivalent schooling as a prerequisite have long been the rule. But these tendencies towards an academic foundation have not lifted the teachers very high in terms of income or status during the last couple of generations. The reverse is rather the case. It is, for example, striking that teaching in primary schools has never been attractive to men of the middle or higher strata in society.

However, if we take a closer look at the academic tendencies of recent decades, we find that teachers' education does not mainly consist in the acquisition of knowledge within the disciplines on the curriculum. Teachers have been educated more and more in the art of teaching. This brings me to the second aspect of the development of the identity of teachers, professionalisation.

Teaching as a profession

It has not been commonplace to speak of elementary school teachers (formerly *folkeskolelærere*, today *allmennlærere*) as a profession. At most one has spoken about the occupation as one resembling a profession or as a semi-profession, in particular when compared to the archetypical profession, medicine, or other professions like lawyers, priests and architects. I would argue that teachers have enough traits in common with the professions for a comparison to be fruitful. How, then, shall we evaluate teaching as a profession?

One of the important characteristics of the self-presentation of professions is that their self-interest is played down in favour of their social contribution. To be honest, all, or most, occupations or groups in society like to enhance their societal importance. The professions, however, will probably even more than other occupations make a strong claim for their uniqueness and indispensability. But in contrast to what I have labelled ordinary trade union policy (inside or outside the working class), where self-interest in the shape of the struggle for higher wages and better working conditions is open and explicit, it is a vital part of the professions' identity that their work is unselfish. In its extreme version we are speaking of a calling or vocation, if not necessarily a sacrifice. An American investigation shows that in particular the semi-professions (teachers, nurses, social workers) emphasise this aspect of their work, although it refers to dedication rather than vocation. This type of motivation has been quite apparent among Norwegian teachers up to this day, but has clearly faded.[29] In a trade union context one ought to hide one's vocation; if not one might be suspected of being ready to work for a meagre material reward. The professional version of this, rather than taking a trade union stand, is probably a transformation of the vocation. One might reasonably interpret the ethical norms of the professions as a secularisation or a bureaucratisation of the vocation. Medicine provides, again, probably the best example.

Already in the early nineteenth century Norwegian teachers legitimised their work in terms of the interest of the people. While the country's first teachers' association, that of Christiania in 1821, solely worked for the benefit of knowledge and the pupils, the local medical association was mainly occupied with the material interests of its members.[30] In the second half of the nineteenth century, Norwegian society had come to value education quite highly, and teachers looked upon themselves as a vital and indispensable group. Those working in the primary schools, of course, were teachers of the whole population, and did not just deal with a small part of it as did teachers in secondary schools and the university, whom they came to view as elitist and even undemocratic.

This wide perspective, the education of everybody, forms a point of departure if we wish to look into the characteristics of the teaching occupation. As soon as the teachers' seminaries (later to be colleges) had furnished the students with a minimum of knowledge in Norwegian, arithmetic, natural history, religion, geography and history, their attention was turned to other occupational goals, namely to perfecting and deepening the role of the teacher. True enough, over the years there has been a tendency towards making teachers slightly more academic. But this tendency was probably slower than the academic trend in the society at large, exemplified by the academic standing of the pupils' parents.[31] As mentioned before, many teachers, often a majority, fought against increasing the professional or academic [*faglige*] content of the education. Introducing English into Norwegian primary schools, for example, was met with strong resistance from teachers in the early twentieth century.

This resistance was not a manifestation of trade union consciousness in the sense that the teachers did not want more, or more difficult, work. It based itself on the conviction that the task of education consisted of much more than furnishing children with book learning. The knowledge ideal among primary school teachers was quite different from, say, that of the grammar schools [*realskolen*] or the *gymnasium*, and was in part developed in public debates with their teachers [*lektorer* and *adjunkter*] educated at the university.

This ideal of knowledge stood against theoretical knowledge. It opened towards the practical aspects of life, making the elementary school a kind of preliminary to the school of life. Teachers having practical experience were best equipped to give the pupils the qualities and attitudes they were considered to need. From this point of view teachers were supposed to be as much educators [*oppdragere*] as teachers. The learning process was considered at least as important as the content of the learning, as the so-called 'reform pedagogy' [*reformpedagogikken*] stressed. The ultimate goal, in an expression taken from newer educational plans [*læreplaner*], was to turn youngsters into 'useful' ('beneficial') human beings [*gagns menneske*]. To achieve this, one had to play down the academic content in school, which, it was thought, had 'overstretched itself as a knowledge-oriented school'.[32]

What sorts of attitudes are we talking about? Teachers characteristically supported egalitarian, democratic, national and rural attitudes. The archetypical teacher hailed from rural districts, above all from Western Norway. Even in school textbooks used in towns and cities until way past the mid-twentieth century, a country childhood was depicted as the typical and normal environment for young people. Until after the Second World War, *Venstre* (the liberal party) was the teachers' favoured political party. The so-called 'work school' [*arbeidsskolen*] and the reform pedagogy of the 1930s onwards took a firm stand against what was seen as the cramming approach of the old school system. In doing this, they reacted more against practice than ideals in the schools. The learning ideal of most teachers during the twentieth century has hardly been that of cramming.

Even though popular education [*folkeopplysning*], the act of providing an uneducated and unenlightened people with basic knowledge, was an important task for nineteenth and twentieth-century elementary schools, it is above all the pedagogical task that has legitimised the teachers' mission. The role of the teacher, as well as the teacher's personality, was placed in the forefront. There was a cultivation of the teacher who communicated well with the children, who radiated confidence and authority (much played down during the last generation!), and who disseminated, also through personal appearance, the qualities endorsed by the teaching culture; Norwegianness, equality, democracy, independence. However, personalities differ, and individuals do not always live up to expectations. Therefore, as Reidar Mykletun wrote in the piece quoted at the beginning of this paper, 'There will be no two school classes in Norway receiving exactly the same instruction, in spite of all efforts to create a uniform schooling [enhetsskole].'

The knowledge of what made a good teacher was not always easy to formulate. It was, supposedly, an integral part of the teacher's experience and behaviour. In many ways it can be compared to the 'tacit knowledge' that has been regarded as part of the ballast of the nurses and pre-school teachers. In this pedagogical praxis lay the distinguishing feature of teachers; herein rested their expertise.

There was a problem, however. The problem, seen from the perspective of professions, was that this expertise was not based on science or scholarship, and therefore not adequately grounded in the eyes of the authorities or the public. The deliverance arrived in the shape of the science of pedagogy. The scholarly pedagogues and the practical pedagogues, the teachers, united at quite an early stage. Already in 1907 the Norwegian teachers' association proposed the establishment of a university chair in pedagogy. The wish was not granted until 1938 with the appointment of Helga Eng as the first professor of pedagogy at the University of Oslo.

With the introduction of pedagogy as an academic discipline, the characteristic ideal of knowledge and competence among teachers was given a scientific anchoring. Their science was that of teaching (and learning), their specialisation was teaching in general. We find a parallel in medicine where general medicine [allmennmedisin] counts as a speciality. With a scientific basis and a status as specialists of a sort, teaching met two of the criteria one normally demands from a profession.

A particularly important criterion for being a profession concerns a long formal higher education. The length of the basic education for (primary school) teachers has never been comparable to the one enjoyed by the university-based professions. The gap is, however, closing and the recently established compulsory four-year teacher courses means that it is only marginally shorter than the education for lower-degree university high school teachers [*adjunkter*], civil engineers or business degrees [*siviløkonomer*]. Quite a few teachers have additional education (in addition to the two, three or four years of basic schooling), often taken at universities or colleges. However, the typical additional education for the occupation consists of various courses in pedagogy. Perfectly in line with the knowledge ideal within the occupation is also the fact that art, besides pedagogy, is the most popular specialist subject in basic teacher training, yet another discipline supposedly furthering the qualities of the human character. Almost no students in teachers' colleges in the 1970s or 1980s voluntarily chose science or languages.[33] Among teachers, the appropriation of knowledge other than pedagogical knowledge has not been in high esteem over the past couple of generations.[34] This has also been the case among university scholars of pedagogy. A debate in a newspaper in 1984 between a university philosopher and a university pedagogue revealed a deep mutual mistrust over the role of pedagogy in the school system. The pedagogue held that knowing one's field (e.g. maths, English, history) well is no longer the decisive issue. What matters is being a good pedagogue. In fact, unless teachers master pedagogy, they are useless. The philosopher finds this preposterous, and blamed the declining standard in pupils' knowledge on this kind of pedagogical thinking.[35]

An archetypical profession delimits entrance into, and insight into, the conduct of professionals. As we have seen, the majority of teachers, the ones hailing from Western Norway [*vestlandslærerne*], preferred the academic requirements for entering college not to be too high. Personality, experience and homeliness should count most. Formal education, however, was important. That is why male teachers long bore a grudge against female teachers. The women were not only mainly town-based, with a solid social background, but until the 1890s they had no formal teacher education, even though they had to pass a teaching test from 1873-74 on. In the nineties female teachers were admitted to the seminaries (colleges), and soon became spokeswomen for a more academic teaching profession.

The majority of teachers also realised that a long education was necessary in order to enhance the teacher's position in school and society. The emergence of the science of pedagogy thus resolved their inner conflict. It was an academic education, which placed the emphasis on the role of the teacher and the teaching process, and not on the knowledge content of that process.

Teachers have only partly succeeded in closing admission to the occupation to the uninitiated. A lack of teachers has sometimes required school authorities to temporarily employ people lacking the necessary pedagogical background. Teachers possessing the necessary pedagogical schooling, led by their association, have long born a grudge against those lacking such schooling, calling them 'unskilled' [*ufaglært*], even in cases where they have possessed excellent qualifications in academic disciplines.[36]

Elementary school teachers have, however, won some of the important battles in the politics of education. I am referring particularly to the struggle over teaching positions in the newly established *ungdomsskole* (from the late 1950s onwards), created for pupils between the ages of 13 and 16, as compulsory schooling was extended from seven to nine years, raising the graduation age from 14 to 16. The predecessor of the *ungdomsskole*, the voluntary *realskole*, had been staffed by university graduates only. With the introduction of the new compulsory school, elementary school teachers gained the right to teach at all levels through all nine years, in principle in all subjects. They did not secure a monopoly, although the teachers' association wanted elementary teachers to have an exclusive right to teach in the *ungdomsskolen*. Many job advertisements in the early years gave the impression that only elementary school teachers were wanted and qualified. The capture of this middle level in the school system (children between the ages of 13 (14) and 16) was for a long time given a high priority in the organisation. No wonder they were at odds with the university educated *lektorer* and *adjunkter*.[37]

In the classroom no one is admitted except the teacher and the pupils, with the occasional exception of the head master and a few others. This means that evaluation of the teacher at work is weak, at most performed by colleagues, a typical professional trait. The evaluation of the teacher by her clients, however, is even more difficult than with clients or patients of lawyers or doctors, because the clients are children. Now, the parents normally regard themselves as clients, too, via their children. But even though co-operation between schools and parents has expanded over the last generation (through parental committees, parent-teacher meetings, information, and so on), parents often get the impression that it is hard to evaluate the teachers. And teachers do not want too much peeking behind the scenes. It is likely that the great parental action taken in 1954 against *samnorsk* (merging the urban and rural Norwegian languages) was not only a fight about language, but also a struggle about influence and openness in schools. The struggle exemplified rather well the fact that many teachers at that stage deviated considerably from large parts of the population in terms of culture. Even town schools were amply staffed with teachers from the West, *vestlandslærere*, understood as teachers favouring rural Norwegian, possibly also being teetotallers and voting *Venstre*, all three being increasingly rare among urban Norwegians.

Independence is another characteristic of professions. Like (other) professions teachers have protected their independence at work with a good deal of success, against parents and bureaucrats in particular. Their independence vis-à-vis the ministry and school administration is partly due to the fact that the bureaucracies have recruited from the ranks of the teachers themselves. In 1940, for example, all provincial school directors [*skoledirektører*] were trained as primary school teachers. To avoid distorting the picture, one must add that teachers in several periods have felt that they have been victims of centralist governing, especially after the 1930s.

Do teachers, then, constitute a perfect profession? Far from it; if that was the case, teachers would probably enjoy more material success, middle-class success if you like. The teaching occupation has always lacked one important characteristic for a profession; it is not very hierarchical. In general, only seniority and additional education will give you a wage rise. A few teachers may achieve superior positions, such as inspectors or head masters. However, becoming a head master is (more than before) seen as leaving the ranks, like when a worker becomes a foreman (the example is not randomly chosen, as we shall see). Head masters, for example, are organised separately. Teachers, then, are not really rewarded for their efforts by advancing in a hierarchy and acquiring more money, power or prestige.

There are several reasons for this state of affairs, many of them historical. Some will say that schools have a flat social structure out of consideration for the pupils, not a very plausible explanation. The flat structure is more on account of the teachers themselves, stemming from the popular-egalitarian tradition among them. And of course the limited possibilities for evaluating their work make it hard to distinguish good teachers from bad ones.

One of the consequences of a flat structure is probably more solidarity within the group (compare the case of workers and the foreman). This is why teachers usually behave almost like workers in questions of pay and working conditions. One can hardly imagine true professions doing something as symbolically devastating as refusing to celebrate the national day with pupils unless paid overtime. But this is what their association tells the teachers to do. Individually speaking, however, teachers have little to gain in terms of advancement by working overtime, especially unpaid overtime. This is in contrast to researchers, for example.

The trade union strategy of course undermines the strength of teachers as a profession. In negotiating wages they will for example argue by stressing their similarity to a profession: 'We get paid so poorly that many of us are about to leave the profession, in spite of our dedication to it [vocation!], and the fact that the children need us badly.' There the threat appears: imagine that there would be a shortage of qualified teachers! Teachers, however, are not professionalised to the degree that education and their occupation are identical. No doctor without a licence may remove your appendix, but for want of qualified teachers, school authorities will employ people lacking formal qualifications.[38]

It also undermines their professional strength, albeit not their trade union strength, that teachers for a long time have prepared their retreat. They have realised that the occupation often becomes a 'cul-de-sac career-wise' [*karrieremessig blindgate*], as a representative expressed it as early as around 1900.[39] This is the reason why education as a primary school teacher counts as part of an undergraduate degree, so that many options remain open for teachers' college graduates. There are high school teachers [*lektorer*] who were first educated as primary school teachers, and even university professors.

Perhaps this vacillating between trade union strategy and profession-oriented tactics may contribute to the teachers' loss of status (as they themselves see it) in the last generation or two. Trade union-wise their market position is not strong enough, particularly because their employers are in the public sector not the private one. But their professional strategy also meets with resistance, among employers and in public opinion.

Ulf Torgersen has categorised what he calls the limits to professionalisation under four headings.[40] The first he calls *populism*. Some people will claim that there is no such thing as expertise in teaching. Teaching does not demand much of you; it can be carried out with a little bit of common sense, that is, if you have something to teach. The classic professions base themselves on the fact that their clients do not know the discipline. If parents think teaching is a piece of cake, while at the same time knowing much more about physics, maths, German or history than their children's teachers do, the latter are in trouble.

A populist view of pedagogy is not confined to parents, but thrives far into the domain of university employees, as we all know. The populist view of the role of the teacher is, by the way, not that far from the teachers' own view more than a hundred years ago, before the discipline of pedagogy entered their world. A good teacher earned his status by virtue of talent, experience and knowledge, not by reading books about teaching.

Torgersen's second limitation is named *innovatism*. Lots of new knowledge appears all the time, but soon becomes dated. It is simply quite impossible for a professional to possess all relevant knowledge at all times. And what is relevant knowledge? Changes in pedagogical ideas and frequent new reforms for schools therefore easily lead to sceptical attitudes towards teachers. Most probably life in the classroom shows considerable stability, but public opinion does not experience that stability.

Specialism is a third limitation to professionalism. The idea is that extreme specialisation threatens the unity of the profession. I do not know pedagogy or teachers well enough to say whether this is a real threat. There are certainly quite a few pedagogical specialities, and there are theories as how to treat pupils at various ages and stages of learning, but I doubt that specialism is a threat to the teachers.

The fourth and last limitation Torgersen calls *personalism*. The quality of the work depends on the personality of the professional. If performances at work differ too much between the professionals, this might threaten confidence in the whole profession. I think teachers easily fall prey to this limitation. While most people do not think it is highly important which accountant one uses or which doctor removes one's tonsils, quite a few would insist that the qualities of the individual teacher are important. That is to say, the formal education possessed by the individual teacher does not guarantee that the child gets the education the parents hope for. And since one can rarely choose the teacher, or effectively evaluate him or her, distrust of the profession may be the result.

Conclusion

The history of teachers up to the end of the twentieth century is a story of contrasts. The pedagogical ideas upon which the teachers built their work have had an impressive momentum in the politics of education. Late in the twentieth century the identity of the primary school teachers was taken over by high school teachers [*lektorer*] as well. Not only have the latter started to call themselves 'teachers' [*lærere*], but some claim that their foremost qualification is experience in the classroom. The greatest threat against teachers at all levels, one *lector* holds, is the attempt at 'destroying [*vingestekke*] the personality of teachers'. The enemy is identified as the school bureaucrats, who not only try to restrain the teachers, but are themselves, unlike teachers, placed in a hierarchical structure giving them higher status and more prestige.[41] It has not benefited the teachers to win the world when they have hurt themselves by falling between the two stools of unfinished trade union affiliation and half-hearted professionalism.

Notes

[1] Until fairly recently, the term teacher (*lærer*) normally referred to elementary school teachers only. Teachers in secondary schools (including the *gymnasium*) had university educations and were called *lektor* or *adjunkt*.
[2] Reidar J. Mykletun, 'Verdier og holdninger i skolen', *Bergens tidende* 1973/204, 2. September. The figures were taken from Tore Lindbekk, Utdannelse, in Natalie Rogoff Ramsøy and Mariken Vaa (eds), *Det norske samfunn*, Oslo 1968.

The full quotation in the first sentence actually reads: 'The teaching occupation in Western Europe is a middle class occupation'. However, figures are given for Norway only.
[3] The Town School Act (*Byskoleloven*) of 1848 and The Rural School Act (*Landsskoleloven*) of 1860.
[4] The farmers' movement (*bondebevegelsen*) developed into the Liberal Party (*Venstre*), which formed a cabinet several times between 1884 and 1935. The citation is from Gro Hagemann, *Skolefolk. Lærernes historie i Norge*, Oslo 1992, p. 328. I owe to Hagemann much of my knowledge of the history of Norwegian teachers.
[5] See e.g. Harold Perkin, *The Rise of Professional Society. England since 1880*, London 1990, ch. 1; Ulf Torgersen, *Profesjonssosiologi*, Oslo 1972; Ulf Torgersen, *Profesjoner og offentlig sektor*, Oslo 1994; Trond Nordby, 'Profesjoner' og 'peofesjonsmakt' som historisk emne. Om begrepsutvikling og analyseopplegg', in Sivert Langholm et al. (eds), *Den kritiske analyse*, Oslo 1994, pp. 212-228.
[6] Jan Eivind Myhre, 'Finding the middle class. Norway in a comparative perspective, 1870-1940', *Scandinavian Journal of History* 3/1994, pp. 237-249.
[7] Øyvind Østerud, 'Nytt perspektiv på hamskiftet', *Historisk tidsskrift* 2/1975.
[8] Brit Berggreen, 'De tre kulturer: søkelys på mellomklassen', *Dugnad* 1/1982, pp. 11-37.
[9] The Norwegian terms being *dannelsesborgerskap* and *næringsborgerskap*.
[10] The term is borrowed from Amatai Etzioni, according to Torgersen 1972, p. 59.
[11] Perkin 1990: especially chapters 1 and 8.
[12] Jens Arup Seip, *Utsikt over Norges historie*, vol. 1, Oslo 1974, ch. II.4; Sivert Langholm, *Elitenes valg*, Oslo 1984, ch. III. Perkin 1990, ch. 1, also makes this point.
[13] Hagemann 1992, p. 126. In this case, the text accompanying the illustrations has a separate author.
[14] Klaus Frode Solheim, *Oppfatningen av forholdet mellom samfunnsklassene slik det kom til uttrykk i stemmerettsdebattene på 1800-tallet*, MA-thesis (*hovedoppgave*) in history, University of Oslo, 1976, p. 68.
[15] O. Welde, according to Solheim 1976, p. 73.
[16] The income limit was set at 800 kroner in towns and 500 kroner in the countryside. The older, and still existing, rules gave the vote to *alle embetsmenn*, the urban burghers (having citizenship as merchants, artisans or sea captains), independent farmers or tenant farmers, or those owning houses in the towns of a certain value. From their implementation in 1814, the rules gave the vote to more than a third of all adult men.
[17] See e.g. Jan Eivind Myhre, *Barn i storbyen*, Oslo 1994.
[18] See e.g. Alfred Oftedal Telhaug and Odd Asbjørn Mediås, *Grunnskolen som nasjonsbygger. Fra statspietisme til nyliberalisme*, Oslo 2003.
[19] Kjell Bjørn Minde & Jan Ramstad, 'The development of real wages in Norway about 1730-1910', *Scandinavian Economic History Review* 2/1986, pp. 117-118.
[20] Male teachers still earned a good deal more than female teachers, who often had to rely on additional income. See Anne-Beate Hagen, *Overgangskvinner. Allmueskolelærerinner i Christiania 1860-1890 – levestandard og sosial status*, main thesis, University of Oslo 1999.
[21] Protocolls of Kristiania Bestillingsmannsforening, *Riksarkivet*, Oslo (The National Archives). *Bestillingsmann* is an older term for a lower public servant or official.
[22] Edvard Bull, Lærerhistorie, *Retten til en fortid*, Oslo 1981, p. 240.
[23] Telhaug and Mediås 2003, p. 79.

[24] Hagemann 1992, p. 101.
[25] Hagemann 1992, pp. 148-149.
[26] Torgersen 1994, pp. 194-198.
[27] Hagemann 1992, p. 119.
[28] Lindbekk 1968.
[29] Richard Hall, 'Professionalization and Bureaucratization', *American Sociological Review*, vol. 33, February 1968, pp. 92-104, according to Torgersen 1972, p. 59; Hagemann 1992, p. 245.
[30] Jan Eivind Myhre, *Hovedstaden Christiania. Oslo bys historie, bind 3 1814-1900*, Oslo 1990, ch. 4.
[31] Relatively speaking, then, the teachers are perhaps less academic than before. However, this is based on impressions, and I have no solid data.
[32] Telhaug and Mediås 2003, p. 115.
[33] NOU 1988:32 *For et lærerikt samfunn*
[34] Hagemann 1992, p. 247.
[35] The newspaper was *Dagbladet*. The articles were by Harriet Bjerrum Nielsen (February 4, March 2) and Atle Måseide (February 13, March 26).
[36] Skolesjefen: 'Ufaglærte' har ofte flere års utdannelse, *Aftenposten* 27.9.1998.
[37] Hagemann 1992, pp. 266ff.
[38] In a newspaper letter, a teacher actually compared teaching without necessary pedagogical qualifications to doing surgery without being a medical doctor. Ufaglært i skolen. Utrolig nedvurdering av læreryrket, *Aftenposten aften* 30.6.1997.
[39] Hagemann 1992, p. 120.
[40] Torgersen 1972, pp. 72ff. Some of the names seem linguistically artificial (as they do in Norwegian), but I believe they convey the right meaning.
[41] Lektor Gunhild Hoem, Lærernes lave status, *Aftenposten*, 11 August 1995.

HANNE RIMMEN NIELSEN

Gender, Class and Culture.
Danish Female Teachers, their Cultural Influence and Integration in the Local Community 1900-1950

Around 1900, village schoolmistresses represented a new element in Danish rural society: women with an education and with the economic and cultural resources to maintain an independent existence.[1] Young girls, the majority of whom came from the peasant community themselves, were given the opportunity to rise to the educated middle class. Basically, this development reflected a need in peasant society for a new type of teacher, one especially suited to teaching small children and girls cheaply.

Generally, village teachers, both male and female, were well equipped to adapt and become cultural leaders in peasant society. On the one hand, most of them were recruited from peasant society and therefore knew the prevailing social norms very well. On the other, they brought with them many new elements of urban middle-class culture that they had learned at training college. They might be seen as agents of middle-class values but they were probably successful only insofar as a real need for change existed among the peasant population.

Danish historians have debated whether the transformation of peasant culture that took place in the second half of the nineteenth century should be seen as a form of urbanisation, a 'peasant adaptation to bourgeois culture',[2] or whether this development should be seen as a transformation from within, as a development of an independent peasant culture, just borrowing urban cultural elements, but in a genuine peasant, Grundtvigian context.[3] What is clear at least is that urban, middle-class cultural elements were introduced into peasant society and that the school system played an important role in this cultural exchange.

As a new element in peasant society, the situation of female teachers was far from being easy or without danger. The basic challenge meeting these women was the necessity of achieving integration into the local community, as opposed to marginalisation or isolation. Because of their isolated situation, they could only survive, professionally and personally, if they succeeded in becoming integrated, at least to a certain extent. Of course, distinguished seclusion, that is, placing yourself in an elevated position, could be an attractive strategy for some female teachers but the costs were enormous. Normally, teachers would have to seek some kind of integration. Integration could be achieved in several ways which are discussed below: through school work, through marriage and through cultural and political activities. Each woman would try to find her own way to successful integration, leading to personal fulfilment and/or a certain social and cultural influence. Some succeeded in achieving integration and influence, others did not.

The main strategies of female teachers related to class, gender and culture. Becoming a teacher must be seen as a class strategy for improving one's situation and moving into the new educated middle class. But it was also very much a gender strategy, aimed at bettering one's material conditions and, above all, escaping the narrow and traditional limitations of a woman's role. Another common gender strategy, joining women's organisations, was very important among female teachers in towns. But in the countryside this strategy was of little use, given the isolated situation of most schoolmistresses.

Instead village schoolmistresses had to use other, more individualistic strategies. Perhaps the first and most crucial demand meeting a new teacher was the need to make herself respected as a competent and popular schoolmistress. A dutiful and understanding schoolmistress would always receive the gratitude of parishioners and at the same time possess the capacity for exerting her cultural influence. The ideal schoolmistress both expressed and contributed to spreading certain new ideas of middle class femininity.

Many schoolmistresses chose to marry, thereby trying to overcome their isolation and raise their social standing, both in a class and in a gender sense. Marrying a wealthy farmer, for example, meant improving one's social standing as well as acquiring the prestige of a married woman which was clearly superior to the status of a spinster. But marrying also involved costs, giving up the newly-won independence or the joy of teaching. On the other hand, many female teachers became pioneers in promoting new ideals of family life in the countryside.

Female teachers also sought integration and influence through participating in cultural and political activities. Even if they were not as active as male teachers, they did participate in a broad range of activities, ranging from feminist work, through church and social work, to local politics. They also propagated new ideas, introducing for example women's rights and social welfare thinking, both of which could be seen as expressions of middle class individualism.

It is not suggested that the small and relatively powerless group of female teachers made a great difference in peasant society. Nevertheless, it is an interesting question what happened when the first group of women with an education and with economic and cultural resources of their own made their entry into rural society, how they sought a balance between their own needs and ideals and the expectations of peasant society. And how new gender and middle-class values were spread and manifested in this process.

Education and social background

Even before 1880 there had been many female teachers in the countryside but our knowledge of them is inadequate and scattered. Some worked as governesses and private teachers in wealthy homes, some as teachers in private infant schools. The private infant schools belong to the nineteenth century. They took care of teaching the smallest children (7-9 years). The teachers in these schools were disabled men, widows in need of support, or young girls, usually without professional education but sometimes with a folk high school course behind them. The wages were poor and the social standing of these teachers was low. To many young girls, teaching was a temporary occupation until such time as they married. The School Act of 1867 admitted female teachers to public schools, including village schools, and a number of Acts and circulars between 1856 and 1893 regulated the organisation of private infant schools and encouraged the conversion of private infant schools into public ones.

The incorporation of female teachers into the public village school had several preconditions. First, the explosion in the number of children in the countryside in the second half of the nineteenth century was an important factor. According to the School

Act of 1856 a second teacher should be appointed when the number of children in a school exceeded 100. Following this Act, it was often decided to appoint a female teacher as a second teacher, especially for economic reasons. Secondly, the establishment of public infant schools was used as a means of shortening long distances to school. Thirdly, the appointment of a schoolmistress also represented an opportunity to introduce needlework for girls. Finally, the tendency to appoint female teachers was connected with the introduction of new pedagogical ideals, ideals that stressed the maternal faculties of schoolmistresses and their supposed special gifts for teaching the smallest children.

Both the introduction of needlework and the stress on the maternal ideal could be seen as reflections of middle-class norms making inroads into the countryside, norms that female teachers were regarded as responsible for introducing. In needlework, girls were to be taught so-called useful needlework rather than the decorative embroidery they had earlier been taught in special sewing schools. Through this they were to learn female middle-class virtues such as 'diligence, watchfulness, accuracy, patience, thrift, cleanliness, and love of order', as one of the textbooks of the period put it.[4]

Carolyn Steedman has shown how a new maternal ideal exerted its influence on the English educational system of this period. The female teacher should be like a 'mother made conscious' [Fröbel]. Among other things the ideal reflected middle-class norms of a more child-centred education. In a Danish context the pedagogical ideas of the Grundtvigian movement could be seen as pointing in the same direction.

In the 1880s a comprehensive pedagogical debate took place on the need for a special education for infant school teachers. Grundtvigian circles in particular argued for the establishment of an education that would meet the scarcity of female teachers in the countryside and at the same time introduce a special infant school pedagogy focusing on maternal care. It was emphasised as a further advantage that infant school teachers would only be entitled to low wages because of their short education. The education was for women only and for use only in village schools and in the teaching of small children under 10 years of age. The State Training College for Infant School Teachers in Vejle was founded in

1893. It was followed by several private training colleges for infant school teachers.

The education of infant school teachers was an immediate success and led to a very significant increase in the number of female teachers in village schools. Thus, in 1905 there were 606 infant school teachers and only 337 so-called permanent female teachers in village schools.[5] But this education was also met with strong resistance, especially from other female teachers and from the women's movement. They saw infant school teachers as a special teacher proletariat and feared that their bad working and economic conditions would undermine the advantages they had fought to achieve.

In the years after 1867 it had become evident that qualified female teachers (three years at college) were not interested in employment in village schools. Most of them preferred town schools where conditions of employment and wages were much better. It is also significant that the great majority of these teachers came from the higher social classes in the towns. Socially and culturally they felt alienated from life and people in the countryside. In contrast, the majority of male teachers had traditionally been recruited from the peasant population, reflecting the very different social and educational opportunities for men and women.

With the establishment of infant school colleges, a new type of female teacher was created, teachers who, like their male counterparts, were recruited from the peasant population and lower social classes. Statistics concerning the 552 students from the Training College in Vejle between 1893 and 1918 show that the large majority, 487, came from the countryside. Of the 552 Vejle students, 144 came from farmer families, 56 from smallholder families. Some 154 were from teacher families, mainly in the countryside. Most of the rest came from artisan families. Infant school teachers were quite clearly recruited from the petite bourgeoisie and the lower middle class of the countryside.[6]

The question is what this meant. First, it must have meant that the future teachers knew from their own experience what conditions were like in the countryside and could settle down more easily there than could teachers from urban, higher social classes. Secondly, you may wonder whether young girls from petit bourgeois backgrounds would be more inclined to achieve economic independence and perhaps marry, compared to girls from higher social classes?[7] This will be discussed later.

The education of infant school teachers was short (a year, later a year and a half) and cheap and it met the need of a group of peasant girls for a theoretical education on easy terms. The education could be seen as the solution to both the economic and the existential problems of a special group. The existential problem is described in several biographical texts. A moving description of the narrow possibilities of eighteenth-century peasant society can be found in the diaries and letters of the farmer's daughter Helene Dideriksen. She never had the chance to attend a college or establish a separate household, partly because of her father's opposition, partly because of advanced tuberculosis that killed her at the age of 31 in 1891. Through her participation in the folk high school and free school movement Dideriksen developed a great existential need for education and new knowledge but the economic and gender specific opportunities required to satisfy this need turned out to be tragically limited for a girl in her circumstances.

The schoolteacher and writer Bolette Sørensen (1856-1931) wrote about the special tension between 'box bed life and poetry', between native soil and longing to travel.[8] In her own life she chose the poetry and left home but at the same time she sought to maintain her attachment to peasant society through impressive efforts as a teacher, writer and organiser. In her novels, she described the old peasant society even if she had personally distanced herself from that way of living. She was both part of and outside peasant society, a particularly marginal and asynchronous mode of existence that is also characteristic of for example the regional writer Helene Strange's life history.

Travelling books[9] from two classes of infant school students (Vejle 1911, Copenhagen 1915), written over a long period of time, describe the time spent at college as the epoch-making event that transformed the lives of these women. The travelling book brought messages of 'the beautiful days of youth' and news of school friends 'who have filled our life with their personality'.[10] Annual gatherings of classes and private visits and holidays also contributed to the feeling of sharing a common history, a common destiny.

During their time at college a new world opened up for these peasant girls and they continued to remember this time with gratitude. But the travelling books also show that their new world was not without its problems. Teachers' lives were filled with challenges of an educational, private and political character. For example, many letters deal with heavy workloads, bad housing conditions, illness, and the loneliness of the single woman.

Integration – marginality

The two concepts of integration and marginality could be used to characterise the situation of female teachers in a village community. On the one hand, teachers had to seek integration in the local community. They had to do this if they were to survive, professionally and personally. On the other hand, they were often placed in a marginal or isolated situation in small, narrow village societies.

A comparison with female teachers in larger towns could be illustrative. In the towns, female teachers functioned within a larger community encompassing their work place, their political and feminist activities and their private housing arrangements. They often worked at girls' schools and in several places, such as Copenhagen and Aarhus, they had their own female teachers' union. Many of them were active in the Danish Women's Society, the YWCA and other women's organisations. Finally, many of the unmarried teachers lived together, sharing flats or houses. In another context, I have described these close working and housing communities as a special women's culture.[11]

In the countryside the situation was totally different. Here the female teacher was often the only schoolmistress within a larger geographical area. She was isolated both in her daily working situation and in her possibilities for social association with other female teachers or other educated women. Many schoolmistresses complained that they were lonely and felt isolated and some of them persistently tried to get away from the village, to get an appointment in a larger town. Only a few of them succeeded in getting away. These teachers had to seek local integration if they were to survive.

Local integration could be achieved in several ways: by obtaining recognition for being a competent and popular schoolmistress, appreciated by pupils as well as parents; by engaging in youth work, popular education and social life in the village; by making a career for oneself in local organisations or in politics. Finally, the female teacher could marry a local farmer or teacher and in this way achieve a special form of social integration. Many female teachers had the skill and good fortune required to achieve integration into the local community. But even the most successful remained stuck in a certain marginal position. They were outsiders in several ways: as newcomers, as educated women, as unmarried women, and in addition, as women with a peculiar position in public life. In some instances, success in public life could even lead to further marginalisation.

How were integration and marginalisation connected? The American historian Margaret K. Nelson offers two explanations in her treatment of village schoolmistresses in Vermont in the first half of the twentieth century. The first explanation concerns symbols of authority, the second notions of power. First, to achieve authority as community builders female teachers had to accept that they functioned as the pure embodiment, the pure symbol of education. Just as priests symbolised the spiritual life, the church, but only by assuming an especially pure or elevated position, so female teachers symbolised education or the school, but again at the cost of an especially secluded, marginal position. This marginality was necessary as a special position guaranteeing the authority of the teacher. This was particularly necessary as many teachers were young and inexperienced. They needed the authority the teacher role or the school as an institution could give them. The marginality and the demand for purity functioned also as an expectation of celibacy or immaculate moral conduct.

Secondly, the female teacher was a potentially powerful person in her local community because 'knowledge is power'. She possessed both the knowledge that is an outcome of education and the knowledge that consists in a close insight into the intimate secrets of family life. Because of this knowledge it was necessary to marginalise or contain her. One of the dangers was that she would become a model to which other women in the village community could aspire. For this reason it was necessary to marginalise her, to place her outside normal social life.

The integration and the authority were necessary in order that she could perform her duties well. But the marginality was just as necessary in order to limit her influence and prevent her from becoming a model for other women in the village. For example, in 1908 Mine Hvid (1885-1970) was appointed schoolmistress at the village school in the remote parish of Pillemark on the island of Samsø.[12] She was quickly recognised as a competent and popular schoolmistress, but privately she did not experience her new life as a success and longed for her family and for colleagues of the same standing. Several times she sought an appointment in the large city of Aarhus. In 1916 the headmaster of Pillemark retired and at about the same time a new school Act made it possible for women to be appointed as head teachers at village schools. In this situation the people of Pillemark requested Mine Hvid to apply for the post as head teacher. She got the post and became the first female head teacher at a village school. She had come as far as it was possible for a village schoolmistress to get.

As head teacher she embodied the school more than anybody else in the local community. But at the same time, she had become even more marginalised: A female head teacher was both a rarity and an anomaly. She was expected to perform the representative functions a male teacher would normally have taken care of. Furthermore, there were expectations that she should remain 'pure', even in a sexual sense. When she married in 1947, this resulted in a sudden fall from public grace, in loss of prestige, even in ridicule. As head teacher Mine Hvid possessed real power but exactly for this reason she had to be represented as a very special person, as asexual, and as somebody who could not serve as a female model.

Integration through school work – motherliness as a profession

'Miss Hansen was a schoolmistress in the true meaning of the word, a woman who was not seeking honour or duties outside the school, an understanding educator, an exceptionally conscientious school worker; Miss Hansen was loved by the small ones who had been entrusted to her care, highly esteemed by her villagers, and her school was a model school. Hardly ever was she absent for even a single hour, before the illness took her, the illness that could be called 'being worn out by her duty'. Her funeral was attended by the majority of the parishioners who in this way paid their last respects to the popular and competent schoolmistress.'[13]

'One of the pillars of the parish has fallen,' was something else they said about Sidsel Hansen, for 25 years schoolmistress in Fuglse, Lolland, who died at the age of 58 in 1929. The description of her personality and work is typical of a great number of obituaries and jubilee articles in *Folkeskolen*, the teachers' magazine. If these do not tell the whole story of a person's achievements, they do at least show us clearly what the ideal schoolmistress was like: competent, popular, loving, dutiful, modest.

In the first part of the twentieth century the typical village school had two teachers: a male head teacher and an infant school teacher who was always a woman. The male teacher taught the older children (10-14 years) and the female one the smaller children (7-10 years). She also taught needlework to all the girls in the school. In many places the school comprised only a single building, with two classrooms and two apartments, one for the head teacher and his family and one for the schoolmistress. The families lived close together and the apartment of the schoolmistress was often just a couple of rooms with a kitchen in the attic. But the main school and the infant school could also be in two separate buildings, either close to each other or separated by one or two kilometres. Instead of or in addition to the infant school teacher there could also be a male or female second teacher who ranked below the head teacher but was entitled to teach all classes and all subjects. From 1916 women could become head teachers but this happened very seldom.

The hierarchy of the teaching staff was well defined. At the top the head teacher, then the second teacher, at the bottom the infant school teacher. The male and female second teachers were regarded almost as equals. The hierarchy was visible to everybody and was expressed in terms of competence, the size of wages and the standard and size of apartments. The head teacher was regarded as an important person in the local community, ranking just below the vicar. Normally, he had important honorary offices in organisations and politics.

However, a female teacher also had the chance to achieve a certain influence and prestige. Not all female teachers refrained from seeking 'honour or duties outside the school'. But normally, it would be a crucial precondition that she had a reputation for being a competent schoolmistress and was generally liked by people. When the above-mentioned Mine Hvid succeeded in getting promoted, it was due to a coincidence of several circumstances, one of which was her own competence and skill as a teacher. 'They always said that the pupils of Miss Hvid were the best, they could become anything.' 'There were several schools over here but we were known to be the best. We had to be, Mine Hvid made it a point of honour.' 'When we came to the vicar to be prepared for confirmation, together with children from other schools, he always said: "Now let us hear the clever Pillemark children." And we normally were well prepared and he knew.'[14]

Mine Hvid is described by former pupils as demanding and strict but also as caring and with social understanding. Besides her competence it was an important prerequisite for her success that she had good personal relations with local farmers with whom she associated socially. Finally, the political situation on Samsø, with the Social-Liberal Party as the dominant party and with a farmer from Pillemark as chairman of the parish council, was crucial in preparing the way for Mine Hvid. Her appointment as head teacher in 1916 was deeply entangled in local party and power politics.

Female teachers who had had three years at college such as Mine Hvid ranked higher and could more easily assert themselves than infant school teachers. In the case of infant school teachers, the expectation of motherly behaviour was even more pronounced: 'When you read the testimonies and references you will find that the words 'practical', 'lively', 'understanding', 'conscientious', 'kind', and 'loving' were especially positive adjectives; without a practical grip on handling a group of children, an infant school teacher was badly off. And without the ability to establish a tie between herself and the small children, she would not be able to manage this kind of work. Competence was of course highly valued, but mostly in connection with a vivid narrative skill and gifts for guiding children.'[15]

One of the women who lived up to these demands was Gudrun Svedstrup (b. 1891). She graduated from the Copenhagen Infant School College in 1915 with the endorsement 'very well qualified'. Her fine reference from the training college testified that she had benefited enormously from the education she had received there. It said she had a good foundation in early years teaching and she was described as very diligent. Her contributions in teaching practice had been careful, kind and co-operative. She was good at telling stories to the children. Later references from local school authorities stressed her close relationships with the children and her popularity among parents and villagers. The education committee had been very satisfied with the achievements of her pupils at the annual examination. In short, she was a competent schoolmistress and people liked her.

Gudrun Svedstrup's letters in the travelling books show that she had a philosophical disposition. She reflected on the short time of human beings on earth, on nature, and above all on the horrors of war. She enjoyed books and the beauty of nature, and she was pleased with her school work and the children's affection for her. But she was also worried because she knew that 'school work wears you out in the long run'. She seems to have been a practical and strong-willed, yet also slightly depressive type of person.[16] When Gudrun Svedstrup retired in 1957, she was 66 years old and had taught for 50 years, a jubilee that apparently nobody felt called upon to celebrate.

Female teachers such as Gudrun Svedstrup belonged to the 'silent workers' of village schools. Their cultural roles originated directly from their school work and consisted mainly in their educational influence and their introduction of middle-class values such as hard work and the suppression of needs, as well as certain ideas of femininity. However, the femininity they represented was always ambiguous: Even if motherliness was a dominant feature of their behaviour, they also represented women's opportunities to get a theoretical education and achieve economic independence.

The concept of the ideal schoolmistress could also be examined negatively, from examples of unsuccessful teachers.[17] The complaint against the schoolmistress Christiane Fold (b. 1858) stated that 'several parents with children in the school have learned that they have been inspired with fear so that they are not accessible to learning.' Later it was reported that there was 'dissatisfaction with the schoolmistress who is thought to be too harsh, that her teaching is too mechanical, that it advances too slowly, particularly in arithmetic, and that the children are inadequately prepared to be admitted to the main school.' The case ended with the dismissal of the schoolmistress in 1913.

In another case against the schoolmistress Marie Pedersen (1872-1926), the complaint referred to her nervousness, her lack of self-control, the bad relationship between her and the male teacher at the school, and finally the general sentiment of a public meeting about school matters. Miss Pedersen, too, was accused of lacking 'the ability, with understanding and love, to take care of the small children'. The case against Miss Pedersen started in 1912 and continued for almost five years, but in the end the teacher was allowed to stay in her office. 'Incompetence' and 'harshness' were among the most common reasons for complaints and dismissals of female teachers. But it was also typical that the cases were entangled in a web of local intrigues, personal antipathy and rumours. In short, these schoolmistresses had never succeeded in becoming fully integrated into the local community.

The question of the dismissal of teachers became explosive after 1908 when the Act on Teachers' Salaries introduced a provision (§8) which stated that a teacher who 'had entered into such a bad relationship with his teaching post that the results of school activities are considerably reduced' could be dismissed on the initiative of the local authorities. The provision must be seen partly as an element in the professionalisation of schools and teachers, partly as a concession to strong, popular and political forces that for many years had demanded more local and parental influence over the management of schools. It appears from many dismissal cases that the parents' ideal was exactly the competent and loving schoolmistress.

Undoubtedly this ideal was shared by the teachers themselves. Their social background and college education had disposed them to similar ideas. Thus it was a widespread ambition among female teachers that 'her school should stand forward as the best'. From the infant school colleges they brought with them the practical, motherly approach. Essentially this moral self-regulation implied that the female teachers internalised the required norms. In this way there was no great need for dismissal cases against female teachers and in fact most cases were conducted against male teachers.

Integration through marriage

Marriage was a possible strategy of integration. By marrying a local man the female teacher would normally raise her social standing because the chosen person would usually belong to the upper or middle stratum of peasant society, and also because a married woman was ranked above a spinster in the division of labour in peasant society. In this way she would also be able to counteract the ingrained prejudices of abnormality or unwomanliness that was part of the marginalisation. Finally, a married woman, despite an almost inhuman double workload, would have far better chances of settling down and being satisfied with her life in the countryside.

In Denmark there was not, as in several other countries, any prohibition against married women working. The problem was dealt with in a number of decisions around the turn of the twentieth century and each time the Ministry of Education stuck to the position that there was nothing to prevent a married female teacher from continuing her work in a public school. On the other hand, local school authorities would be entitled to pass over an already married woman when appointing a new teacher.

According to the census of 1911, there were 724 married female teachers and 426 widows employed in elementary education in Denmark. This means that just under 9 per cent of the teachers were married and 5 per cent were widows. In 1930, 12 per cent of the female primary school teachers were married, in 1940 24 per cent. The great leap in the number of married teachers happened in the 1930s, despite the fact that the campaign against married women's work reached its peak at exactly the same time. Consequently, the campaign was not effective, but probably the true facts of the case were that the campaign was started *because of* the rise in the number of married women while many male breadwinners were unemployed. In 1960, 56 per cent of female teachers in the countryside were married.[18]

The census of 1930 informs us whom female teachers married. About half the schoolmistresses (700) married teachers. The rest mainly married self-employed people and white-collar workers in trade, craft and industry. In the countryside in particular there were two large groups, the teachers and the farmers.

These figures raise the question under what circumstances it was appropriate for a married village schoolmistress to continue to work. First, it is obvious that everybody looked favourably upon widows as teachers. Before the First World War, teaching was one of the few means of self-support for single middle-class women. Secondly, it was sometimes convenient for a school to be looked after by a couple and there are examples of advertisements requesting the appointment of a married teaching couple. Thirdly, it was often pointed out that married female teachers would be steadier or more settled than unmarried women who would be inclined to move when offered higher wages and urban conditions. Fourthly, there are accounts of popular opinion accepting that a married schoolmistress should continue to work simply on the basis of her strong inclination for school work. Fifthly and generally, it seems that if a female teacher was broadly respected and popular, villagers would prefer to keep her, even if she married. The precondition was that she married a local man. Female teachers who had to move in connection with marriage might have great difficulty in finding a new job. As mentioned above, it was not permissible to dismiss a teacher who married. But in the countryside public opinion could be a forceful factor and very difficult to defy if people did not want the schoolmistress to stay.

To throw further light on this problem, it is necessary to examine the group who married and gave up their jobs. The investigation of 552 students from the Infant School College in Vejle between 1893 and 1918 shows what happened to students after college. Some 352 worked at public and private schools and 26 had died. A total of 178 or 32 per cent of the students had married. Of course, in 1918 the youngest of the women might yet marry at a later date. As regards the group educated before 1910, as many as 40.5 per cent had married. We are not told exactly how many of the 178 continued to work but it appears from the total number of employed and from the individual biographies that the majority stopped working. For example, only one continued to work of the nine married from the 1894 class. Of eleven married from the 1910 class only two went on working.

According to the investigation, it was not surprising that so many teachers married. This reflected 'what is generally said, that is, that many infant school teachers married.' Implied in this was also that the majority of female teachers with the longer education did not marry. This is confirmed by other sources and probably reflects the different economic and mental conditions of the two groups. Infant school teachers had less to lose and a lot to gain from marrying. The implication is that many of these teachers chose to stop working or quietly accepted such an option.

This conclusion is sustained through a reading of the travelling books from two infant school colleges. When the teacher Anna Høy married a local farmer and widower with three children in 1933, there was apparently no argument or doubt that she had to leave her teaching post. She found that it was 'strange to let go of her work' and very sad to say goodbye to her small pupils. But when she gave birth to a son the following year (at the age of 44!) all doubt and sadness evaporated. Anna Midtgaard, as she was now called, described herself as a very privileged woman who had been allowed to experience a late and unexpected happiness. It is also very striking that all her unmarried college friends expressly stated how lucky they considered her to be. The writers in the travelling books clearly regarded marriage as the favoured state. Having a 'real' home was contrasted with the loneliness, illnesses and nervous disorders of the unmarried teachers.[19]

The question is in what sense marriage functioned as integration. Looking at the large group of female teachers marrying local teachers, farmers and artisans and giving up their jobs, this was a process that in fact obliterated the professional identity of the teacher and made her into a housewife. Yet the process was not complete, as many of these women became unusually active in organisational and political work. They had at their disposal two important resources, first their own educational backgrounds, secondly the social prestige of their husbands. The married former-teachers were at one and the same time a well-integrated and organisationally active group.

The case is more complex if we turn to teachers who tried to combine marriage and school work. In peasant society it was the rule that women worked and, like farm work, teaching was accepted as women's work. So it was not necessarily wrong for a married teacher to work. The precondition was that she was able to manage both teaching and housework. There are examples of complaints against female teachers whose school work allegedly suffered from their household duties.[20]

Conversely, the teacher was also judged by her ability to take care of her own children and housework in an adequate way. Before 1919 there were no special provisions regulating maternity leave for teachers or other civil servants. The norm was four weeks' leave and the teacher had to pay her substitute out of her own wages. The Act on Teachers' Salaries of 1919 introduced regulations for maternity leave and the rule was now six weeks' leave, against giving up half of the salary.

Many married teachers had maids so that child care and housework were not necessarily overwhelming tasks, or at least any more overwhelming than they are today. The problem was above all an ideological one. Was the working teacher able to look after her children properly? And how should the relationship between the spouses be? An old-fashioned complementary relationship or a modern companionate marriage? These questions were the subject of a debate between two village schoolmistresses in 1913.[21]

Rigmor Vigild (b. 1881) had as a young woman worked as an infant school teacher but she had resigned her teaching post when marrying a teacher at the same school in 1905. Over the years she had six children. The other participant in the debate, Lilly Plet (b. 1883), had also worked as a teacher before marrying. When she married she made the 'sacrifice' of giving up her teaching post. One of the reasons was that there was already a schoolmistress employed at her husband's school. Later, when this schoolmistress left, the villagers requested Lilly Plet to apply for the post. She did so and got the job. She too had children (we are not told how many) and a maid to look after them.

The fundamental attitude of Rigmor Vigild was that it was not possible for 'any woman to be at the same time a competent teacher and a fine mother for many years, as the present demands are on a permanently employed teacher and a dutiful mother with more than one child.' The schoolmistress who married should give up her work unconditionally for the sake of her children. Rigmor Vigild would not go as far, though, as to forbid the work of married teachers. The women themselves ought to regulate their behaviour. She described herself as an ardent supporter of the women's cause and the chairman of the local branch of the Danish Women's Society. In fact, Rigmor Vigild is a good example of those married former teachers who actively engaged in public life.

Lilly Plet was of the opinion that a woman should be allowed to choose to give up her job or go on working when she married. Personally, she had preferred to continue working. She felt that she was able to manage her housework as her salary allowed her to hire a maid. She described her life as greatly satisfactory: 'Madam, if you knew what satisfaction it gives me to be the colleague of my husband, to have the time after school to go for a long walk with my husband and my children. Then, when the children are put to bed, we old people (I am 30) are in a wonderful mood to study for a couple of hours at the office. We discuss the burning questions of our time or we take turns at reading aloud for the grown-up members in the home.'

The question was whether the woman could primarily fulfil herself through motherhood, or whether she had several identities as working woman, mother, wife and citizen. Both the cult of motherhood and companionate marriage were recent phenomena, originating from middle-class ideology. According to Rigmor Vigild, 'most men' wanted their wives to concentrate fully on performing their tasks as wives, mothers and housewives. This idea of the complementary, in fact unequal, marriage seems old-fashioned. But the core of her thinking was the cult of motherhood and this was a modern idea. Lilly Plet's example points towards the much discussed companionate marriage of the 1920s and 1930s. Companionate marriage was based on the spouses' equality in a community of work and thought. Teacher couples were pioneers in promoting the new ideal of marriage, most noticeably in Copenhagen and other large cities. But as this example from the countryside shows, young working couples everywhere would tend to practise equality in marriage relations. In this way married female teachers and their husbands could function as important models for others. From the perspective of class, you could say that the cult of motherhood was characteristic of the petite bourgeoisie whereas companionate marriage rather represented the ideals of the educated middle class. The central role of the mother in the petite bourgeoisie probably reflected the fact that she bore and reared the next generation for the family enterprise. In the educated middle class, child rearing became in a way subordinated to the sexual and intellectual needs of spouses.

Married female teachers were often forceful personalities and in some cases they would achieve prominent positions, respected for their personal qualities. One example was Marie Askgaard, who with 'unyielding force and energy' taught for more than 25 years, while at the same time raising 11 children. Another example was Nicoline Nielsen Dahl who taught at the same school as her husband and after his death was requested to take over his post as head teacher. Not only did she replace her husband as head teacher, she also took over his many honorary offices.[22] Even if married female teachers were a rather small group, they attract our attention because these women were a new element in peasant society, an element pointing towards modern society.

Integration through political and cultural activities

You might wonder whether the invisibility of female teachers reflected an actually insignificant role in the cultural and political life of local society. It is a fact that female teachers were generally overshadowed by the male teachers and that many of them were not really interested in undertaking public duties. But a large group were in fact active in various fields and the pattern of their activities might tell us something about on the one hand the schoolmistresses' role as community builders, and on the other hand the conditions of women's political work in the countryside generally.

From biographical reference works it is possible to get a certain impression of the extent of female teachers' activities and the most important fields of work.[23] No doubt, these works underestimate the total extent of activities, partly because they mainly include chairmanships and not rank-and-file memberships, partly because there are gaps, oversights and omissions in the communications of the informants. The *Reference Work of Danish Teachers*

(1933-34), which is the most comprehensive and informative of the works, is used as a starting point for the following discussion.

It appears that female teachers were elected primarily to the following public boards: parochial church councils and child-welfare committees, and to a lesser extent relief committees and town councils/parish councils. The general pattern was that female teachers concentrated on social policy tasks, church work, the women's movement, and cultural and educational activities. But there were also women who moved into male domains, as for example local and party politics. And I have found several examples of tasks and offices of a more unconventional kind, such as in smallholders' organisations, village halls, and local newspapers. One schoolmistress was the accountant for a fishing sales corporation, another ran a meteorological station.

On average the women undertook fewer tasks and offices than the male teachers. In the countryside female teachers were primarily active in church and social work, whereas the sphere of action of male teachers was broader and included political and economic offices (for example in parish councils, local party organisations, co-operative societies, dairies, and savings banks). One explanation for these differences could be that the genders encountered different local expectations. Another possible explanation is that schoolmistresses were socialised into being more reluctant to undertake public tasks and offices.

It is instructive to compare village schoolmistresses with two other groups, first female teachers in the towns, secondly farmers' wives. Female teachers in the towns were part of effective women's networks. Through their activities in the women's movement they achieved a certain success at the municipal elections in 1909 (the first elections with votes for women) at which 127 women were elected, including at least 22 female teachers. Most of the female teachers (18) were elected in towns. Even if the farmers' wives did not play a major political role, they were quite successful at the first elections to public relief committees in 1908. At these elections women's representation in the countryside was as high as 36 per cent.[24] The position of farmers' wives in relief committees can be seen as a counterpart to the dominant position of farmers in parish councils. Female teachers in the countryside had access to neither effective women's networks nor class networks and so were seriously handicapped.

The following discussion examines the opportunities that the female teachers did have and tries to evaluate the results of their work, seen in relation to their own integration and influence, as well as the development of local society as such. On the basis of archival material, three cases are examined, each of which focuses on the career of a number of individual schoolmistresses.

The first case focuses on a group of female teachers who, through a broad involvement in trade union work, the women's movement and local politics, achieved a respected and powerful position, both in the local community and in broader organisational contexts. They were the most *feminist* among the teachers, active in a broad spectrum of women's organisations.

When Lucie Jensen (1862-1935) was elected as the first village schoolmistress to be on the executive committee of the Association of Danish Teachers in 1909, it was neither a coincidence nor a surprise that the choice fell on her. She knew from her own experience about the hard and changing conditions of village schoolmistresses. After her teacher education she became schoolmistress in a small village, first at the private infant school from 1889 to 1891, then at the public infant school from 1891 to 1900, and finally she secured a post as second teacher in the same parish from 1900. Her own experiences with bad housing conditions, long hours and low pay prompted her to start a battle to improve the conditions of village schoolmistresses. From 1906 she was active in trying to organise the village schoolmistresses on Funen, writing letters to *Folkeskolen* and running for election to the executive committee of the Association of Danish Teachers. She was not elected in 1906 but she and her Funen colleagues continued their struggle. In 1909 she spoke about 'The Demands of the Village Schoolmistresses' at the ordinary educational meeting in Copenhagen. The same year she was elected to the executive committee of the Association of Danish Teachers and was a member from 1910 to 1919. She was one of the founders of the League of Village Schoolmistresses in 1910 and was the chairman of the Relief Fund of Female Teachers from 1910. In 1909 she was the only woman appointed to the state commission concerning the supervision of schools. She seems to have been generally liked and respected, including among male colleagues, because of her energetic work and upright character. Besides her extensive trade union work, she was also active in local, social and political contexts. She was the co-founder and chairman from 1908 to 1912 of the local branch of the Danish Women's Society. She was also elected chairman of the public relief committee in her municipality in 1908. Like many active female teachers, she was inspired by a strong social commitment to the poor and weak, both among teachers and in peasant society.

Lucie Jensen's strategy can be described as an effort to mobilise a women's network for herself and village schoolmistresses. Her most important contribution was her effort to organise village schoolmistresses and improve their living conditions. Locally she also contributed to organising and raising the consciousness of women in the crucial phase of the battle for female suffrage and full civil rights. Her appointment as chairman of the relief committee showed that she enjoyed the confidence of local people. More generally, she might be seen as one of the many women who made an important, yet unnoticed contribution to shaping local social politics in the transitional stage from philanthropy to the welfare state. She resigned from her teaching post in 1919 and moved to the nearest town, perhaps evidence that she preferred to live in a larger town despite her apparently successful integration into a village community.

Marie Hansen (1872-1951) made a similar contribution to the organisation of infant school teachers. She was the first infant school teacher elected to the executive committee of the Association of Danish Teachers in 1915. She was aggressive in style and far from loved by other groups of female teachers or male teachers. But she did excellent work for her own group and had a considerable share in the work of mobilising and consciousness-raising among infant school teachers. She too rose to local leadership positions, among other things as chairman of the child-welfare committee in her municipality. She founded a branch of the National League of Woman Suffrage and was one of the first women elected to the executive committee of the Danish Temperance Society. Marie Hansen resigned from her teaching post when she married and moved to a larger town in 1919. Her husband was A.C. Mortensen, a newspaper editor and Social Democratic member of parliament. But even as an older woman, she seems to have been restlessly active in organisations and public life in her local community.

Many other success stories like those of Lucie Jensen and Marie Hansen could be told. Generally, female teachers were a very active and numerous group in both the Danish Women's Society and the suffrage organisations. This was particularly the case in larger towns, but also to a certain extent in the countryside. Many local branches of the Danish Women's Society were started with the local schoolmistress as the driving force and first chairman. Activities in the women's movement often went hand in hand with trade union work among schoolmistresses. The women's cause and trade union politics were seen as two sides of the same coin, as part of the same struggle for the emancipation of women. Finally, several women in this resourceful group were also active in social work or local politics.

At a personal level, these women achieved a respected and sometimes powerful position in organisations and local communities. They established a social network around themselves, thereby overcoming isolation. These women did not lack self-confidence. The picture you get is that they wanted or accepted a public role, that they stuck to their rights and could be tough negotiators. But their relations with other women were often characterised by close and affectionate feelings.

The second case deals with those female teachers who were active in *church and social work*, primarily in local contexts. Motivated by their Christian faith and social commitment, these women made impressive, often prolonged contributions to philanthropic societies and public social boards.

Two schoolmistresses and colleagues in the same village exemplify typical careers of this group. Nicoline Rasmussen (b.1866) came to the parish in 1893 and taught at a somewhat remote infant school until 1936, that is, for more than 40 years. Laura Boeskov (b. 1870) was employed at the other school in the parish in the period between 1901 and 1935. Both schoolmistresses 'survived' a number of male head teachers and the very duration of their employment and efforts obviously contributed to the strong and independent positions they reached.

The activities of Rasmussen were characterised by great continuity and faithfulness. For example, she became the leader of the Sunday school as early as 1893 and continued at this post for more than 40 years. When the Act on foster children came into force in 1895, she was attached to the supervisory committee of foster children, an office she kept till 1933 when a new Act on child welfare was passed. Beginning in 1898, she taught at evening classes for young girls for many years. Furthermore, she was a member of the regional committee for the Christian Association for Home and School from 1906 till the 1930s. Finally, she was a frequent and active participant in the meetings of the local branch of the teachers' association.

The activities of Boeskov took place in somewhat different, but related contexts. She was a member of the first child-welfare committee according to the new Act on child-welfare committees of 1905. This office she kept till 1917. In that year she was elected to the public relief committee and was a member from 1917 to 1925, and its chairman from 1921 to 1925. She was also a member of the parochial church council for many years and had a number of organisational posts. For example she was a member of the committee of the local nursing association which had hired a nurse to take care of the sick people of the parish. She was a co-founder of the local temperance society and a co-founder and manager of the parish library (established in 1905). For a number of years she assembled the young girls for reading and recreation and she also held women's meetings as part of missionary work. Boeskov, too, was active in the teachers' association and a member of the committee from 1919 to 1920.

The sources for the information on the social work of these two women are the surviving minute books of the supervisory committee of foster children, the child-welfare committee, the relief committee, and the parish council. It is far from being an easy task to examine women's work in local boards of social work. For one thing, the material is scattered and often of a primitive nature. Secondly, the individuals are not particularly visible in the material. For example, it appears from the minute book of the supervisory committee of foster children that Nicoline Rasmussen paid frequent visits to foster homes and that her evaluations of the homes were often critical. No doubt she was zealous in what she did but it is almost impossible to determine how she was regarded by the unmarried mothers she controlled. Former pupils have described her as a somewhat strict and awe-inspiring lady.

The cases taken up by these boards were often difficult and sad. The preliminary investigations included among other things visits to the homes of clients. The teachers often knew the clients from school work and were able to exploit this knowledge. In this way they could achieve important insights as well as a certain power. Thus, memberships of public boards placed the two teachers in a central position in local social work. They were typical by virtue of their Christian and social commitments, their broad and varied contributions, and impressive continuity in their work. Through their contributions, they also achieved personal advantages. They won the respect of their contemporaries and achieved a strong integration in local community. But their contributions were made quietly and left few traces. At a personal level, they solved their family needs in ways that were also typical. Nicoline Rasmussen took a foster daughter into her home and Laura Boeskov lived with her sister who ran the house.

Honorary offices on social boards often functioned as stepping stones to proper political careers. Most did not go that far. But almost as a universal rule, the first women elected to town and parish councils and to parliament had previously been members of local social boards.

The third case deals with a little group that moved into a traditionally male domain, *municipal politics*, and became members of parish councils. In a very few instances female teachers were also elected to the Danish parliament from 1918.

According to the English historian Patricia Hollis, municipal politics was exactly the field where women's philanthropic or social work and their feminist involvement in the struggle for woman suffrage converged. In municipal politics women wanted to realise both goals of social policy and feminist hopes of political rights and influence. At the first municipal elections (with votes for women) in 1909 a notable group of at least 22 female teachers were elected, most of them in towns. In the countryside very few women were elected, most of them farmers' wives. As late as 1950 the percentage of women in parish councils was only 3 (compared to 12 per cent in towns and 27 per cent in Copenhagen). In 1966 the percentage of women members in the countryside was 9. Work in parish councils was clearly regarded a male monopoly and it required strong personalities and effective women's networks to get access to these councils. This state of things reflected partly a complementary ideology of gender, partly economic and power realities. As the women themselves pointed out, it was the parish councils that controlled the purse. Women were allowed to display their skills in the field of social policy but only within the economic limits set by the men in the parish councils. To get a share in real power, the power to reform social politics and school matters for example, women had to fight to get access to municipal councils, to party machines, and to parliament. But very few women had the courage or drive needed to go that far.

Already at the first municipal elections in 1909 a few female teachers were elected to parish councils. One of them was Thora Nielsen (1873-1951) who was a Social Democrat and a parish councillor from 1909 to 1913. The facts known about her life and political activities are very few, we only know that her career as a teacher was long and successful. She was celebrated at her 25th anniversary in 1927 and again in 1942 when she resigned after 40 years of teaching. In both cases her ability to understand and take care of small children was stressed and it was said in 1942 in the speech of the chairman of the education committee that she had been 'unequalled' in her calling.[25]

Laura Markmann (b. 1891), who was elected to the parish council of her municipality in 1929, seems to have been an unusually resourceful woman. Glimpses of her activities appear from the travelling books of the class of 1911 from the Training College in Vejle. Her classmates wrote in their letters of their great admiration for her great energy and many activities. After teacher education she continued to study and took courses in areas such as domestic science, English and physical education. Gymnastics was also one of her great interests and the occasion of many travels, both in Denmark and abroad. She was an instructor of gymnastic teams for young girls and was also active in the local lecture society. Apparently she managed an incredible amount of work. Besides her 40 hours of weekly teaching, she was, for example, the deputy chairman of the local branch of the Danish Women's Society. She was one of the driving forces behind the founding of the

League of Infant School Teachers in the region and was also a member of the committee of the local branch of the teachers' association.

Laura Markmann's career in municipal politics began when she was elected to the public relief committee in 1925. In 1929 she was elected to the parish council, representing the Social-Liberal Party as did many feminist female teachers. She lived with another woman, a living arrangement very common among female teachers, but less common in the countryside than in towns. Around 1930 the couple were the happy owners of a car, a very modern phenomenon according to her classmates. A car was a means of mobility and so of overcoming isolation in the countryside. In 1957 she was the only teacher left from the class of 1911 who was still teaching. She was still tirelessly energetic, for example participating in the work of the Missionary Society of Female Teachers, an organisation supporting the sending out of female teachers as missionaries.

Ingeborg Lindby (1907-99) was elected to the parish council of her municipality in 1950 as its first woman member. She represented the Liberal Party and was a member until 1963. For 36 years (1934-70) she lived 'a plain and toilsome life' as an infant school teacher. She grew up in the area and it seems that she became deeply rooted in the local community. For example, she arranged reading evenings for housewives for 31 years, went on bicycle rides with the oldest school children, and was an organist in church. Her relationships with neighbours and parents was excellent, and in her own words, she developed a very strong sense of 'belonging' to school and neighbourhood over the years.[26] Regarding women and municipal politics, there were few changes from 1909 to the 1950s. Still, only a very few resourceful women were able to overcome the strong barriers against women's involvement in local politics.

Feminist struggle, social work, and local politics, three different ways of displaying a commitment to public affairs, and at the same time ways of achieving or consolidating local integration. Elections to local, honorary offices were both signs that teachers were respected and means of achieving further insight and influence on local matters.

Conclusion

The cultural influence of these female teachers, its extent and character, is not easy to evaluate. On a structural level, it is important to realise that the institution of the infant school lacked prestige and that infant school teachers saw themselves and were seen by others as a proletariat among teachers. This weakened the possibilities of this group and it is clear that female teachers with the longer education were far better equipped for achieving prestige and influence. On the individual level, however, things may have looked different. As active individuals, a number of strategies were at the disposal of teachers when they tried to achieve integration and influence.

One group of teachers almost abstained from public activities. They asserted themselves primarily through their conscientious work in school. These teachers were often respected but their personal influence was limited to their educational efforts and status as role models. By representing certain pedagogical models, especially the ideal of the competent and motherly teacher, they may have contributed to propagating new middle class norms in the countryside. As professional women, they personified new opportunities, new images and ideals of women in peasant society. More generally, a teacher's competence and popularity was also the basic precondition when she aspired to public offices outside school.

Female teachers who married were probably the most successful in fulfilling ambitions of integration and a good life. Because of the possibility of hiring domestic servants, women's dual roles were not necessarily harder then than they are today. Married teachers, too, introduced a modern ideal of woman, the married working woman. But in peasant society this ideal was not as new or controversial as it was in the urban middle class, for example. Married female teachers were among the most successful in public life and a special group, the married former teachers, were sometimes capable of exploiting their resources in conspicuous ways.

The organisational and political activities of female teachers present a varied picture. The most numerous and most accepted group were the Christian and socially committed teachers. You could argue that these teachers, together with other socially committed women in local communities, have played a greatly overlooked, but nevertheless important part in the creation of the modern welfare society. They were the infantry of philanthropy and social politics who introduced and adapted social policy to local conditions, often under difficult circumstances.

Those involved in trade union and feminist work constituted a kind of elite among female teachers. Their main contribution was that they were active in obtaining better material conditions for schoolmistresses. Better conditions meant higher prestige and increased scope for action. Many in this resourceful group were also active in local politics. On the whole, they displayed an impressive, broad-spectrum commitment. Much the same is true of the last group, the local politicians, who had to overcome powerful barriers in order to move into the predominantly male domain that the parish councils constituted. In addition to their direct influence through political work, this group is also important because it contributed to changing perceptions of what women can do. The breakthrough for women's political representation came as late as the 1970s and 1980s but the first women in local politics had done important preliminary work.

Finally, it is important to emphasise the differences between different generations of female teachers which can be seen as stages in the development of modern middle-class femininity. The oldest teachers (born before 1860) were often not formally qualified but recruited directly from the peasantry, typically with a course at a folk high school as an intermediate station. These women were difficult to organise because of their scattered and isolated situations. From the end of the 19th century a process of professionalisation began, involving among other things demands for formal teacher training. This was also the start of a very difficult process of organisation for female teachers. This generation of teachers (born 1860-1890) was often very active in women's organisations and primarily took an interest in church matters, social work and the women's movement. The third generation (born 1890-1920) had lives and careers that are more recognisable from a contemporary perspective. They were more likely to marry and the tendency was that they preferred to work in contexts involving both men and women. Some of them made brilliant political careers for themselves but of course this was still the exception. For most female teachers the reality was still 'a plain and toilsome life' in the village school.

Notes

[1] This essay is a revised version of my paper 'Danish Female Teachers, their Cultural Influence and Integration in the Local Community 1900-1950', presented at the Third Conference on the Middle Class in the Nordic Countries, in Helsinki 21-23 April 1995. In the essay references are kept to a minimum and interested readers are referred to the original paper for further documentation. Most names of geographical localities are omitted as they are presumably of interest only to Danish readers. A shortened version of the essay has been published in Adda Hilden and Grethe Ilsøe (eds), *Veje at vandre* [Roads to Follow], Roskilde 2003.

[2] Palle Ove Christiansen, 'Peasant adaptation to bourgeois culture. Class formation and cultural redefinition in the Danish countryside', *Ethnologica Scandinavica,* 1978; Bjørn 1988, p. 410.

[3] The clergyman N.F.S. Grundtvig (1783-1872) gave his name to the Grundtvigian movement, a popular, religious and cultural movement with a strong influence on the peasant population. A bright Christian faith and an educational programme founded on national and historical traditions were some of the elements of the movement. The Grundtvigian movement served as the starting point for an extensive private school sector comprising free schools and folk high schools. Grundtvigian pedagogy, which stressed among other things the free development of the child, became influential also in the public school system.

[4] The quotation is from Minna Kragelund, *Opdragende håndarbejde.* [Educational Needlework], PhD thesis, Copenhagen 1989, p. 192.

[5] According to *Statistiske Meddelelser* [Statistical Information] 1908, p. 242, the 1,208 female teachers in the countryside were: 337 permanent female teachers, 606 infant school teachers, 64 private infant school teachers, 185 winter teachers and 16 other teachers. Not all the permanent female teachers had a formal teacher education. In 1905 female teachers constituted a quarter of the total number of teachers in the countryside, in 1941 a third and in 1965 a little more than half.

[6] The fathers' occupations were: teacher 154, farmer 144, smallholder 56, artisan 93, white-collar worker 32, grocer 20, worker 6, fisherman or sailor 15, clergyman 5, other occupation 27. P. Elmquist, *Statens Forskoleseminarium Vejle 1893-1918* [The State Training College for Infant School Teachers Vejle 1893-1918], Vejle 1918, p. 108.

[7] Dina M. Copelman ('A new comradeship between men and women' in Jane Lewis (ed.), *Labour and Love.* Oxford 1986) has argued for this connection between social background and lifestyle as regards English female teachers, especially in London.

[8] Inger-Lise Hjordt-Vetlesen, 'Alkoveliv og poesi' [Bed box life and poetry], in J. Holmgaard (ed.), *Det grundtvigske bondemiljø* [The Grundtvigian Peasant Life and Culture], Ålborg 1981.

[9] Travelling books were books that circulated around a group of classmates, constantly being passed from one to another over and over again, with each contributing to it before passing it on to the next. This would go on for years.

[10] Kristine Ejstrup, 3 April 1957, in the travelling book of the class from Vejle 1911.

[11] Hanne Rimmen Nielsen, 'Troende og dygtige lærerinder' [Christian and Competent Schoolmistresses], PhD thesis, Århus 1990; and Hanne Rimmen Nielsen, ' Christian and competent schoolmistresses' in Tayo Andreasen (ed.), *Moving on. New Perspectives on the Womens Movement.* Århus 1991.
[12] Hanne Rimmen Nielsen, 'Mine Hvid, Samsø', *Den jyske Historiker* [The Jutlandian Historian], vol. 62, 1993.
[13] *Folkeskolen* [The Folk School], 1929, p. 385.
[14] Interviews with former pupils of Miss Hvid, cited in Nielsen 1993, p. 79.
[15] Adda Hilden and Erik Nørr, *Lærerindeuddannelse* [Female Teacher Education], Odense 1993, pp. 195-196.
[16] Travelling books of the class from Copenhagen 1915.
[17] The following examples of dismissal cases are from my unpublished 1995 article, 'Teacher dismissals and local conflicts in Danish schools, 1900-1933', in Kate Rousemaniere, Kari Dehli and Ning de Coninck-Smith (eds), *Discipline, Moral Regulation and Schooling. A Social History,* New York and London 1997. The cases mentioned below are in the Archives of the Ministry of Education, cases no. AO 2650 and AO 2947.
[18] Census figures in *Statistisk Tabelværk* [Statistical Tables] 1914, 1935, 1949, 1964.
[19] Travelling book of the class from Copenhagen 1915, 12 October 1933, 24 October 1933, 10 November 1933, 17 February 1934, 12 July 1934, 11 February 1935.
[20] Two cases of complaint are referred to in my unpublished 1995 article, 'Teacher dismissals and local conflicts in Danish schools, 1900-1933'. The cases are in the Archives of the Ministry of Education, AU 1733 & 2461/1921 and 2157/1922.
[21] *Folkeskolen,* 1913, pp. 286-287, 399-400, 433-434, 548-549. See also the memoirs of Rigmor Vigild: *Nogle korte - maaske foreløbige – Optegnelser* [Some short - maybe provisional - records], Aarup 1940.
[22] *Folkeskolen,* 1917, p. 59, 1919 p. 582.
[23] The following works are used: *Dansk Skolestat* [Directory of Danish Teachers], vols. 1-4 1933-34; Elmquist 1918; *Danmarks Kommunale Forvaltning* [The Municipal Administration of Denmark], vols. 1-11 1928-30; *Kvindernes Aarbog* [Women's Yearbook], 1912; *Danske Kvinders Aarbog* [Danish Women's Yearbook], 1947. Dansk Skolestat has information on approximately 5,700 female and 8,000 male teachers in primary schools.
[24] *Statistiske Meddelelser,* De kommunale Valg i Marts 1909 [The municipal election of March 1909], 1909 p. 105. *Tidsskrift for Forsørgelsesvæsen og Filantropi* [Journal of Public Care and Philanthropy], 1908, pp. 225-237.
[25] *Folkeskolen,* 1927 p. 339, 353; 1942 pp. 777, 895; *Venstres Folkeblad, Ringsted og Omegn* [The Popular Newspaper of the Liberal Party for Ringsted and District] 26 April 1927, 23 November 1942.
[26] Ingeborg Lindby, 'Et jævnt og virksomt liv som lærerinde i Hvilsted' [A plain and toilsome life as a teacher in Hvilsted], in Gerda Reppke (ed.), *Fire sogne omkring Solbjerg* [Four Parishes around Solbjerg], vol. 1, 1979, pp. 67-71.

JØRGEN SMIDT-JENSEN

Retailers in a Danish Town: The Streets of Århus 1860-1900

Introduction

An early portrait of the retailers of Århus in the 1850s delineates them as merchants with 'low-ceilinged business offices [and] insignificant old fashioned shops [where] ... the economic history of the town was written in these years.'

This may be quite a representative illustration of the provincial towns at the middle of the nineteenth century when the retailers were still a minor social group. The merchants were the dominant element of the commercial world, and the large merchants' houses still formed a characteristic part of the street scene near the town gates. But during the second half of the nineteenth century the group of retailers, both in Århus and in other Danish provincial towns, was radically changed. The number of shopkeepers proliferated, and new categories of retailers appeared in new quarters of the towns. If in the first half of the nineteenth century retailers had been characterised by a certain degree of homogeneity, in the 1890s they were conversely characterised by their differences in economic and social conditions as well as in social identification.[1]

A more adequate portrait of the economic and social conditions of the great majority of the retailers in the second half of the nineteenth century than the quotation above can be seen in the minutes of the administration of tobacconist Christian Jensen's bankrupt estate (1877): 'Jensen has dealt in cigars and tobacco etc. without having a trade licence and justifies himself by saying that he has not been able to gather together enough money for the licence and the stamp duty. It is this trade that has made him go bankrupt, while he has not been practising his profession (as a moulder) in the last half year.' Several similar reports indicate the emergence of a large group of retailers beside the wealthy merchants. This new group of retailers apparently had nothing in common with the merchants except that their rooms were presumably low-ceilinged too.

This essay is an analysis of the economic development and social composition of the group of shopkeepers in Århus in the four decades from the passage of the Trades Act in 1857 to the turn of the century. The aim is to demonstrate the economic and social diversity among the shopkeepers, and to analyse the relationship between their political attitudes and their social and economic positions including the types, sizes and locations of their businesses.[2] You can assume the shops of the working-class districts to be smaller and less specialised than shops in socially heterogeneous areas, and you can assume the larger and more specialised shops to be situated in districts largely dominated by a middle- and upper-class population where purchasing power was greater and consumer demands more varied. The essay will concentrate on the retailers of four streets of the town: Fiskergade, Mejlgade, Sjællandsgade and Søndergade. These four streets do not make up a strictly representative section of the streets of Århus, but each typifies one of the four different neighbourhoods of the town.

Mejlgade and Fiskergade are both old streets with relatively heterogeneous buildings, large and small houses mixed together. They represent the pre-industrial town which was not yet divided into residential quarters, and where the population was socially as heterogeneous as the buildings. Yet Mejlgade was a street with the character of being one of the principal streets of Århus with a large number of merchants' houses and a relatively large number of retailers and master artisans among the residents. Still a relatively large proportion of the residents were workers: 25 per cent at the beginning of the 1860s. At the end of the century this rate had decreased. Fiskergade was one of the less fashionable streets of the older part of Århus. The workers amounting to 40 per cent of the residents were the largest section of the population in 1860 and even increased their share in the last decades of the century, when the town was split up into residential quarters.

In contrast to these two streets, Søndergade and Sjællandsgade represent the new dynamic industrial town that is divided into several different residential quarters. The first houses in Sjællandsgade were erected in the 1850s, and right from the beginning it was a working-class street. Throughout the entire period workers made up more than 80 per cent of the population. This makes Sjællandsgade typical of the large number of working-class streets that grew up in the outlying districts of the town, partly around Sjællandsgade to the north of the centre, and partly on Frederiksbjerg to the south. Just like Sjællandsgade, Søndergade was built from the 1850s onwards. Originally the street was inhabited by quite a varied population: skilled and unskilled workers, shopkeepers, master artisans and (owing to its location near the railway station that was opened in 1862) quite a number of railway employees. However the social composition of the population of Søndergade changed radically in the last half of the century. In 1884 the building of a bridge over Århus River turned Søndergade into the main street of the town connecting the old town centre by the cathedral with the new town centre by the railway station. This totally changed the character of the street and made it probably the most fashionable one in the town. The workers disappeared. In 1880 they had made up a third of the street's inhabitants; 20 years later their share had decreased to just 10 per cent. The proportion of shopkeepers and master artisans in these years increased from barely 30 per cent to almost 50 per cent in 1900. At that time there were not many small houses left in Søndergade. The street had become middle- and upper-class.

These four streets represent four different neighbourhoods: Mejlgade and Fiskergade belonged to the old streets of Århus with a socially mixed population. Mejlgade was more fashionable, Fiskergade less so. Both streets became socially more homogeneous in the years between 1860 and 1900, Mejlgade becoming more and more middle-class, Fiskergade more and more working-class. Sjællandsgade and Søndergade belonged to the new part of the town, the former representing the recently formed working-class quarter, where the working class was totally dominant, whereas Søndergade came to represent the new fashionable shopping centre of the town, where tradesmen became the dominant section of the population.

The shopkeepers of Århus 1860-1900

Århus was one of the most rapidly growing Danish towns in the second half of the nineteenth century, when the population increased from 7,886 to 51,814. The working class was the fastest growing social group, but the number of retailers increased rapidly too, from 222 in 1860 to 891 in 1900. This is an increase of more than 300 per cent, and it was accompanied by profound structural changes in the retail trade and a growing social differentiation among shopkeepers.

In 1860 the merchants who were licensed for both wholesale and retail trade had been the dominant group and had made up almost 50 per cent of the 222 retailers, but at the end of the century they were reduced to less than 10 per cent. The absolute figures did not change noticeably during these 40 years, but as a whole the group was undergoing considerable changes in its internal structure. The old-fashioned merchants' houses that combined wholesaling and retailing, and where different sorts of trade were united under one roof, had almost disappeared at the turn of the century. Some of them concentrated on the wholesale business but a fast-growing majority became retailers. As they multiplied so did the number of branches and kinds of trade. In the 1860s shopkeepers such as chemists, fuel merchants, bread sellers, milk sellers, ship's chandlers, gentlemen's outfitters and general shopkeepers appeared in Århus.[3] The next decade saw needlework dealers, sand dealers, stationers, hosiers, wool dealers, lingerie dealers, lamp dealers and cheese mongers establish their shops. The 1880s found room for florists, coffee dealers, a tea dealer, footwear dealers and egg dealers, and in the last decade of the century butter retailers, confectioners and bicycle dealers were added to the multitude of shopkeepers.

While in 1860 the merchants, ironmongers, second-hand dealers, drapers, milliners, greengrocers and small tradesmen accounted for almost 90 per cent of the shopkeepers, these 7 branches were reduced to 25 per cent of the total number of retailers at the turn of the century. On the other hand there had been an enormous rate of increase in the shops whose articles appealed to the rapidly growing group of consumers in the working class and which were normally small undertakings. The number of beer retailers, fuel dealers, general shopkeepers, fishmongers and tobacconists increased from 28 to 321 in the 30 years from 1870 to 1900, and these 5 categories of shopkeepers made up more than a third of the retailers in Århus by the end of the century.

In 1860 the commercial activity of Århus had been concentrated in the old town centre around the cathedral except for the great merchants. They traded with farmers and the peasants of the countryside and placed their great houses on the main roads leading to the south, north and west (to the east is the sea). Forty years later the merchants who traded with the peasants had almost disappeared. In the town centre a more specialised and diversified retail trade was to be found including drapers' shops, wine shops, ironmongers, bookshops, outfitters and grocers that primarily appealed to the growing middle class of the town. The shape of the town centre was changed as a secondary centre emerged at the railway station and became connected to the still existing centre at the cathedral by the new fashionable street Søndergade, mentioned above. However it was in the outskirts of the town in the new quarters, mainly populated by the rapidly growing working class, that the main increase in the number of shopkeepers took place. Thus by the turn of the nineteenth century more than half of the retailers in Århus were located in the densely populated working-class quarters. They were shopkeepers who tried to satisfy the demands of the working class for daily supplies in small quantities of necessities such as foodstuffs and solid fuel.

Quite a number of these small shops of the working-class districts served a new function as an extra source of income for distressed workers or as an emergency occupation. This sideline shopkeeping accounted for approximately 8 per cent of the shopkeepers of Århus. Three-quarters of these shopkeepers were skilled or unskilled workers, who supplemented their income in this way. Typically they established shops that did not demand a large initial capital, as for example general shopkeepers, small tradesmen and second-hand dealers. The working-class quarters had the largest share of people with sideline retailing. In Fiskergade and Sjællandsgade the proportion fluctuated between 20 and 45 per cent of the shopkeepers, while it did not exceed 10 per cent in Mejlgade and Søndergade, and in Søndergade this sort of retail business had totally disappeared by 1900.

The growth in the number of shopkeepers was very uneven. The 1870s had the greatest growth rate: 94 per cent compared to an increase in the population of 75 per cent. The second half of the 1870s was a time of general recession, and the extraordinarily high growth in the number of shopkeepers was caused by a large number of emergency shops established by those in social need. The numbers of merchants and grocers were almost stable, while the number of small shopkeepers such as fuel dealers, general shopkeepers, fishmongers, greengrocers, small tradesmen, secondhand dealers, milk sellers, beer retailers and dealers in articles of wood skyrocketed. None of these undertakings demanded more than a small initial capital, nor did they necessarily presuppose a vocational training. Besides it was possible to run the business from home, from an inexpensive basement shop or a barrow. Thus they were all suitable alternatives for supporting a distressed family fighting against unemployment and low wages, or for satisfying a need to supplement the income, and for exploiting the working capacity of women and children.

The function of the small shops as an emergency occupation made the years of depression into years of growth for the retail trade, measured by the number of shopkeepers.[4] As a consequence of this a relatively large number of not very permanent shops were established, and of course this influenced the overall stability of the retail business. Less than a third of the shops of Århus had a life of more than ten years in the period 1860-1900, and this instability actually increased and was more noticeable in the working-class districts than in the fashionable shopping streets.[5] As a consequence of this there was a large turnover at the lower end of the shopkeeper scale.

The income and capital of shopkeepers

There were great varieties in levels of income between the different branches of trade. In 1890 many shops were at the top of the income scale, clearly separated from the rest. Ironmongers, drapers, leather goods dealers, wine merchants, booksellers and merchants licensed for both wholesale and retail trade all enjoyed annual incomes of more than 4,000 crowns. At the bottom of the scale with an average annual income of below 1,000 crowns were those with embroidery shops, sand dealers, small tradesmen, milkmen, fishmongers and shopkeepers with a free trade licence. Real average incomes at this end of the scale were even lower because almost half of the shopkeepers here did not register their incomes at all because they were below the level at which they had to pay tax.

Income levels also varied with the location of the shop. Shopkeepers' average incomes in the four streets Mejlgade, Søndergade, Fiskergade and Sjællandsgade, as they can be read from the municipal registers of tax-payers, are listed in Table 1.[6]

Table 1. Average and variation (difference between highest and lowest) of incomes in crowns of the retailers in Mejlgade, Søndergade, Fiskergade and Sjællandsgade 1870-1900

| | Mejlgade | | Søndergade | | Fiskergade | | Sjællandsgade | |
	Av.	Var.	Av.	Var.	Av.	Var.	Av.	Var.
1870	2100	2500	817	900	1000	800	600	-
1880	1893	4800	1769	4300	1150	1200	892	700
1890	1870	5000	2609	6200	1013	700	1121	1300
1900	3036	11300	4181	14200	1145	1300	1533	2900

Av. = Average; Var. = Varitaion. Source: Jørgen Smidt-Jensen.

It is evident that as regards level of income it was important in which quarter retailers established their shops. Of special interest is the tremendous growth in average income in Søndergade, clearly reflecting the fact that this became the most fashionable shopping street in the town. In other streets changes were less dramatic. Income levels in Fiskergade show a tendency to stagnate connected with the fact that the street itself was in a stagnant state, slowly turning into a working-class street and so losing social prestige during the period. As far as Mejlgade is concerned, the table also shows a stagnation in incomes, apart from the last decade of the century when a couple of extraordinarily prosperous shopkeepers brought the average up. Rising incomes in Sjællandsgade are due partly to the general population growth in the surrounding area, and partly to the fact that Sjællandsgade was the first built-up street in the neighbourhood and so developed into the main street of this working-class district with a more diversified selection of shops than the surrounding streets had.

However, having a shop in Søndergade did not automatically ensure a shopkeeper a high income. In 1900, for example, the two tobacconists on the street made only 1,000 and 900 crowns respectively, while two of the three hosiers and the florist on the street had an income of 800 crowns each. Location could not neutralise the importance of which branch of trade was concerned. For instance, in Mejlgade a whole group of shopkeepers never enjoyed incomes above 1,000 crowns over a long period. These included fishmongers, milliners, small tradesmen, second-hand dealers and dealers in articles of wood.

Similarly, there were shopkeepers in the less fashionable streets of Sjællandsgade and Fiskergade who had incomes that rose above the average. An ironmonger in Sjællandsgade earned 2,400 crowns in 1900, while two grocers had incomes of 2,000 and 2,400 crowns respectively. In 1880,there were two grocers making 1,800 and 1,900 crowns respectively in Fiskergade, while in 1900 a stationer made 1,600 crowns. It appears that the shopkeepers exceeding the normal income level of 1,000-1,100 crowns in working-class streets were either in businesses that usually enjoyed a high level of income (like grocers) or had highly specialised shops (like stationers and ironmongers).

Apparently it made no difference, in terms of income, whether one was a fishmonger, a beer seller, a fuel dealer, a tobacconist or a milliner in a fashionable street or in a working-class street. Irrespective of location these groups of retailers had very low income levels, and they noticed no significant increase in average income from 1860 to 1900. The only difference was that while an income of 700 to 1,000 crowns was in accordance with general income levels in the working-class districts, these shopkeepers in middle- and upper-class districts had a low economic status compared to their neighbours. To the retailers in the more prosperous retailing areas, such as ironmongers, drapers, paint dealers, and grocers, location was of greater importance. It made quite a difference whether an ironmonger, a draper or a grocer had a shop in a working-class street or in a middle/upper-class street, although their levels of income compared with that of their neighbours were usually fairly high wherever they traded. The outcome was increasing economic differentiation between retailers throughout the second half of the century. In 1900 a small group became separated from the rest by having incomes close to upper-class levels, while the incomes of the great majority of retailers were low and stagnant.

When it comes to property ownership, the picture is less clear when looking at retailers in the four streets than it is when incomes are concerned. This can be seen from Table 2.

Table 2. Retailers in possession of real property 1860-1900

	Mejlgade	Søndergade	Fiskergade	Sjællandsgade
1860	15 (19)	1 (1)	8 (9)	- (-)
1870	11 (21)	2 (8)	6 (9)	- (4)
1880	6 (29)	5 (14)	10 (20)	7 (13)
1890	8 (30)	10 (37)	5 (10)	10 (20)
1900	9 (30)	11 (47)	4 (16)	18 (35)

Note: The figures in brackets indicate the total number of retailers in the street.
Source: Jørgen Smidt-Jensen.

Table 2 shows a more frequent occurrence of property-ownership in the less fashionable streets of Sjællandsgade and Fiskergade than in the other two streets, and also a relatively stable tendency in the number of property owners. It may seem strange that so many retailers in working-class streets owned property, but this does not necessarily mean that they were wealthy, although property-owners normally had a larger income than tenants. Much of the property was heavily mortgaged, and properties varied in value enormously. In working-class districts properties were generally small and humble and so shopkeepers could more easily afford to buy them.

Stability in the proportion of property-owning retailers is not found in Mejlgade. Here the proportion of property-owners was clearly declining throughout the entire period. This was connected with the decrease in the number of old fashioned merchants who had been both wholesalers and retailers. The merchants were the group of shopkeepers with the highest level of property ownership and the value of their property was way above the average. In 1860 the average value of merchants' properties in Mejlgade was 15,000 *rigsdaler* (30,000 crowns). The same year a small tradesman owned three houses in the street, and they were all of very modest value, 600, 900 and 950 *rigsdaler* (1,200, 1,800 and 1,900 crowns) respectively.

Even if a relatively large proportion of shopkeepers both in the main streets and in the working-class quarters owned their own properties, certain groups of shopkeepers never or rarely were registered as property-owners: fishmongers, fuel dealers, secondhand dealers, milliners, milk sellers, tobacconists, fruit dealers, beer sellers and dealers with a free trade licence. Shopkeepers of these kinds belonged to the lowest stratum of shopkeepers, economically as well as socially.

Domestic servants and shop assistants

Because domestic servants and shop assistants normally lived in the houses of their employers, it is possible to get an impression from the census of the number of shopkeepers having domestic workers, shop assistants and apprentices in their service. The number of shopkeepers employing domestic servants in the four streets is listed in Table 3.

Table 3. Retailers in Mejlgade, Søndergade, Fiskergade and Sjællandsgade employing domestic servants 1860-1900

	Mejlgade	%	Søndergade	%	Fiskergade	%	Sjællandsgade	%
1860	11	58	1	100	1	11	-	-
1870	11	52	1	25	1	11	-	-
1880	20	69	5	36	5	25	2	15
1890	11	37	12	32	1	10	6	30
1900	12	40	22	47	3	15	6	17

Source: Jørgen Smidt-Jensen.

Domestic servants were concentrated in the two fashionable streets, where between a third and a half of shopkeepers employed servants. Yet some of the shopkeepers in Fiskergade and Sjællandsgade kept servants too. This was most evident in 1890 when almost a third of the retailers in Sjællandsgade kept servants. Presumably the majority of these servants were working at least part-time in the shops. In terms of the different areas of trade, the largest number of servants was employed by the wealthiest shopkeepers: the merchants and grocers, paint dealers, chemists, ironmongers, and drapers. This of course is what was to be expected. Compared to other households the proportion of shopkeepers who employed servants was rather high. In Copenhagen 12 per cent of all households kept servants in 1900. Among the shopkeepers in the four streets of Århus, the rate in 1900 was between 17 and 47 per cent.

While the employment of servants depended partly on personal practical circumstances, for example a widower's or bachelor's need for a maid to be in charge of the household, the employment of shop assistants seems to be a more reliable indicator of the size of a shop and of the economic status of the shopkeeper. Much more than in the case of servants, shop assistants were concentrated in the two fashionable shopping streets of Mejlgade and Søndergade. The number of and the percentage of shops employing shop assistants and apprentices is shown in Table 4.

Table 4. Number and percentage of shops with shop assistants employed 1860-1900

	Mejlgade	%	Søndergade	%	Fiskergade	%	Sjællandsgade	%
1860	8	42	1	100	1	11	-	-
1870	11	52	1	13	2	22	-	-
1880	12	41	2	14	2	10	-	-
1890	6	20	9	24	-	-	1	5
1900	9	30	15	32	1	6	2	6

Source: Jørgen Smidt-Jensen.

Broadly speaking, the figures for shop assistants reveal the same trend as the figures for incomes. This suggests a more or less stable situation in Mejlgade, a rising trend throughout the period in Søndergade, and a constant absence of shop assistants in the working-class streets of Fiskergade and Sjællandsgade. Even more than in the case of servants, shop assistants were employed by very few categories of shopkeepers. Almost all of them were employed by grocers, ironmongers, drapers, and paint dealers. For other than these groups of shopkeepers the employment of a permanent staff remained more the exception than the rule.

The analysis of the economic status of shopkeepers in Århus has revealed a group characterised more by dissimilarities than by similarities, and where the dissimilarities became more pronounced as time went on. Grocers, drapers, ironmongers, paint dealers, booksellers, and wine dealers were located at the top of the scale. They had high incomes, they were often property-owners, they normally kept servants, and they almost always employed shop assistants. At the lower end of the scale were fishmongers, fruit dealers, dealers in articles of wood, beer sellers, thread dealers, milliners, and dealers with a free trade licence. They had the lowest level of income, only a few of them were property-owners, and they hardly ever employed servants or shop assistants. This group of rather poor shopkeepers, and the intermediate stratum of mainly small general shopkeepers, grew enormously during the whole period numerically, and because of that the group of shopkeepers became more and more divided socially and economically in the second half of the century. A contributory cause was that retail trade, especially in times of economic distress, became an emergency occupation for workers affected by unemployment or who for other reasons needed to supplement their incomes. This meant a large turnover, especially at the lower end of the shopkeepers group. The largest increase in the number of shopkeepers took place in the newly-built working-class districts on the outskirts of the town. The meagre incomes of the workers did not form the best basis for running shops. Consequently most of the shopkeepers operating in the working-class districts remained in the lowest stratum of retailers, with an economic status close to that of the workers of the neighbourhood.

Shopkeepers and general elections

Before the secret ballot was introduced at general elections in 1901, a voters' register was kept. It contained information on the voting record of each voter. Some of these registers have survived and consequently it is possible to see whether the social and economic heterogeneity of the shopkeepers influenced their political attitudes.

For Århus as a whole the proportion of shopkeepers voting for the Conservatives [Højre] was higher than that of the electorate as a whole. At the general elections in the period from 1879 to 1892 the number of votes for the Conservatives fluctuated between 39 and 54 per cent. At the same time between 59 and 69 per cent of the shopkeepers voted for the Conservatives. On the other hand, the proportion of shopkeepers voting for the Liberals

[*Venstre*] was lower than average. In the town as a whole between 26 and 33 per cent voted for the Liberals, while only between 21 and 27 per cent of shopkeepers voted for this party. When the Social Democratic Party started standing for parliament in 1892, the Liberal votes decreased to only 4 per cent, while the Social Democratic Party gained 21 per cent. Among shopkeepers, only 11 per cent voted for the Social Democrats, while 8 per cent still voted for the Liberals.[7]

In the four streets of Mejlgade, Søndergade, Fiskergade and Sjællandsgade voting has been examined for 1881, 1890 and 1898. On the first two occasions the general election was a straight fight between the Conservatives and the Liberals, but in 1898, when Århus had been divided into two constituencies, the Social Democratic Party had gained so much strength that the former political enemies, the Conservatives and the Liberals, arranged not to fight each other, nominating candidates for one constituency each. The Social Democratic Party had candidates in both constituencies. The votes of the shopkeepers in the four streets at the general election of 1881 is shown in Table 6.[8]

Table 6. Votes of shopkeepers at the general election 1881

	Mejlgade	Søndergade	Fiskergade	Sjællandsgade
Conservatives	16	5	6	1
Liberals	2	3	2	7
Abstained	2	-	4	2
Unregistered	4	1	5	1

Source: Jørgen Smidt-Jensen.

As can be seen, shopkeepers in Mejlgade, Søndergade and Fiskergade had a tendency to vote for the governing Conservatives, while almost all of the shopkeepers in the working-class street Sjællandsgade voted for opposition candidate. If the distribution on the basis of trades is analysed, it becomes apparent that the merchants were the most loyal Conservative voters. Out of 17 merchants, 13 voted for the Conservatives, while only one voted for the opposition. With the small general shopkeepers the situation was just the opposite. All four registered voted for the Liberals.

At the general elections of 1879 and 1882, the figures of the merchants matched the tendency for the town as a whole. In

1879, 82 per cent of the grocers voted for the Conservatives, and in 1882, 85 per cent.[9] The votes of the small shopkeepers in the four streets differs from those of the town as a whole. The small shopkeepers in the four streets were more inclined to vote for the opposition. But as most of them were located in the working-class street of Sjællandsgade, it is not possible to tell whether it was their location or the tiny size of their businesses that made them vote for the opposition. Table 7 shows how the elections turned out among the shopkeepers in the four streets in 1890.

Table 7. Votes of shopkeepers at the general election of 1890

	Mejlgade	Søndergade	Fiskergade	Sjællandsgade
Conservatives	14	10	5	3
Liberals	7	10	2	5
Abstained	1	3	2	3
Unregistered	5	5	1	4

Source: Jørgen Smidt-Jensen,

The pattern is the same as it was in 1881. The majority of shopkeepers voted for the Conservative candidate (who nevertheless lost the election) and only in Sjællandsgade did the Liberal candidate get the majority of the shopkeepers' votes. Again it was the merchants who had the largest proportion of Conservative voters, as everyone in this area of trade voted for the right. For most of the other shopkeepers the picture is less clear. However the Liberals' share of the votes rose from 28 to 37 per cent, while that of the Conservatives decreased from 56 to 49 per cent. This change was caused by the large increase in the number of small shopkeepers such as fishmongers, beer sellers, small general shopkeepers and the like, while the number of merchants decreased during this period. The 'natural' electoral potential of the opposition was thus growing, while that of the Conservatives was stagnant.

The result of the general election of 1898 is probably more representative than the previous two as regards the differences in political attitudes among the shopkeepers, because now the Social Democrats were standing for parliament in both constituencies of Århus, while in one of the constituencies the Liberals did not contest the seat, and in the other there was no Conservative but only a Liberal candidate to challenge the Social Democratic rival. The shopkeepers in the four streets voted as shown in table 8.

Table 8. Votes of shopkeepers at the general election of 1898

	Mejlgade	Søndergade	Fiskergade	Sjællandsgade
Conservative/ Liberals	13	12	4	7
Social Democrats	7	2	2	10
Abstained	4	6	1	7
Unregistered	2	6	5	6

Source: Jørgen Smidt-Jensen.

The Conservatives' share of the shopkeepers' votes in the constituency where they had nominated a candidate remained unchanged at 49 per cent, while the share of the opposition decreased from 37 to 27 per cent. This was most likely due to the shopkeepers' aversion to the Social Democratic Party. Shopkeepers, who formerly would have voted for the Liberals, at this election preferred to vote for the Conservatives or to abstain rather than give their vote to a Social Democrat. This is most obvious in Søndergade where in 1890 there had been an even distribution of votes between the Conservatives and the Liberals. In 1898 this distribution was replaced by a strong predominance of the Conservatives, when only two of 22 registered electors voted for the Social Democrats. This development has to be seen in the light of the transformation of Søndergade into a fashionable shopping street with a large share of economically high status shopkeepers.

At the election of 1898 the shopkeepers in the working-class street of Sjællandsgade once more differed from the others, as the majority voted for the Social Democrats. The pattern of voting among the various areas of business was the same as earlier. Merchants and the majority of larger shopkeepers (drapers, paint dealers, stationers) voted for the Conservatives. The small shopkeepers (small general shopkeepers, fishmongers, beer sellers, second hand dealers, dealers in articles of wood and fuel dealers) were in a greater degree disposed to vote for the Social Democrats. While all nine merchants and grocers in the four streets voted for the Conservative candidate, only five out of sixteen small general shopkeepers did so. In this context it is remarkable that all three tobacconists voted for the Conservatives, as tobacconists economically belonged to the lower end of the shopkeepers, and so were potential Social Democratic voters. That the opposite appears to be the fact in this case was probably because the goods they dealt in, cigars and choice tobaccos, were luxury goods which primarily appealed to middle- and upper-class clienteles. This combined with the location of their shops in the fashionable shopping streets might have given them a feeling of being natural Conservative voters.

As has been shown with respect to political attitudes, retailers did not form an homogeneous group. Their voting at the general elections was determined by both social and geographical elements. A majority of shopkeepers at the higher end of the economic scale voted for the Conservatives. As far as the merchants and grocers were concerned, in the town as a whole the vote ran as high as 85 per cent, and in Mejlgade, Søndergade, Fiskergade and Sjællandsgade in one case (the elections of 1898) the ratio attained 100 per cent. This orientation towards the right took place despite the fact that some of the grocers had very low incomes. Yet none of them seems to have inclined towards the opposition. The area of trade here seems to have been important. To be a grocer, apparently was to be a Conservative.[10] Among shopkeepers at the other end of the scale a larger proportion voted for the opposition, the Liberals and the Social Democratic Party. So in the case of the small general shopkeepers the votes for the opposition amounted to 25 to 47 per cent.

The voting, however was not only determined by the economic and social status of shopkeepers, but also by the quarters in which they lived and operated. So at the elections of 1895 no less than 45 per cent of small general shopkeepers in the southern constituency of Århus voted for the Social Democrats.[11] In this constituency the shopkeepers' votes approached the working-class votes, as 56 per cent of the workers voted for the Social Democrats.[12]

The same pattern was to be observed in Sjællandsgade in 1898, where 42 per cent of the shopkeepers voted for the Social Democrats, only 29 per cent voted for the Conservatives, and another 29 per cent abstained from voting. In Søndergade only 9 per cent of the shopkeepers voted for the Social Democrats, while 64 per cent voted for the Conservatives, and 27 per cent abstained from voting. This difference in the shopkeepers' voting between working-class districts and socially more heterogeneous areas was partly due to the differences in economic status of shopkeepers from different parts of the town. Thus Sjællandsgade had a far larger share of small shopkeepers than Søndergade, and a shopkeeper's average income was more than two and a half times as high in Søndergade as in Sjællandsgade.

Income and the area of trade were, however, not the only reasons the retailers in working-class districts were more inclined to vote for the opposition than their colleagues in the fashionable shopping streets were. The location of their shops in working-class districts and a clientele primarily composed of workers made them apparently more attached to the working class than other shopkeepers.[13] This tendency can be seen by comparing the voting in Sjællandsgade with that in Fiskergade, where the humbler shopkeepers were in the majority, but where the income level was also considerably lower than in Sjællandsgade. It appears that the majority of shopkeepers in Fiskergade nevertheless voted for the Conservatives, no matter whether the opposition was Liberal or Social Democrats. Fiskergade was, despite a relatively large working-class population, not to be considered a working-class street. The population of the street was relatively heterogeneous with a large number of master artisans, whereas Sjællandsgade was totally dominated by workers. Consequently Fiskergade in general had a larger potential of Conservative voters. It was quite natural for shopkeepers to identify with them and so vote for the Conservatives. In Sjællandsgade shopkeepers, because of the dominance of the workers, were more open to working-class points of views and working-class policies, and so were more disposed to vote for the Social Democrats. At the same time it must be recalled that Sjællandsgade was the street with the largest proportion of shopkeepers having another profession beside retailing. So in 1900 23 per cent of shopkeepers had more than one profession, and most often the sideline was working as an unskilled labourer. Finally it must be taken into consideration that a large proportion of shopkeepers in those areas of business that did not demand any vocational training (small general shopkeepers, small tradesmen, fuel dealers, dealers in articles of wood, and so on) were workers who supposed that they could make a better living by establishing a small retail shop. Naturally this direct contact between the working class and shopkeepers was instrumental in the extension of the Social Democratic point of view to the shopkeepers of Sjællandsgade as well as those of other working-class districts in the town.

Conclusions

As the town expanded, the population increased, and industrialisation gained momentum, the shopkeepers of Århus proliferated. Around 1860 they were a relatively small group dominated by a small number of merchants licensed for both wholesale and retail trade, having their shops situated in the centre of the town or near the town's gates (which were not far from the centre of the town anyway); 40 years later they had become a large and heterogeneous group socially as well as geographically. This group consisted partly of shopkeepers who ran some kind of specialised shop in the fashionable shopping streets, and partly of a large number of small shopkeepers dealing with mixed goods in the growing working-class districts, where retailing became to a significant extent an extra source of income for skilled and unskilled workers, the unemployed, and wives or widows of workers.

At the economic level there was a three-way division of shopkeepers, which to some extent was constituted by the different areas of trade. However, a shop's location might modify the importance of the kind of business it was. The upper middle class of shopkeepers were the merchants/grocers, ironmongers, drapers, book sellers, wine merchants and paint dealers, who all had large incomes that allowed them to invest in real property, to keep servants and to employ shop assistants. The shopkeepers' middle middle class, which was less numerous than the upper middle class, consisted of haberdashers, stationers, hosiers, chemists, flour dealers and a few others having incomes that provided them a reasonable standard of living. Both the upper and the middle strata of shopkeepers had their shops in the centre of the town. At the bottom of the scale, composing the large majority of shopkeepers (around two-thirds) with incomes usually not exceeding those of unskilled workers, were the beer sellers, the small tradesmen, the fishmongers, the small general shopkeepers, the fuel dealers, the milk sellers, the milliners, the dealers in articles of wood, the fruit dealers, and the dealers with a free trade licence. Most of these lower middle-class shopkeepers were running their business in the working-class districts, and they did not normally employ a permanent staff. If they owned any property at all, it was of small value.

The economic heterogeneity of the shopkeepers and the positions and types of shops appears to have had an influence on shopkeepers' political attitudes. Even if the majority voted for the Conservatives, nevertheless between 20 and 30 per cent voted for the opposition (Liberals and Social Democrats), and in the working-class districts close to 50 per cent voted for the Social Democrats. In the more fashionable parts of the town almost all shopkeepers irrespective of their area of business or economic status voted for the Conservatives. Socially and politically it seems as if the shopkeepers were influenced to a rather high degree by their customers in their neighbourhoods. Politically they did not necessarily side with their colleagues and fellow middle-class citizens elsewhere in town.

Thus the retailers of Århus did not at all constitute an homogeneous group at the end of the century. They were divided with regard both to economic and social status and to political attitudes and social identification.

Notes

[1] The results presented in this essay originate from an unpublished paper produced at the University of Århus in 1986: Jørgen Smidt-Jensen, *Detailhandlerne i Århus ca. 1860-1900. En lokalhistorisk undersøgelse af en middelklassegruppes økonomiske, sociale, politiske og organisatoriske differentiering* [Retail Trade in Århus 1860-1900]. The paper, which is mainly based on research of unpublished source material, is available at Erhvervsarkivet in Århus.

[2] The geographical object of this research, Århus, is not a typical Danish market town. On the contrary this town was characterised by an extraordinarily high increase in population in the second half of the nineteenth century. It will therefore not be reasonable to draw too general conclusions from this research. Furthermore it must be expected that there will be large local and regional variations (P. Boje, *Danske provinskøbmænds vareomsætning og kapitalforhold 1815-1847* [The Trade and Finance of the Danish provincial Merchants 1815-1847], Århus 1977, p.13). The advantage of restricting the research to only one market town is on the other hand that it has been possible to use more, and more varied, source materials and thereby to carry out a more detailed and varied examination of the shopkeepers.

[3] The Trade Act of 1857 made it possible to take out four different kinds of trade licence: merchant's licence which allowed only whole-sale trade, grocer's licence which allowed both whole-sale and retail trade, shopkeeper's licence which allowed only retail trade and small tradesman's licence which allowed retail trade

in small quantities of domestic provisions. Furthermore it was possible to obtain a free trade licence which allowed trade in a number of articles as bread, candles, yarn, thread, soap, cakes, and toys.

[4] A similar increase in the number of shopkeepers during the recession of the 1870s can be observed in Copenhagen. J. Warming, *Gode og dårlige Tider* [Good Times and Bad Times], Copenhagen 1903, pp. 75 and x.

[5] Similar tendencies are seen elsewhere. In about 1905, 16 per cent of the shops in Copenhagen closed down each year (Vagn Dybdahl, *De nye klasser* [The New Classes]. *Politikens Danmarkshistorie* vol. 12, third edition, Copenhagen 1978, p. 250; Vagn Dybdahl, *Det nye samfund på vej* [The New Society Dawning]. *Dansk socialhistorie* vol. 5, Copenhagen 1982, pp. 66- 67). In Paris one third of the grocers' shops changed hands in 1910 (Heinz-Gerhard Haupt, 'The petite bourgeoisie in France, 1850-1914', in Geoffrey Crossick and Heinz-Gerhard Haupt (eds), *Shopkeepers and Master Artisans in Nineteenth-Century Europe*, London and New York 1984, p.107).

[6] 1860 is omitted as the register for this year does not specify the incomes but only tax rates. The figures of 1860 are therefore not comparable to the figures for other years.

[7] Vagn Dybdahl, *Partier og erhverv* [Political Parties and Business], Århus 1969, pp. 43-54, tables VI-X; Finn Odgaard, Handelsstanden i Århus og folketingsvalgene 1852, 1876 og 1879 [The Merchants of Århus and Parliamentary Elections 1852, 1876 and 1879], in *Erhvervshistorisk Årbog 13*, 1962, pp. 165-169.

[8] Of course the numbers of votes should be read with certain reservations. It is possible that there was some intimidation of electors (see Vagn Dybdahl, *Partier og erhverv* [Political Parties and Business], pp. 27-30), and it must be taken into consideration that the franchise was withheld from women, and men had to attain the age of thirty to get the vote. They also had to have the right to manage their estates, and were not allowed to be in receipt of poor relief. In at least one instance it is found that a shopkeeper was not able to vote because he was in receipt of poor relief (a fishmonger in Fiskergade in 1880).

[9] Finn Odgaard, *Handelsstanden i Århus*, p. 167; Vagn Dybdahl, *Partier og erhverv* [Political Parties and Business], pp. 48-53.

[10] This distribution regarding areas of trade is expressed in the organisation of the middle class too. See Jørgen Fink, 'Middelklassen' (The Middle Class), in *Socialhistorie og samfundsforandring* [Social History and Change of Society], Århus 1984, p. 211.

[11] Vagn Dybdahl, *Partier og erhverv*, p. 52.

[12] Ibid., p. 51, table 8.

[13] See Jørgen Fink, *Middelklassen*, p. 219. Thea Vigne and Alun Howkins assert that, because of their relatively high social position, shopkeepers in socially homogeneous areas like working-class areas dissociated themselves from the working class (Thea Vigne and Alun Howkins, 'The small shopkeeper in industrial and market towns', in Geoffrey Crossick (ed.), *The Lower Middle Class in Britain 1870-1914*, London 1977, pp. 190-195). The opposite seems to have been the case in Århus.

Contributors

Lars Edgren is Associate professor of history at the University of Lund. His main field of interest is Swedih urban artisans during the eighteenth and nineteenth century. His publications include *Lärling, gesäll, mästare. Hantverk och hantverkare i Malmö 1750-1847*(1987) and Die schwedische Zünfte im 18. Jahrhundert, in *Das Ende der Zünfte. Ein europäischer Vergleich*, Heinz-Gerhard Haupt, ed., 2002.

Tom Ericsson is Professor of history at Umeå University. His main field of interest is social history. He has published books and articles on the lower middle class and the petite bourgeoisie in Sweden, including *Mellan kapital och arbete. Småborgerligheten i Sverige 1850-1914* (1988). His most recent article in English is 'Women, family and small business in late nineteenth century Sweden', *The History of the Family* 6, 2001.

Jørgen Fink, Dr. phil., is Director of Centre of Business History, established in 2003 in a cooperation between University of Aarhus and The Danish National Business Archives. He has published numerous books and articles including *Middelstand i klemme? Studier i dansk håndværksmestres ökonomiske, sociale og organisatoriske udvikling 1895-1920* (1988), *Butik og værksted. Ehrvervslivet i stationsbyerne 1940-1940*(1992), and *Storindustri eller middelstand? Det ideologiske opgør i Det konservative Folkeparti 1918-20* (2000)

Christina Florin is Professor of history at Stockholm university and a Research Fellow at the Institute for Future Studies in Stockholm. She has published widely on womens history including *Kampen om katedern. Feminiserings- och professionaliseringsprocessen inom den svenska folkskolans lärarkår 1860-1906* (1987). Her current research deals with gender and politics.

Jan Eivind Myhre is professor of modern history at the University of Oslo. Life member of Clare Hall, Cambridge university. His principal interests lie in the fields of social history (classes, migration, urbanisation, childhood), historiography and university history. Among his books are *Norsk innvandringshistorie. Bind II 1814-1940* (Norwegian immigration history, Oslo 2003, coauthored): *Nordic Historiography in the 20th Century* (Oslo 2000, co-edited and -authored); *Making a Historical Culture. Historiography in Norway* (Oslo 1995, co-edited and -authored); *Barndom i storbyen* (Urban childhood, Oslo 1994); *Hovedstaden Christiania. Oslo bys historie, bd. 3 1814-1900* (History of Oslo, Oslo 1990).

Hanne Rimmen Nielsen (1953-2002), PhD. She was a Member of the editorial board of Den Jyske Historiker [The Jutlandian Historian]. Reader at The National Encyclopedia of Denmark, and Co-editor of Biographical Dictionary of Danish Women 1996-2000. She has published numerous biographies and articles on educational and gender history, among them are *Troende og dygtige Lærerinder". Lærerindeuddannelse og -fællesskab på Århus (Kvinde)-seminarium 1909-1950.*

Jørgen Smidt-Jensen, M.A., is Director of the Museum of Cultural History at Randers. He has published books and articles on the Danish industrialization and on Danish local history. His publications include *Detailhandlerne i Århus ca. 1860-1900 - En lokalhistorisk undersøgelse af en middelklassegruppes økonomiske, sociale, politiske og organisatoriske differentiering (1986)* and *Randers - Fra handelsplads til storkommune (2003).*

Index

AFL (Arbeidernes faglige landsorganisasjon);126
Agrarian Party;42; 139
Agri;166; 169
Akersbanene;228; 230
Andersen, Hans Christian;59
Andersson, C.A.;166; 169
Antonsson, A.;166; 169
Arbeiderbruk- og boligbanken (bank, Norway);228
Arbeidernes faglige landsorganisasjon;126
Arbeiderpartiet (The Labour Party) (Norway);139
Aschehoug, Torkel Halvorsen;242
Association of Lower Public Officials;123; 126; 130
Back, Pär-Erik;33
Ballin, Max;192; 194
Bergmann, Jürgen;168
Bestillingsmændenes Forening (Association of Lower Public Officials) (Norway);123
Betjeman, John;229
Birck, L.V.;189; 191; 192; 193; 194; 195
Blackbourn, David;171; 173
Boeskov, Laura;283; 284; 285
Bondepartiet (The Agrarian Party) (Norway);139
Bouvin;166; 169
Braudel, Fernand;219
Briggs, Asa;113
Bull, Olaf;224
Central Bureau of Statistics (Norway);114
Centre Party;40
Chayanov, A.V.;239
Christian Association for Home and School;284
Christian People's Party;139; 247
Christiania Bestillingsmannsforening;131
Christiania Haandværkerforening (C. Association of Artisans);131
Communications from the Swedish Retailers' Association;38

Conservative Democratic Party (Denmark);3; 11; 12; 88; 96; 97
Conservative Party;12; 40; 138; 186
Correus, Carl;22
Crossick, Geoffrey;4; 113
Danish Protestant Church;72
Danish Temperance Society;282
Den frisinnade valmansföreningen;165
Det frisindede Landsparti;89
Det konservative Folkeparti;185; 313
Det Nya Sverige;22
Dideriksen, Helene;266
Edgren, Lars;3; 11; 313
Emanuelsson, Agneta;208
Eng, Helga;251
Erhvervspartiet;88; 190
Ericsson, Tom;153; 158; 160; 161; 162; 313
Fahlbeck, Pontus;21
Ferrin Weber, Adna;234
Fink, Jørgen;3; 12; 313
Florin, Christina;3; 13; 314
Fold, Christian;272
Foss, Alexander;78; 186; 187; 194; 195
Fraenkel, Arnold;189; 190; 191; 192; 194; 196
Geijer, Erik Gustaf;20
General Swedish Union of Dairy Managers;209
General Trading Association of Sweden;35
Greve, Knut;104; 110; 111
Hagemann, Gro;241
Haggard, H. Rider;75
Hansen, Marie;282; 283
Hansen, Sidsel;270
Hantverkarnas läse- och klubbsällskap;175
Hantverks- och Industritidning;35
Haupt, Heinz-Gerhard;173; 175; 176; 313
Hoel, Sigurd;224
Hollis, Patricia;285

Holmenkollbanen;228
Huldén, O.T.;35; 36; 37
Hvid, Mine;269; 271
Højre;60; 67; 68; 88; 185; 304
Høverstad, Torstein;241
Høy, Anne;276
Høyre (Conservative party) (Norway);113; 138
Industriföreningen;175
International Bureau of the Middle Class;8
International Order of Good Templars;43
Jensen, Lucie;281; 282; 283
Jaabæk, Søren;244
Kant, Immanuel;8
Karstensen, Asger;185; 186; 189; 190; 191; 192; 193; 195; 196
Keilhau, Wilhelm;104
Kjeldstadli, Knut;106
Kristelig folkeparti (The Christian People's Party) (Norway);139
Kristiania Bestillingsmannsforening;244
Labour Party (Denmark);14; 87; 88; 139
Landsorganisasjonen;126
Langholm, Sivert;241
Lenger, Friedrich;168; 173
Liberal Party;14; 42; 139; 287
Lindby, Ingeborg;287
Lithander, Per E.;38
Ljunggren, C.J.F.;22
LO (Landsorganisasjonen) (Norwegian Federation of Labour);126
Löwenstern, Alf von;40
Malmö Association of Industry;170
Malmö detaljistförening;39
Malmö Hantverksförening;163
Malmö industriförening;170
Malmö Retailers' Association;39
Malmö Workers' Association;164
Mannsåker, Dagfinn;105; 106
Markmann, Laura;286; 287
Martin, Jean-Claude;29
Marx, Karl;8; 189
Meddelanden från Sveriges minuthandlares riksförbund;38

Medelklassens politiska organisation;40
Medelklassens riksförbund (National Association of the Middle Class);11; 40
Michelet, Jon;224
Ministry of the Interior;65
Missionary Society of Female Teachers;287
MWA;164; 168
Myhre, Jan Eivind;13; 14; 313
Mykletun, Reidar;251
National Organisation of Swedish Retailers;39
National Organisation of the Middle Class;40
National Swedish Union of Clerical Employees;211
Nelson, Margaret K.;268
Nielsen Dahl, Nicoline;279
Nielsen, August;222; 225
Nielsen, Hanne Rimmen;3; 13; 314
Nilsen, Rudolf;224
Nilsson, Bengt;210
Norwegian Federation of Labour;126
Palm, Conrad;35; 36
Paulsson, Gregor;31; 45
Pedersen, Marie;273
Perkin, Harold;241
Petersen, H.C.;220
Plet, Lilly;277; 278
Political Organisation of the Middle Class;40
Qvam, Anton Fredrik;244
Rasmussen, Nicoline;283; 284; 285
Rolfsen, Erik;231
Saldern, Adelheid von;170
Schulze-Delitzsch, Hermann;164
Schück, Henrik;19
Seip, Jens Arup;241
Sejersted, Francis;7
Semmingsen, Ingrid;105
Skjæraasen, Einar;224
Social Democratic Party;10; 33; 38; 41; 50; 62; 96; 98; 305; 307; 308
Social Democrats;33; 34; 39; 40; 41; 165; 166; 305; 306; 307; 308; 309; 311

Socialdemokraten (newspaper, Norway);225
Social-Liberal Party;271; 287
Sommestad, Lena;209
Steedman, Carolyn;264
Steen, Sverre;103; 104; 105; 114
Stores-project;68
Stortinget (Norwegian parliament);116; 242
Strange, Helene;266
Strindberg, August;20
Sundt, Eilert;116
Svedstrup, Gudrun;272
Svensk Hantverkstidning;37
Sveriges Hantverks- och Industriorganisation;157
Sveriges hantverksorganisation;22
Sveriges Köpmannaförbund;39
Sveriges Minuthandlares Riksförbund;22
Swedish Association of Female University Graduates;212
Swedish Association of Nurses;208
Swedish Handicrafts Association;22
Swedish Journal of Handicrafts;37
Swedish Order of Good Templars;43
Swedish Organisation of Crafts and Industry;157
Swedish Retailers' Association;22
Sæter, Svein;241
Söderberg, Tom;41; 154; 158
Sørensen, Bolette;266
The Broad-minded National Party;89
The Conservative Democratic Party;96; 97; 98; 186; 188; 190; 191; 194; 197
The Danish T.U.C.;75
The Educational Circle;163
The Industrial Council;78
The New Sweden;22
The Norwegian Teachers' Association;243
The Radical Left;87; 88; 96; 97
The State Training College for Infant School Teachers;265
Therborn, Göran;41
Thompson, F.M.L.;218; 229
Thörnberg, E.H.;21
Torgersen, Ulf;256; 257
Torstendahl, Rolf;161
Tschudi, Anton;225; 227
Ueland, Ole Gabriel;244
Venstre (Liberal national party) (Denmark);60; 67; 87; 88; 305
Venstre (Liberal national party) (Norway); 117; 138; 139; 247; 250; 254;
Vigild, Rigmor;277; 278
Wahrman, Dror;113
Wallengren, Hans;46
Wergeland, Henrik;112; 219
Women in Government Service;210; 211
YWCA;267
Öberg, Lisa;205
Öhngren, Bo;28; 31

Extended Table of Contents

Preface   3

Introduction   7
    A tale of three nations   9
    The themes   11

PART 1
NATIONAL PERSPECTIVES

A Silent Class. The Lower Middle Class in Sweden, 1840-1940   19
    Introduction   19
    Early understandings of the lower middle class   20
    The lower middle class in official statistics   24
    Social mobility and recruitment   27
    Politics and ideology   30
    Popular movements and the lower middle class   42
    Family and the urban environment   44
    Conclusion   50

The Middle Class in Denmark 1840-1940   57
    A portrait of a nation   57
    The transition to a capitalist economy 1870-95   60
       Population growth   60
       Socio-economic development   61
       The middle class   63
       Politics and Culture   66
       Middle class ways of life   72
    The good old days 1895-1920   73
       Economic Background   73
       Socio-economic development   74
       The middle class   76
       Patterns of organisation in industry and handicrafts   77
       Pattern of organisation in the commercial trades   85
       Political and cultural development   87
       The middle class ways of life   91
    The inter-war years 1920-1940   92
       Economic background   92
       Socio-economic development   92
       The middle class   93

The old middle class	94
Pattern of organisation	95
Political and cultural development	96
Middle class ways of life	98
100 years of the middle class	99
The Middle Classes of Norway, 1840-1940	**103**
The middle class in history and historiography	103
Norway in Europe: mainstream and periphery	106
The language of the middle	110
Criteria for the social middle	115
The rise of the middle classes	118
Diverting experiences: the middle classes at work	125
The middle classes in public and private	129
The social middle as a political project	137
Conclusion	139

Part 2
Themes

Craftsmen and Political Consciousness in Sweden 1850-1900	**149**
In Defence of the Middle Class. But who and how?	**185**
The ideologies of the middle class wing	189
The antitrust Act and the decline and fall of the middle-class wing	194
Multiple Identities. Female Professional Strategies in an Historical Perspective	**199**
Introduction	199
The gender-structure imbalance	201
Professionalisation patterns of some different female professions	205
Multiple identities	213
Middle Classes and Suburban Lives: Norway 1840-1940 in a Comparative Perspective	**217**
Introduction	217
Pre-modern suburbs	218
The modern suburb	220
The rise of suburbia – a middle-class phenomenon?	221
Suburbs as nature	223

Planning and commuting	225
Social and geographical distances	228
Families, individualism and ownership	231
Conclusion	234
Uncertain Status: Norwegian Teachers between Professions and Middle Classes	**237**
Two perspectives	237
The teachers and the middle class	242
Teaching as a profession	248
Conclusion	257
Gender, Class and Culture. Danish Female Teachers, their Cultural Influence and Integration in the Local Community 1900-1950	**261**
Education and social background	263
Integration – marginality	267
Integration through school work – motherliness as a profession	269
Integration through marriage	274
Integration through political and cultural activities	279
Conclusion	288
Retailers in a Danish Town: The Streets of Århus 1860-1900	**293**
Introduction	293
The shopkeepers of Århus 1860-1900	296
The income and capital of shopkeepers	298
Domestic servants and shop assistants	302
Shopkeepers and general elections	304
Conclusions	310
Contributors	313
Index	315